T0298550

Endorsements

"*Practical Customer Success Management* is a must-read playbook for all business leaders and customer success-focused professionals. It imparts a solid grounding in what customer success is and why it is so important, whilst highlighting key challenges and how to respond to them. In addition it provides a detailed practical framework that explains both what to do and how to do it at every stage of the customer success engagement."

Jason Noble
Global Customer Success and SaaS Leader

"*Practical Customer Success Management* is unique from any other customer success management book I've read in that it bridges the gap between the theory of customer success and the reality of actually implementing a customer success program. The templates provide the jumpstart needed to either stand up a new framework or to bridge gaps in an existing framework. This is a welcome addition to my customer success library!"

Theresa Campbell
Customer Experience Executive
Presidio

"This book contains so much common sense that my neck was getting tired from nodding my head in agreement so often. As you read the material, and especially if you're a seasoned customer success professional, you immediately recognize that it was written by someone with many years of deep experience working with clients. And I think that's where Rick Adams' book is differentiated from most of the other customer success content that has been published. He's clearly coming at this from years of customer leadership in real life scenarios, from the trenches in which it seems he was able to work with customers week by week to help them methodically advance in their ability to adopt more of a product or service in order to achieve their goals. And that's what customer success is all about."

Peter Armaly
Senior Director Customer Success
Oracle

"As a relative newcomer to Customer Success, I have found this book to be an invaluable resource. Customer Success as a function within my organization is still in its infancy, and for that reason, there is much that remains to be built out and standardized. I feel as though we've done a good job of making the best with what we have, but I am someone that thrives when there is a structured roadmap to follow. That is precisely what this book offers, and does so with great detail. I found so many of the scenarios and examples to be extremely relatable, and the recommended processes highly applicable. I plan to implement Rick's framework not only to my day-to-day activities, but also to serve as our Customer Success team's playbook and guide."

Dan Louks
Customer Service Manager
Hiring Solved

"I wish a book like this existed when I started in Customer Success! I've been in the role for more than half of my career and I was impressed with the book's vast coverage of the multiple facets and nuances of the Customer Success position. *Practical Customer Success Management* is a great foundational book for learning the principles and applications of Customer Success and a good practical guide, well laid out enough to be easily referenceable and easily digested."

Cyn Taylor
Enterprise Customer Success Manager
LogicMonitor

"This book provides a comprehensive review of the Customer Success role and responsibilities as distinctly different from overall customer experience and applicable to any business, not just SaaS. Onboarding, adoption planning, and adoption implementation are described in depth and there are immediately usable recommendations to execute each phase effectively."

Anne Marie Ponder
Senior Manager, Enterprise IT Infrastructure,
Astellas Pharma US

"An actionable and to-the-point 'gospel' of customer success management. In his book, Adams not only clarifies what customer success management is, but he also provides all the ingredients to create the right customer success strategy. If you need to implement customer success within your own company, or if you are a CSM who simply wants an authoritative guide to customer success management best practices then dive in!"

Baptiste Debever
Head of Growth & Company Founder
Alkalab

"It is refreshing to see a book that articulates easy-to-follow concepts of customer success management using real-life examples on how to perform the role more effectively and efficiently. Adams' style of writing is entertaining and very simple to digest, and what I particularly appreciated is the way in which he has broken down complex challenges and made them easy to understand for customer success managers to apply in everyday situations when serving their customers."

Samuel Parri
Global Success Manager and Senior Program Leader

"The growth of Customer Success as a corporate discipline has been remarkable and continues unabated. Rick's excellent book is an invaluable resource for anyone with an interest in Customer Success. Whether you are contemplating your first foray into Customer Success or are a seasoned executive, this book provides both the framework and practical guides to help ensure that you have the best-practice structures and processes in place for both today and the future."

Adam Joseph
CEO
CSM Insight

"A structured and logical approach that will help new and experienced CSMs to bridge the gap between Customer Success theory and practical application."

James Scott
General Partner
Success Hacker

Practical Customer Success Management

Management

A Best Practice Framework for Rapid Generation of Customer Success

Practical Customer Success Management

Management
A Best Practice Framework for
Rapid Generation of Customer Success

Rick Adams

Routledge
Taylor & Francis Group

A PRODUCTIVITY PRESS BOOK

First edition published in 2020
by Routledge/Productivity Press
52 Vanderbilt Avenue, 11th Floor New York, NY 10017
2 Park Square, Milton Park, Abingdon, Oxon OX14 4RN, UK

International Standard Book Number-13: 978-0-367-18276-2 (Hardback)
International Standard Book Number-13: 978-0-429-06045-8 (eBook)

Library of Congress Cataloging-in-Publication Data

Names: Adams, Richard, 1967- author.
Title: Practical customer success management : a best practice framework for rapid generation of customer success / Richard Adams.
Description: New York, NY : Routledge, 2020. | Includes bibliographical references and index.
Identifiers: LCCN 2019008115 (print) | LCCN 2019010743 (ebook) | ISBN 9780429060458 (e-Book) | ISBN 9780367182762 (hardback : alk. paper)
Subjects: LCSH: Customer relations. | Customer services.
Classification: LCC HF5415.5 (ebook) | LCC HF5415.5 .A343 2020 (print) | DDC 658.8/12—dc23
LC record available at https://lccn.loc.gov/2019008115

Visit the Taylor & Francis Web site at
http://www.taylorandfrancis.com

and the CRC Press Web site at
http://www.crcpress.com

Contents

Acknowledgments

Thanks go to my two sisters Susan and Janet for their love and moral support, and to my friends Gus and Brendan for the practical help and advice they have given me here in Ireland. I really appreciate it. Thanks are also due to everyone in the Cisco Customer Success team that I met during 2016 and 2017 who shared their knowledge and insights with me so generously. Special thanks go to my very good friend Sam who painstakingly read every word of the manuscript and provided so many excellent suggestions for its improvement. This book would be half as good without his valuable input.

Who Is This Book For?

We Are All Beginners, But We Are Also All Experts

A good friend of mine recently asked me what type of person my book is aimed at—the brand new customer success manager (CSM) who is looking for an introduction to the basics, the expert who wants access to the latest thinking on customer success tools and best practices, or the intermediate who has a strong foundation in customer success and is looking to build upon this to help move their career to the next level.

The short answer is *all of them and more.*

The long answer is that in reality it's just not that simple. The vast majority of people coming to the CSM role are not first jobbers fresh out of college—far from it. Generally speaking, CSMs enter into this role from a breadth of other previous careers ranging from sales to customer service to technical subject matter expertise to project and program management and many others. It is not uncommon for me to meet people with 5, 10 or even 15 or more years of solid previous career experience behind them who have recently made the move to customer success management. Naturally, these people most definitely do not come without a wealth of knowledge, skills and experience that they can apply to their new role.

Few if anyone therefore starts from the beginning and needs to build their knowledge and skills from scratch, instead they come with their existing expertise. Of course, the specific knowledge, skills and expertise differs from person to person, so that, for example, someone with a sales background might already be great at communication and stakeholder management, whereas someone with a technical background might already be fantastic at data analysis and problem-solving. But here's the thing—the role of CSM is so broad in terms of the required knowledge and skills that few if anyone is going to come with *all* of the necessary expertise.

In addition, this book is aimed both at CSMs themselves who need the skills and knowledge to get out there and engage with customers to deliver customer success for them and at their managers and leaders who have to determine customer success strategy, provide appropriate resources and support and measure and report on the activity of their customer success teams to show the return on investment that is being produced by them.

Why Purchase This Book?

This book presents an entire, end-to-end, best practice framework to the user in just the same way as I present it in my training, coaching and consultancy courses. It is not just another book about customer success management, it is an in-depth manual that provides detailed explanations on customer success practices and provides step-by-step guidance for CSMs to fulfill their role in a productive, efficient and high-quality manner. It provides an entire methodology for you to follow in your role as CSM and also gives you access to multiple downloadable tools including templates and checklists that you can customize and use within each customer engagement.

How to Use This Book

This book aims to provide a way to fill the gaps—whatever those gaps are and however many or few you have—by providing a comprehensive coverage of *all* the tasks that CSMs are generally asked to perform in a clear, concise way and presented in a logical order of progression. Readers are welcomed and indeed encouraged to start from the beginning and work through the entire book from beginning to end to gain the maximum benefits from understanding the entirety not just of the Practical CSM Framework but also of the philosophy of customer success that lies behind it. However, some readers might choose instead to jump straight to the descriptions and explanations for those tasks that they are not already familiar with and need help to perform immediately.

Foreword

Helping to guide people toward success is our most noble calling, and I have been fortunate enough to have built my career around just exactly this. When I worked at Lands' End in 1983, reporting to its founder and owner Gary Comer, the concept of a chief customer officer (CCO) did not yet exist, and this meant I was at the forefront of pioneering the role and of defining what it should be. I very much see the role of the CCO as one of working across the organization to unite the entire company behind the delivery of the best possible experience to customers. Gary described me as *the conscience of the company* and putting the customers' needs first in order to earn the right to customer-driven growth is a key concept behind both customer experience and customer success. I feel very fortunate to have been one of the architects of the customer experience movement and I remain passionate to this day about the need for driving a customer-first culture through the entire organization.

When I wrote my first book, *Chief Customer Officer*, in 2006, I had to convince my publisher to name it that. By 2015 the role of CCO had become widely accepted, and the world had changed, including the economic downturn and the rise of social media. Additionally, I had over the intervening years distilled my concepts for achieving customer-driven growth into a best practice methodology called the *Five Competency Model*, so I took a year out of work to sit down and write a new book called *Chief Customer Officer 2.0*. The concept of the *Five Competency Model* is to provide clarity around what a company and its people must do to build a business that's truly customer driven. All my books have been very "tool heavy" and they intentionally focus on providing practical help and guidance to readers that can be taken and applied to their own situations.

The concept of customer experience is now a critical component of most successful businesses. One aspect of customer experience is customer success management, which focuses specifically on helping customers achieve their goals. For many companies and perhaps especially (though not only) those with a business-to-business focus, the need not only to ensure customers attain value from the products and services they buy and use but actually *measure* and *realize* this value has become increasingly important. While the concept of helping customers to achieve their desired and needed outcomes is not a new one, what is relatively new is the specific role of Customer Success Manager or CSM. What Rick sets out to do in his book *Practical Customer Success Management* is to provide the framework, the tools and the guidance to help CSMs perform their specific, customer success-related activities in the same way that I have set out in my books to provide the framework, tools and guidance for business leaders to align the entire organization behind a customer-centric model.

In conclusion, I know that Rick shares my own passion for putting the customer first in all activities and for ensuring that businesses are truly aligned behind the need both to better understand customers' desires and needs, and to use that understanding to help customers achieve their goals. I hope that all who read this book are similarly inspired to put the customer first and in so doing to earn the right to customer-driven growth.

Jeanne Bliss
March 3, 2019

About Jeanne Bliss

Jeanne Bliss is one of the foremost experts on customer-centric leadership and the role of the chief customer officer. For over 20 years, she led customer experience at Land's End, Coldwell Banker, Allstate, Microsoft and Mazda. Since 2002 she has guided customer experience transformations for major global organizations through her firm, CustomerBliss, and has inspired audiences through her keynote speeches. She is the cofounder of the Customer Experience Professional's Association and has been called the "godmother of customer experience." Her latest book is called *Would You Do That To Your Mother?*; in it she explains how to cut through the rigmarole of business to give customers the treatment they desire and employees the ability to deliver it. Her most recent thinking on customer experience can be learned by visiting her website https://make-mom-proud.com/.

Author

Rick Adams is an independent author, trainer and consultant specializing in helping companies deliver measurable business value for their customers. Adams has over 25 years of experience working with companies of all types to improve outcomes for their customers. He also founded a software-as-a-service startup which he sold in 2012 to focus on writing, training, and consulting. Having delivered training and consultancy services to thousands of professionals working for hundreds of different companies in over 30 countries across four continents, Adams is now based in the rural west coast of Ireland where he lives with his two dogs Zeus and Terri.

Adams' recent work includes the development and delivery of a global certification program on customer success management for Cisco Systems, Inc. His current interests include helping individuals and companies develop best practices in innovation, in customer success management and in business outcomes focused selling.

He can be contacted via LinkedIn at https://www.linkedin.com/in/rickadams01/, Twitter at https://twitter.com/RickAda84728077 or email at rick.adams@practicalcsm.com.

Introduction

In a Perfect World We Would Not Need Customer Success Management

In an ideal world, there would be no need for customer success-related activities and so there would be no need for CSMs to perform those activities. In this perfect environment, customers would already know exactly what they need and would understand both how to go about getting it and how to measure it afterwards, salespeople and design teams would already have fully understood the customer's outcome requirements and built the sales proposal in a way that best enables the attainment of those outcomes, products and services would perform exactly as intended, communications between people, teams and companies would be unambiguous and harmonious, and end users would be champing at the bit to get going with using the CSM's company's products and services to realize the value necessary to ensure their company gets the best possible return on their investment.

Welcome to the Real World

Meanwhile, back on planet Earth we find that the above scenario is not how it actually is. In reality—or at least in *my* reality—customers are not clear about what it is they have purchased, stakeholders are difficult to manage and disagree between themselves as to what is important, outcomes are at best hazily defined, strategies and initiatives get changed all the time, and end users are, let's say, "less than enthusiastic" about embracing change.

So They Bought the Solution, Now What?

The point of the above description of the difference between the ideal world and the real world is to illustrate the concept that the purchase or even the installation, configuration and integration of a solution does not guarantee that the customer will attain the results they are hoping for, even if they purchased the right solution and deployed it perfectly. There is almost always much more to be done than just "provisioning", and this is where the CSM steps in.

Explaining the SPL or Senior Project Lead

This term SPL or Senior Project Lead is my own, and I have used it in this book as a shorthand way to describe whoever it is in the customer's organization that has direct responsibility for making the utilization of the CSM's company's products and services that have been purchased a success. This person might be the sponsor (i.e. the person who provided the budget), the decision maker (i.e. the person who approved the purchase) or very commonly someone else such as a project manager, a process owner or a team leader who has been given the task of making the initiative work. Whoever they are in terms of their job title and level of seniority, they will be the CSM's principal contact for this particular initiative, and it is likely that the CSM will be working closely with them throughout the engagement. They are therefore a very important stakeholder for the CSM to form a good working relationship with and to establish regular and high-quality communications with.

The Role of the CSM… It's Complicated

The role of the CSM is to act as a friend, adviser, counselor, coach, consultant and subject matter expert as appropriate to the customer's lead stakeholder—the person I describe as the customer's senior project lead or SPL. The CSM helps the SPL to understand what they bought and why. The CSM provides best practice process and tools to helps the SPL develop high-quality onboarding and adoption plans and to implement and project manage those plans to a successful conclusion. The CSM acts as a conduit to all sorts of resources from subject-matter expertise through to existing generic training content from both the CSM's own company and third-party organizations as appropriate. The CSM helps the SPL to determine KPIs and to take measurements, analyze and report on results and where necessary take corrective actions to get the initiative back on track. In a nutshell, the CSM is there to help the customer realize the maximum possible value from the purchase of the CSM's company's solution—*whatever* that takes.

Where Does This Book Come In?

Customer success management as a profession is still in its infancy, and just like most infants is growing and maturing rapidly. As it grows and matures, it will begin to develop its own language, its own best practices and its own tools and templates to help CSMs with being as effective and productive as possible. This book sets out to further this maturing process by providing just such best practices and tools in the form of a framework called the Practical CSM Framework. This framework takes readers through the entire end-to-end experience of engaging and working with customers to help them actualize their successes and in so doing help the CSM's *own* company attain its successes through maximum renewals and expand opportunities. The purpose of this framework and the step-by-step processes it contains, together with the tools and templates it provides, is to impart the *what to do* and the *how to do it* information for CSMs who free their time so they can get on and actually *do* those things, instead of having to work them out from first principals every time.

What Is in the Book?

The first three chapters of this book set out the basic concepts of customer success management as a professional practice and explain what customer success management is all about, how it helps

Figure 0.1   The Practical CSM Framework.

the company that the CSM works for and how it helps that company's customers to realize more value from the products and services they purchase from that company. These initial chapters also explain how to prepare for the CSM role and how CSMs should go about managing their time, as well as explaining the role of research, analysis and planning within the context of customer success management and the critical path for CSMs to follow to maximize their effectiveness.

The major part of the book provides a detailed review of the Practical CSM Framework itself (Figure 0.1). Each phase within the framework gets its own chapter, which describes what happens within that phase, lists and explains the steps within it and provides recommendations and instructions for the best way of fulfilling each step. Additionally, a series of downloadable templates and checklists have been created to assist the CSM with their tasks, which are explained within the book and can be downloaded from the www.practicalcsm.com website.

1: Overview	7: PCSMF Phase 4: Adoption Planning Part 1
2: Readiness	8: PCSMF Phase 4: Adoption Planning Part 2
3: Tasks, Tools & Techniques	9: PCSMF Phase 5: Adoption Implementation
4: PCSMF Phase 1: Preparation	10: PCSMF Phase 6: Value Realization
5: PCSMF Phase 2: Commitment	11: PCSMF Phase 7: Engagement Evaluation
6: PCSMF Phase 3: Onboarding	12: Concluding Thoughts

Figure 0.2   Chapters within the book.

The final chapter provides some concluding thoughts on how CSMs can best prepare themselves for their role and how they can avoid some of the most common customer success pitfalls and traps. The chapter also discusses how customer success fits within the overall concept of customer experience and concludes by providing some ideas around how the customer success management profession might evolve and adapt in the future.

Outcomes from Reading This Book

Customer success management is all about outcomes—outcomes for the customer and outcomes for the CSM's own company. This book is also all about outcomes—outcomes for the CSM and for managers who need to set the customer success strategy, provide the resources and lead the team.

The outcomes that CSMs can expect from reading this book include a deeper understanding of the following:

- The nature of customer success management and its role within a modern business
- What skills, knowledge and experience the CSM needs in order to be effective in their role
- The types of research, analysis, planning and action-taking activities that CSMs get involved in
- The need for a customer success strategy and what should be in that strategy
- The Practical CSM Framework, its benefits to the CSM and how CSMs can engage with it to maximize the quality and efficiency of their work
- What the CSM should do to prepare for engaging with a new customer initiative
- Approaches to onboarding and the role of the CSM in ensuring that onboarding takes place and is relevant to each customer's needs
- How to engage with customer stakeholders and how to create meaningful stakeholder management plans and utilize those plans to develop high-quality relationships
- How to understand the customer's business vision and strategy, and how their business capabilities relate to that vision and strategy
- How to help the customer understand which users will be impacted by the change and what those users' needs are
- How to help the customer build an adoption roadmap that includes a communication strategy, a training plan and a user support package for all impacted users
- The role of the CSM in helping customers track and measure activity and to analyze and report on these measurements to show the value being realized
- The role of the CSM in helping customers identify and overcome adoption barriers and deal with risks
- How the CSM can develop their own knowledge, skills and experience over time to fully realize their potential as a highly competent and successful customer success professional

For customer success senior leaders, the specific outcomes from reading this book are twofold:

The first specific outcome is that they will have a ready-made, complete, end-to-end, best practice framework for conducting customer success management-related activities, which they can either give to their teams to use as it is or adapt and customize to meet their own organization's specific customer success-related requirements.

The second specific outcome is that they will gain an understanding from the book on how to create and develop a customer success team, how that team can integrate and work with colleagues from other departments to ensure maximum benefits, what resources that team will need to be able to fulfill their roles, how to set targets and activities for individual team members, how to measure team and individual CSM performance and finally how to improve that team's performance over time.

The End Game: Increased Revenues and Greater Profits

Of course, the ultimate outcomes for CSMs and senior managers alike will be the increased revenues and greater profits that will flow from having a productive, efficient and high-quality customer success organization. But sadly those are not outcomes that you can attain just from reading the book. Having read the book, you then need to *take action* to put the concepts and ideas you have learned into practice. That of course is the hard part and also the lengthy part. Reading the book is the start of your journey, but the ongoing application of the tools, techniques and best practices you learn from the book in each customer engagement you work on will help you to attain these ultimate outcomes of higher revenues and higher profits.

Chapter 1

An Overview of the Customer Success Manager's Role

1.1 What Is Meant by "Customer Success"?

1.1.1 Defining Customer Success

Before we discuss the details of customer success management, it makes sense to pause for a moment to reflect on what we actually mean by the term "customer success." There are various definitions that I have seen being used, and without a doubt the concept of customer success has evolved over the years, but the essence of it remains the same. At its heart, customer success occurs when the customer gets to realize a satisfactory (or better) level of return on their investment in the company's products, services and solutions (Figure 1.1).

So, for example, let's say we sold our customer a fleet of delivery vehicles to replace their old fleet on the basis perhaps of reduced running costs (such as parts, maintenance, fuel and road tax) and increased reliability (less breakdowns and less time off road for servicing and repairs) compared with their existing, aging fleet. If after, say, 5 years the customer could calculate that the combined purchase or lease price plus ongoing costs of their new fleet comes to less than what they would have had to have paid out to keep their old fleet on the road then we could argue that the purchase was a successful one for the customer, all other factors being equal.

Of course, the way success itself is defined will differ from situation to situation, and will not necessarily always all be just about cost savings or revenue increases. For example, alongside the

customer success	Helping customers to maximize the value they attain from our products

Figure 1.1 Defining "customer success."

reduction in overall costs, what might be the value to the above customer of an increased reputation for always delivering their products to their customers on time, now they have a more reliable delivery fleet? Or how might their brand reputation increase by reducing their carbon footprint through using more energy efficient vehicles that also produce less toxic pollution?

1.1.2 Customer Success Management Is about Realizing Value

The concept of customer success is more complicated and varied than it might first appear. Oftentimes I have seen vendors and customers calculate the return on an investment just purely on what we might consider to be the hard cash only. This happens either because neither party has uncovered the additional, hidden value in other areas outside of just cost savings or increased revenues or (more commonly) because although they have recognized that there are other benefits, they do not know how to measure or calculate those benefits in any meaningful way. From our perspective as customer success managers it is most definitely in our interest to make sure we have identified *all* of the value that our customer will realize from buying and using our company's products and services, and that we help our customers to find ways to measure and calculate (and ultimately to report back to senior management) on this value. I would say that being able to do this is a critical skill for every CSM, and is one that needs to be honed and improved over time, based upon the experiences that each of us will encounter as we go through our careers.

1.1.3 Customer Success Management Should Focus Primarily on Product (or Service) Value

Recently, it has become fashionable to widen out the definition of customer success (and therefore the role of the CSM) to include not just the value that customers receive from buying and then using our products and services, but from any other way in which we might be able to help them as well. I do not have a big problem with this wider definition, but I do think it is important to recognize that the primary role of the CSM is not just to make the customer successful, but to make them successful *through the utilization of the products and services that they have purchased from us.* Helping our customer in other ways may play a role in rapport building and relationship management with customer stakeholders, and may also contribute to enhancing the overall customer experience (of which more will be discussed below) but ultimately it is only when our customer can see that our *products and services* are generating value for them that they will consistently want to continue to buy them and buy more of them. And getting customers to continue to purchase our products and services is exactly what customer success management is all about.

1.2 Understanding Outcomes and KPIs

1.2.1 Defining "Outcomes"

The concept of outcomes is a really important one to the CSM and indeed to the whole philosophy and ethos of customer success management. As we saw in the previous section, the role of the CSM is to help customers to realize value from their purchases of the CSM's company's products, services and solutions. To perform this role successfully, the CSM needs to understand what the term "value" means to each customer that they engage with.

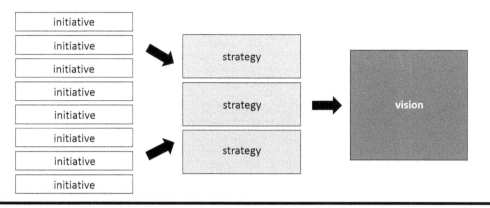

Figure 1.2   Outcomes occur at all levels within the business.

Of course the details of what specific value is being sought will differ from customer to customer, but what we can say is that every customer will have (or at least should have) a set of clearly defined goals or objectives for the initiative that the CSM's company's products, services and/or solutions have been purchased to support, and which will mean that the initiative has been successful if they can be shown to have been attained. These objectives are what we mean by the term "outcomes." To put it another way, an outcome can be thought of as an end result that the customer hopes to achieve over time through the work that the company will perform as they utilize the products, services and solutions they have purchased from the CSM's company (Figure 1.2).

Outcomes occur at all levels within the customer's business, and outcomes from the lower, tactical levels generally combine to create the outcomes for higher, more strategic levels. In this way, the outcomes from each individual project or initiative that might each, for example, be run by a particular department head or process owner combine to generate the overall outcomes of departmental or corporate strategies. In turn, the outcomes from each strategy are what drives the company forwards toward the attainment of its overall business vision. Indeed the business vision itself can be thought of as a statement of the outcomes that the whole company is working toward achieving in the long term.

1.2.2   Identifying and Documenting Outcomes

It is useful to the CSM to try to understand not only the specific outcome requirements of the particular initiative that they are engaged to support but also how the success of that initiative supports wider strategic outcomes and ultimately the overall corporate vision. Understanding these connections can be very powerful for the CSM, since it helps with gaining support and sponsorship from the customer's senior leadership team and with ensuring that the initiative (and therefore the CSM's company's products and services) is seen by the organization as important in contributing to the company's overall success.

A customer may have multiple outcome requirements for any particular initiative, and it is important for the CSM to make sure they understand all of these outcome requirements and to document them for future reference. In order to serve as a useful target, they need to be defined by at least three properties, as shown in Table 1.1:

Table 1.1   Properties of a Well-Defined Outcome

Property	Description
Quality	The type of result that is desired (for example, "Revenues generated from sales of Product X within the EMEA region")
Quantity	The amount of result that is required. This can be described in either absolute or relative terms (for example, "$20m gross takings" (absolute) or: "average 15% per annum increase over the period" (relative)
Deadline	The time limit by which the result must have been attained. This can also be described in either absolute or relative terms (for example, "By the end of the Financial Year ending 2025" (absolute) or: "Within eighteen months of implementation" (relative)

Not all customers are good at explaining their outcomes in these terms (though many are excellent at it). If a customer is struggling it is worth persevering with because a clear understanding of the initiative's goals makes it much easier to work out what action must be taken in order to realize the desired value. It may require some work on the part of the CSM to help the customer with these definitions, although typically this is something that would have been addressed already at the pre-sales stage. If the outcomes have not yet been fully identified, then the CSM needs to ask the relevant stakeholders within the customer's organization questions such as "What results do you need to achieve from this initiative?," "How much of it do you need to achieve in order to be successful?" and "By when must you have achieved this result?" By defining each outcome by all three of these properties, the CSM and the customer will be able to clearly understand what needs to be achieved in order to be able to state that the initiative has been successful, and how to calculate how much value the customer has already attained and will ultimately attain from the initiative.

1.2.3 Defining "KPIs"

There are usually plenty of ways in which a company might measure its performance on an ongoing basis, but what is of most interest to learn is the level of progress being made toward outcome attainment. Key performance indicators (KPIs) are measurements that are taken that show this progress toward the attainment of each outcome. Generally speaking, it may take several different KPIs to fully understand just how much progress is really being made, and where any problems may be lying that need to be addressed in order for further progress to be made.

To understand how multiple KPIs can help to build up a more complete picture of the true progress toward a specific outcome, we will use an example. Let's say that the customer has stated an outcome requirement as follows:

> A minimum of $15m in Product A sales revenues to be achieved within eighteen months.

One obvious KPI to use would be "monthly revenues." If we divide the target of $15m by the number of months within the period, we can see that assuming a linear relationship between time and revenues, this company needs to achieve an average of around $830,000 in sales revenues per month. But is the monthly revenues figure enough on its own to understand what is happening so that if the target is *not* being met the appropriate corrective action can be taken? Let's say we take this measurement for the first 3 months and we find that monthly sales are currently only averaging at around $650,000, which is substantially less than what needs to be seen in order for our 18-month outcome to be achieved. Do we have enough information just from measuring sales revenues alone to know where the problem lies and therefore what corrective action to take? The answer of course is "no," so what other measurements might be useful to take as additional KPIs?

Perhaps alongside sales revenues, the company could also measure the number of sales proposals written and the number of sales proposals accepted each month which we will say is 20 and 12, respectively. This will tell us a whole lot more than just the revenues on its own. For example, if we divide the average monthly revenues by the average number of sales made per month we will learn the average size of each sale, which turns out to be roughly $54,000. If we then divide the *target* monthly revenues by the average number of sales made per month we will learn what the average size of each sale *needs to be* for this number of sales, which is about $69,000. So we can see that the average sale size is about 20% less than what it needs to be if the company makes this same number of sales per month in the future. Additionally, we can now calculate that the company is currently only closing around 60% of sales proposals. We can also calculate that if the current average deal size of $54,000 remains the same then increasing the number of sales by another three customers per month to raise the number of deals to 15 per month will bring in the shortfall needed.

So now we have three KPI measurements—monthly revenues, monthly sales and monthly proposals—and just this information alone has started to provide useful data from which the customer can start to formulate strategies for taking any necessary corrective actions to ensure their outcome is met. Of course, there are other measurements that could be taken—for example, around marketing activity to increase the number of prospects to sell to, or around product quality to ensure the product is desirable.

1.2.4 Selecting and Understanding Outcomes and KPIs Is Important (But Not Always Easy)

Each KPI that is measured brings useful information that contributes to the overall picture. More KPIs make for a high-definition picture that in turn allows better quality management decision-making to take place. On the other hand, too many KPIs and/or the wrong KPIs will become expensive and time-consuming to measure and analyze, and may result in increased confusion rather than better decision-making. The customer will (or should) have plenty of expertise in knowing which KPIs are meaningful and important to measure, and it is strongly recommended that if the CSM is not already familiar with them, they should perform some basic research on the typical KPIs used to measure performance within the industry that their customer operates in.

In short, the CSM must understand both what *outcomes* the customer needs to attain from their initiative and which *KPIs* could be used to measure progress toward the attainment of those outcomes. If the CSM is not aware of this information, then they will struggle to understand what activities the customer needs to perform in order for their outcomes to be attained and how they themselves can be of use to the customer. Therefore, they will be less well positioned to ensure that the customer will realize all of the value that could be realized from the products, services and/or solutions that the CSM's company has sold them.

1.3 Treating Your Customer as Your Business Partner

1.3.1 Customer Success Management Is a Business Partnering Approach

I'd like to make a suggestion to you. My suggestion is:

> If you are selling business outcomes to your customer then you are effectively going into business with them.

As soon as you stop selling the products and services themselves and start selling results, you have changed the relationship between your own company and your customer. Effectively it's as if you are going into business with them. You have made the business case that they should invest in your products and/or services and they have done so. To continue to use those services and purchase further products the customer will need to see that value is being realized. The more value that gets realized, the more they will continue to invest. Therefore, it is in the interest of your company for their company to succeed—your two company's interests are aligned. When they win, you win, and therefore you have effectively gone into business together and the more success they get from this partnership the more success your company will get.

This is why selling business outcomes is so powerful and it is also one reason why customer success management is such an important part of the business to get right.

1.4 Why Is Customer Success Management becoming More Important?

1.4.1 Customer Success Management—A New Role, but not a New Concept

The CSM as a formal job role has only existed for a relatively short time, but the core concept of helping our customers to gain value from using our products and services is of course something that has been around for a long time. Traditionally, it would form a part of service managers' and support managers' roles to provide assistance to customers around product and service utilization. Additionally, there may be further help in the form of chargeable professional services that customers can avail themselves of should they wish to. These might include consultancy around requirements analysis and building the business case, and/or assistance with implementation and change management. It could also include aspects of customization or systems integration, for example.

1.4.2 Recent Rapid Growth in Customer Success Management

That being the case, why are we only now seeing customer success management being formalized into its own, separate departmental unit with its own workforce, budget, strategy, targets and managers? The business social media site LinkedIn places customer success management as No.3 in their top ten list of most promising jobs for 2018 (https://blog.linkedin.com/2018/january/11/linkedin-data-reveals-the-most-promising-jobs-and-in-demand-skills-2018), so we can see that customer success management is growing in its importance. What is causing this increased focus on creating customer value through customer success management? These are good questions to ask, since an understanding of why customer success management is important and what is causing its importance to grow helps us to understand what that role entails and also how it might continue to grow and develop in the future.

1.4.3 Increased Customer Agility Is Driving the Need for Customer Success Management

The answer comes from the change in the way customers now purchase products and services. Taking the technology industry (from where customer success management as a formalized job role first came) as an example, traditionally customers would need to make a fairly significant, up-front capital investment whenever they wished to buy new technology. This might be an investment in new hardware such as servers, routers, switches, data centers and so on and in new software such as operating systems and applications. Once these capital items were purchased they became assets of the customer, which could be used over a period of time and ultimately scrapped or sold for a small residual value when it became time for the company to reinvest in new replacement technology. Assuming (as typically would be the case) the initial up-front investment together with the ongoing management and maintenance expenses is high and the residual value is either very low or even nonexistent, to realize a return on their technology investment the customer will need to use this technology to increase revenues and/or decrease costs to a level that exceeds the combined initial outlay plus ongoing management and maintenance costs.

This model can work well where companies know in advance what their technology needs are now *and* what their ongoing needs will be over the term of the use of the technology they purchase. The problem, however, is that capital purchases of technology can be very expensive and so it may take many years of ongoing use of the technology before the customer breaks even on the deal. In this day and age, many companies find that the amount of change that they experience on an ongoing basis makes it very difficult for them to plan ahead for that sort of time period in any reliable way. Many things can happen in this time period—customers may have new requirements, new laws may be passed, new competitors may arise, the financial climate may change, and of course new technology innovation may occur.

So with this background, company executives might have to think very carefully about making any significant capital investments which tie them into having to use the products they have purchased for many years before they will realize any profit from their purchase. Far better perhaps, to wherever possible purchase their technology *as a service* instead and pay only for the *use* of it on a monthly, quarterly or annual contract without ever actually owning it outright. What this provides the management team with is *agility*—the ability to make the decision to purchase less of a particular service or more of a particular service or even cease using it entirely each time the contract comes up for renewal (Figure 1.3).

This agility brings significant value to the customer organization since from that company's perspective it reduces risk. However, in reality, it does not reduce risk, instead it transfers it. Some of the risk still remains with the customer of course, but a significant proportion of it transfers across from the customer to the vendor. This is because in the old model the vendor received all (or at least a large part) of their overall remuneration from the deal straight away when the customer made their initial purchase. Now however there is no large capital purchase and instead the customer pays a regular fee on a monthly, quarterly or annual basis over the lifetime of their use of the technology, which will over a number of years finally add up to a similar amount as that which they would have paid via the old method.

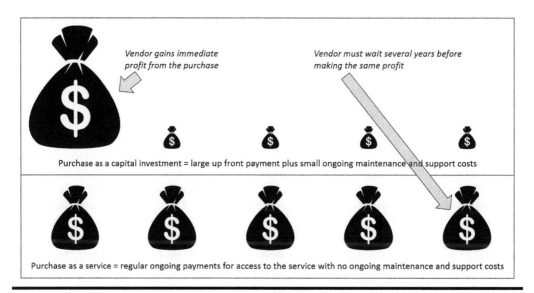

Figure 1.3   Delayed vendor profitability from X-as-a-Service.

In the new world of X-as-a-Service, it may take, for example, up to 5 years or more for a vendor to generate the same revenues from an as-a-service sale that they used to make straight away from a capital outlay sale. This means that whereas previously the vendor made pretty much all of the profit from a new sale straight away, now the vendor has to wait several years before they get the same level of value from the deal. This is the reason why for companies who wish to sell their products as a service, it is essential not just to help the customer to make the initial purchase in the first place (which of course is the domain of the sales executive) but also to generate real and measurable value from *using* those products so that the customer continues to renew their contract (which is the domain of the customer success manager).

There are other aspects to the CSM's role, but in a nutshell this transfer of risk from being entirely or at least almost entirely the customer's risk to having the risk split more equally between the customer and the increase in selling as-a-service style contracts is why customer success management is increasing in importance for many companies.

1.5 How Does Customer Success Management Help to Realize Business Value?

1.5.1 How Does Customer Success Management Work?

Now that we have defined what customer success is and why it is important, let's turn our attention to how it works. When a customer purchases a product, service or solution (a solution being multiple products and services that have been combined and packaged together as one purchase to solve a problem or overcome a business challenge), it is likely that they will know a lot less about the product, service or solution than the vendor does. The vendor has researched, developed and created the product itself and then ultimately it has been marketed and sold to its customers and perhaps installed and configured it for those customers and maybe provided management services but almost certainly supported those customers afterwards.

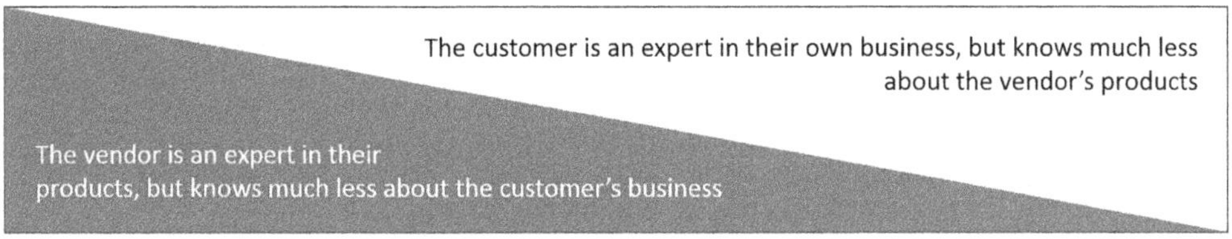

The customer is an expert in their own business, but knows much less about the vendor's products

The vendor is an expert in their products, but knows much less about the customer's business

Figure 1.4   Customer and vendor knowledge.

It makes sense therefore that after all these efforts the vendor has become an expert in its own products. Similarly, a particular customer organization is an expert in its own business. It knows its vision and strategy, its systems and processes, its resources and capabilities, its knowledge and experience, its customers and competitors, and its *own* products and services. Each of the two parties knows one part of the picture very well, but has a less profound understanding of the other part (Figure 1.4).

When a customer purchases a product, service or solution from us, a good question for them to ask themselves would be "How are we going to integrate this new product into our company so that it enhances what we do and generates measurable value for us?" Given that at this stage the customer has little or no experience of using the product, it might make sense for the customer to turn either to the vendor or a third-party company with similar knowledge and experience (such as a reseller or systems integrator) to help them.

If they are purchasing this product outright as a one-off capital investment, there may be less pressure or necessity experienced by the vendor to provide this sort of post-sales assistance without charging for it as a separately billable professional service. However, if the customer is purchasing this product as a service on a renewable contract or indeed if this customer may be making additional purchases of the same or other products in the medium- to near-term future based upon their experiences with this initial purchase, it may be worthwhile for the vendor to provide this assistance at no additional charge to the customer. This, of course, is because it is in the vendor's interests to make sure that the customer realizes a good return on their investment in order to maximize the likelihood of them renewing their contract for this product and/or purchasing additional products.

1.5.2 What Does Customer Success Management Do?

Customer success activities tend to commence after the purchase has been agreed, and the CSM would typically start to get involved after whatever was purchased has been customized, installed, configured, integrated, secured and had any other work completed that is necessary to make it ready to be used. The core purpose of customer success is to generate customer value (both as much as possible and as soon as possible) in order to maximize the likelihood of that customer renewing their existing contract and/or making additional purchases. To do this, the CSM will need to focus their efforts on the core activities shown in Table 1.2.

These are the core activities that CSMs tend to get involved in, which directly contribute to the generation and realization of value for customers, and of course as we have already seen, by creating value for the customer the CSM creates value for their own company. However, the CSM may also commonly be involved in realizing additional value for their own company in three other ways, as shown in Table 1.3.

Table 1.2 Core Customer Success Activities

Activity	Description
Onboarding	Making sure that relevant customer stakeholders understand what they have bought, why they have bought it, how it works and what (if anything) needs to be done to get it up and running
Adoption	Helping the customer to plan for whatever is necessary to get the product or service into use, and then helping the customer to implement that plan. The plan might include aspects of research and analysis on the impact of using the new product/service and then the creation of communication, training, support and (where relevant) incentives for end users, as well as documentation of new processes and tasks
Ongoing value creation	Providing ongoing assistance to customers to ensure they continue to access the product/service and continue to use it to generate value. The CSM might be tasked with helping the customer to identify barriers that are preventing that value from being created and plan how to overcome those barriers
Measurements and reporting	Ensuring that once the customer is up and running with the new product/service, measurements are regularly taken to prove the level of value that is being generated. The CSM might also be involved in preparing reports based upon those measurements and communicating the information within them in meetings
Adapting and fine-tuning	Helping the customer to refine the way that the product/service is used to maximize its value, and to adjust that usage in the light of change occurring either at the customer end (for example, due to a new corporate strategy) or at the vendor end (for example, a "dot x" upgrade that provides new features and functions)

1.6 Where Do CSMs Fit within the Wider Organizational Structure?

1.6.1 Customer Success Management in Different Companies

Not every business is the same in the way in which they organize their workforces and neither should they be. Each company is unique in terms of what it does, why it does those things and how it goes about getting them done. With this in mind, it would be unreasonable to expect CSMs to fit in exactly the same way within every company.

The biggest difference is whether or not the company has created a separate department or team that is dedicated to customer success management and that employs workers whose time is committed only to customer success-related activities. If that is not the case, then this may be either because the company does not see a need for a full time, dedicated customer success team or because while they do see the need for it, they do not (or do not as yet) have the available management time, financial resources, personnel, systems and processes and/or experience around customer success management best practice to get a full time, dedicated customer success team up and running.

Table 1.3 Additional Value from Customer Success

Value	Description
Advocacy	Because the CSM works with the customer stakeholders to generate value, the CSM may be well positioned to know when to ask for advocacy (such as referrals, testimonies, appearing in a case study, etc.) and who to approach within the customer organization to gain the necessary permission and assistance
Sales	Because the CSM experiences how the customer really uses the product/service they may be well placed to identify additional opportunities for increased use of this product/service (upselling) or for using additional products or services that their company also sells (cross-selling). These opportunities would typically be passed to the Sales team for them to follow up as appropriate
Product improvement	Because the CSM experiences how the customer really uses the product/service they may be well positioned to understand which features and functions work well, which are just OK and which ones are not so great—perhaps because they are too complicated, or time intensive to use, or reduce the quality or for many other reasons. Passing this information on to the R&D team is an important aspect of the CSM role that contributes to the ongoing efforts to continually refine and improve the company's products

Not every company needs or can afford a dedicated customer success team. Where a business is not selling anything that is complicated to deploy, adopt and use, and/or where they are not selling their products on renewable as-a-service style contracts there may be less of a requirement for a dedicated customer success team. In these types of situations, it may not be financially viable or worthwhile to invest in an entire customer success department, but it might still be useful for an existing team such as sales, product support or service management to take on some of the responsibilities and duties of a CSM. This to my mind may be a very sensible and pragmatic approach that helps the company to gain some of the benefits of a customer success-driven approach to their customers without the concomitant costs associated with a dedicated customer success team. This decision is of course one that needs to be made at the executive or "C" level, and should be reviewed from time to time as the business changes and grows.

1.6.2 Customer Success Management as One Aspect of Customer Experience

For organizations that do sell products, service and/or solutions that are complicated to deploy, adopt and use, and especially if they are sold either wholly or partly on renewable as-a-service style contracts there may well be a much stronger business case for creating and running a dedicated customer success department. Assuming this to be the case, there can still be large differences between such organizations in how they go about managing that team and its responsibilities alongside other parts of the business, particularly other departments that interact directly with the customer. Let's very briefly examine the role and function of each of these departments alongside customer success management so we can see more clearly how they differ and where they overlap (Table 1.4).

Table 1.4 Customer-Facing Departments

Department	Responsibilities
Marketing	Making prospective customers aware of the company and its products, services and solutions and helping them to understand the features, advantages and benefits of them. Helping customers to relate the potential value they might receive from purchasing these products to their own business challenges and opportunities.
Sales	Engaging with new and existing customers to understand their needs. Identifying new sales opportunities within both new and existing customers. Developing sales proposals that support a customer's needs and communicating those proposals to relevant customer stakeholders. Negotiating and agreeing sales contracts. Winning new sales. Managing and recording sales.
Product support	Helping the customer to use the products they have purchased by providing support services (typically either by telephone, email or online). The support service will typically help the customer to resolve technical problems they encounter and/or provide end-user advice on how to perform a specific task or use a specific feature or function of the product or service.
Service management	The primary role of service management is to ensure that the services they are responsible for are available and working so that customers who have paid for those services can log in and use them. Service management is typically responsible both for service availability and for service quality, and may be involved in routine reporting to prove and justify the availability and quality that was experienced over the preceding period.
Professional services	These are additional, chargeable services that the customer may decide to purchase alongside the core product/service and which enhances the value for the customer in some way. These may include consultancy to help the customer with requirements analysis and/or with business case development. It may also include more practical services related to customization, configuration, project management and integration. It may additionally include services relating to user training, adoption and change management.
Customer success management	This is generally a non-billable service that provides post-implementation assistance to the customer to help them generate value from the products/services they have purchased. It typically provides advice, assistance and resources relating to adopting and using the products/services and to measuring and reporting on the value attained from their use. (Although most companies do not charge for customer success management, some companies do charge for it. Arguably in that situation customer success management becomes another professional service.)

1.6.3 Customer Success Management Is Still Growing

It is important to recognize that customer success management is currently still growing and has not yet matured as a profession. For example, Totango is a software vendor that specializes in customer success management tools and they undertake an annual global survey of the industry. Their 2018 survey report showed 83% of customer success management teams were growing in size (www. totango.com/content/totango-customer-success-salary-and-state-of-the-profession-report-2018). This means that there are many new or relatively new customer success management teams out there who are currently going through the process of growing in size, experience and their own maturity.

1.6.4 Customer Success Management Is Still Maturing

Like many activities in business, it would be great if we could work out exactly what to do and how to do it first before getting on and doing it, but life rarely gives us that luxury. The reality therefore is that many companies are implementing customer success within their businesses without a fully formed strategy and without having created all of the resources and got all of the systems and processes up and running that they would ideally make available for their CSMs to use. I see this as being a reasonable and pragmatic way forwards, although I also recognize that this can potentially make the life of the individual CSM who works for that company that much harder. I certainly do not think I have all the answers, but if you find yourself in this situation then hopefully this book will provide you with some of the structure you need, fill some of the knowledge gaps you may have and give you access to some downloadable resources that will help you become more effective and productive in your role.

1.7 The 14 Tenets of Customer Success Management

There are 14 tenets (or principles) by which a CSM should live. Some of these may be obvious, but it is worthwhile reviewing all of them carefully as these explain both the role of the CSM and how that role can be successfully performed. Absorbing and understanding these tenets and then applying them in your work will go a long way toward helping you become an effective and productive CSM (Table 1.5).

Table 1.5 The 14 Tenets of Customer Success Management

	Tenet	Explanation
1	The CSM exists to create value for their own company	The reason why your company has decided to invest in customer success management (either as a fully fledged, separate department or as tasks to be performed by people in other existing roles such as customer services) is because it expects to see a financial return from that investment. Usually, this financial return comes from increased product/service sales and contract renewals from customers, but it may also include additional customer advocacy levels and/or a deeper understanding of customer needs to help with product development

(Continued)

Table 1.5 (*Continued*)   The 14 Tenets of Customer Success Management

	Tenet	Explanation
2	The CSM's primary task is to help customers attain measurable value from using their company's products and services	Customers expect to see a return from their investment in our products/services. The primary task of the CSM is to help customers to attain the maximum returns possible and to make sure they are measuring and reporting on these returns so that it becomes known and understood by the relevant decision makers within the customer organization
3	The CSM is a subject matter expert in how to adopt, use and realize value from their company's products and services	The customer is already a subject matter expert in how to run their own business, but the reason why a CSM can add value for a customer is that they have subject matter expertise in the products and services that this customer has purchased. Specifically, that expertise lies in the adoption and value generation processes that customers need to undergo in order to attain the maximum return on their investment
4	The CSM understands the customer's business	While the CSM may never know as much about a customer's business as the customer themselves, they need to make sure they know enough about that business to be able to understand how their own company's products and services can add value for that business and to provide contextualized help and assistance to the customer in planning for and undergoing product/service adoption and in measuring the value gained from doing so
5	The CSM is a researcher and an analyst	In order to plan for and take effective action, the CSM must first understand the situation, which means the CSM needs to be able to uncover the right information and to make sense of it. The information that needs to be researched and analyzed includes that which relates to the customer's business strategies and outcome requirements as well as its current situation. It also includes that which relates to the CSM's own products and services and how they might be adopted
6	The CSM is a consultant and an adviser	For each customer engagement, the CSM's role is to act as consultant and adviser, rather than as the decision maker. It is the customer's money that is being spent to pursue the customer's own strategic outcomes by engaging the customer's workforce to use the customer's new products and services (that they have bought from us). Our responsibility is to provide timely and useful information and guidance and to lend a practical hand where necessary to help them get our products and services adopted

(*Continued*)

Table 1.5 (*Continued*) The 14 Tenets of Customer Success Management

	Tenet	Explanation
7	The CSM is an educator	Key stakeholders within the customer organization may not always know everything that they need to know about the products and services they have purchased from us, or about the activities that need to be performed to get them fully adopted. While the CSM should make sure not to take on a formal training role, it is definitely part of their role to provide informal training and related activities to help these stakeholders understand the situation more completely in order that they can make well-informed decisions
8	The CSM is a communicator	Communication is at the heart of customer success management. This includes verbal communication in meetings, workshops and presentations as well as written communication in reports and on management systems (such as a CRM tool). Needless to say it also includes active listening. The CSM needs to have excellent communication skills and must be versatile enough to communicate with a wide range of stakeholders from a variety of cultural and job role-related backgrounds from within their own and the customer's companies and sometimes from third-party companies as well
9	The CSM is an influencer and an enabler	While the CSM is not generally the formal leader within an engagement, they most definitely need to have strong leadership qualities, especially the abilities to influence people and to enable activities to occur. Strong interpersonal skills including rapport building and forming trust relationships are also important, perhaps especially because the CSM may not be seen as the "person in charge" but yet still needs to influence others in order to get the job done
10	The CSM is a planner and a project manager	Not all activity is equal. Before taking action it is imperative that time is taken to formulate a well-thoughtout plan that adequately manages risk while maximizing efficiency and effectiveness in getting things done. Once the plan is in place, it needs to be followed and outputs measured and where necessary adjustments made to ensure that the project remains on track to deliver the desired results. The CSM may not be a formally qualified project manager, but should definitely be comfortable with planning and managing activity

(*Continued*)

Table 1.5 (*Continued*)   The 14 Tenets of Customer Success Management

	Tenet	Explanation
11	The CSM is a problem solver	There are many potential barriers to customer success that CSMs may come across. These may relate to very practical problems such as a lack of information or insufficient resources, they may relate more to conflicts of interest and/or opinion between stakeholders or they may come from outside the project itself such as a change in corporate strategy or a new piece of legislation. Whatever the situation, CSMs need to be good at viewing problems logically and rationally and determining the right course of action to overcome those problems
12	The CSM is a pragmatist	It is perfectly reasonable for customers to desire to see a return from their investment in our products/services. But sometimes the customer (or specific stakeholders within the customer organization) may have unrealistic expectations. Perhaps sometimes even our own colleagues may also have ideas that are impractical or unworkable for one reason or another. The CSM needs to remain realistic about what can be achieved within the timeframe, budget and whatever other resources and situational limitations exist
13	The CSM proactively seeks further sales opportunities	While I am not an advocate of turning CSMs into sales people per se, I do very much believe that it is the duty of every CSM to use their knowledge and understanding of both their own company's products and services and the customer's business and technical needs to identify further opportunities for which the CSM's company's products and services might be used by the customer to gain additional value. These opportunities should be passed to the Sales team to follow up with the customer as necessary
14	The CSM should do as little as possible—ideally nothing at all	This final tenet is partially humorous but also partially a truism since in an ideal world there should be little or nothing that the CSM needs to do. In this ideal world, much of the work that a CSM is normally involved with will already have been completed during the pre-sales process, and much of the remaining work will be completed by a well informed and sufficiently skilled and resourced customer adoption/change management team. It may not come as a surprise to learn however that we do not live in an ideal world, so in reality there will generally be plenty of work for the CSM to do. The secret of a good CSM lies in spotting where the knowledge and skill gaps lie and what hasn't been done that needs to be done, and in doing the work to plug the gaps and get the necessary tasks completed

Chapter 2

Readiness for Customer Success Management

2.1 What Is Your Organization's Customer Success Strategy?

2.1.1 Understanding Your Own Company's Context

Context is always important, and no more so than when performing the role of CSM. The most obvious context for any customer success engagement is of course the *customer context* and we will be examining in detail how a CSM should go about researching and analyzing each specific customer's situation, requirements and needs in later chapters. However, there is another context that is also important for CSMs to understand and take guidance from, this being the context of the CSM's own company, which is what we will be exploring in this section.

As we discussed in Chapter 1, the reason *why* CSMs exist is to generate value for their own company, and *how* they do this is primarily by helping customers to attain success through their use of the products and services they have purchased. But precisely what this "value for their own company" might be will vary from organization to organization. While superficially the strategy of every customer success team might look very similar, the details may be quite different. If the individual CSMs within a team do not understand that strategy and/or their own roles in fulfilling it, then they are very unlikely to generate the same level of value for their own company as they would if they did have this understanding.

2.1.2 Creating a Customer Success Strategy

An initial customer success strategy will typically be set by the senior management team, along with a budget and a set of targets to achieve. These are the "C" level executives who decided to create a customer success department within their business and who will continue to fund that department (assuming the department hits its targets of course). They will have selected an overall leader as the head of the department either from within the company's own ranks or by recruiting someone from outside of the business. Alongside the financial budget, they will have given that leader a certain amount of corporate resources including existing personnel, HR support, IT systems and so on. And they will also have provided that leader with this strategy and targets (or goals), which the leader will strive to achieve through the wisest possible use of the resources that have been made available to them.

Of course, the strategy the customer success leader (let's call this person the Head of Customer Success) will have been given will likely be high level only, and it will be up to them to create a more detailed plan that will include the specific objectives that they will set for their team and the tactics they will employ to attain those objectives. But whatever the detailed plan might look like, it will of course directly reflect the strategy and goals they were handed down from the senior executive team.

So what might influence this variation in strategy and goals from company to company? The answer is twofold. Firstly, they will be influenced by the overall aspirations of the business as a whole including its corporate vision, mission, goals and strategies. Secondly, they will be influenced by the current situation of the business in terms of what the business does; how it does those things; what financial, personnel and other resources it has access to; what level of experience and maturity around customer success it already has; who its customers are; what products and/or services it sells to them and so on.

So, for example, a newly formed company in a high-growth industry with strong financial backing and an innovative but relatively inexpensive and simple to use product or service may want its CSMs to focus strongly on winning new customers through gaining increased advocacy from its existing customers, in order to grow its market share. On the other hand, an established market leader in a highly competitive but slow growth industry that sells very expensive and complex solutions may be much more concerned about retaining its existing customers in order to protect its current market share and defend its revenues. These are just examples, and yes of course both companies will wish to retain as many existing customers as possible and win as many new customers as possible; however, the emphasis within each company's strategy is likely to vary— perhaps quite wildly—and this variation in corporate vision will be reflected in the goals each company sets for its customer success department.

2.1.3 Knowing Your Own Company's Success Strategy

Every CSM should know their company's vision, mission and corporate-wide goals and strategies, and should understand why those goals exist and how those strategies will achieve those goals. Every CSM should know this information well enough to be able to explain it to an outsider in a few simple sentences without recourse to complex language or diagrams and in such a way that the outsider "gets it" without the necessity of having any background knowledge about the company in question. This is a good exercise to test yourself with. Try right now to explain the above information to a third party (this can be a fictitious third party) either verbally or by writing on a whiteboard or with pen and paper (or digital equivalent) and see how far you get. The best CSMs, the best salespeople and the best executive decision makers can do this…can you? If not then your task is to go and do whatever research, analysis, thinking and practicing need to be done in order to be able to do it, and to do it well enough that if a customer stakeholder was to ask you to explain your company's vision, mission, goals and strategies you would be able to respond to them without hesitation.

Once you know this, the next step is to understand the specific goals and strategies of your customer success department, together with the detailed objectives that your department is working on and the tactics that it is employing to fulfill those objectives—especially of course those objectives that you personally have a role to play in their fulfillment. As discussed, it should be evident to you that these goals, strategies, objectives and tactics reflect and support the overall strategic direction of the business as a whole (and if they do not then perhaps there is something

Figure 2.1   The context for your role as CSM.

wrong or missing with your understanding that you should re-examine). As before, the test of your understanding is whether you are able to explain your departmental strategy and tactics to a third party. Again, this is a great exercise to try out either verbally or written and either to a real person or to a fictitious third party if no one is handy as your guinea pig. As with the overall corporate vision and strategy, if you find that you are unable to explain your departmental vision and strategy in simple terms then do whatever you need to do to rectify this (Figure 2.1).

2.1.4 Using Your Success Strategy

Now you have that all-important context as to what you are supposed to be doing in your role as CSM. This context should inform *everything* you do, sometimes directly and obviously but at other times gently and subtly, but always there in the mix somewhere. If you have ever practiced martial arts then I would liken it to having a grounded core or "chi" that means you are always well balanced and firmly positioned but also agile and ready to move in whatever direction is necessary. All decisions should stem from a consideration of this "core" of your departmental strategy, which in turn is a reflection of your corporate vision. The best CSMs understand this and allow their knowledge of the goals and direction of their department and their business as a whole to guide their decision-making in terms of how they prioritize and divide their time between tasks and what specific results they pursue with (and from) their customers.

2.2 What Is Your Role in Helping to Fulfill Your Organization's Customer Success Strategy?

2.2.1 Defining the Role of the CSM

Everyone who works for a company should know what their job role is. This goes without saying. However, because customer success management as a separately defined job role is very new to many companies and many individuals, there is a certain amount of confusion and/or ambiguity around the role and duties of a customer success manager. My experience of working with and delivering training to many hundreds of customer success managers leads me to conclude that as things stand, there is a significant proportion of CSMs who are in fact *not* clear on what their role is or what expectations their company has of them. I therefore think it is worthwhile to have a brief discussion about it here in this book.

As we know, the primary role of the CSM is to help customers maximize the value they gain from the products and services they have purchased from the CSM's company. This primary role supports increased renewals (generally considered to be the primary way in which the results of customer success activity is measured) and increased levels of upselling. Secondary roles typically include spotting additional (i.e., net new) sales opportunities, gaining customer advocacy for marketing purposes and assisting with understanding actual product and service utilization and product and service requirements, in order to help the R&D team refine and improve those products and services in the future.

Although the essence of customer success management remains the same, the specific job role and the particular duties and responsibilities of CSMs will vary from company to company, depending upon differing needs, differing capabilities and differing existing levels of customer success maturity. For larger, more complex companies there may be more than one CSM role. For example, at Cisco Systems in their FYE (financial year ending) 2018 there were three types of CSM. First was the Virtual CSM who managed many hundreds of customers which had direct contracts with Cisco for relatively simple services that had been purchased online. Second was the High Touch CSM who worked with either just one or a very small number of important customers. Only the very largest customers with the most complex needs and with a direct purchasing relationship with Cisco was provided with their own High Touch CSM as this was a relatively expensive resource. Finally, there was the Partner CSM. This type of CSM worked alongside Cisco's large reseller channel network and was assigned to one larger or a few smaller reseller partners. The role of the Partner CSM was to support and assist both the reseller partner and that partner's customers. While the customer success organization within Cisco Systems has subsequently changed, the approach shown above is illustrative of how a large vendor might arrange their customer success activities to suit a wide range of customer sizes and needs.

2.2.2 Understanding Your Own Specific Job Role

The obvious starting point for CSMs to understand their specific role is to review their written job description. In theory at least, this job description should give a reasonably detailed and accurate account of what tasks the CSM should perform in their day-to-day activities. While the written job description may be a great starting point, there are a number of considerations that should be borne in mind. First and most obvious is the age of the job description and/or the length of time since it was last reviewed and updated. Needless to say, if the job description was either written or updated recently then it is much more likely to be an accurate reflection on the job role itself than if it has not been recently written or updated. Another consideration is the level of detail with which the job description has been written.

Many job descriptions give a useful list of tasks and duties, but there are plenty out there which have (deliberately or otherwise) been couched in vague terms and which are open to various interpretations. This can put the CSM in a difficult position if their understanding of their role and the tasks and duties they should perform within that role differ from the understanding held by their colleagues or manager. Finally comes the well-known "caveat clause" that is found in many of today's job descriptions which will state something along the lines of "…and any other duties that your manager may request you to perform." This catch all clause means that in effect the CSM might be asked to do anything whatsoever, although HR best practice would of course ensure that all core tasks and duties are correctly and accurately documented within the job description and that any additional duties that are not specifically documented make up no more than a small proportion of the overall workload and are reasonable requests to make given the skills and experience of the person the request is being made of.

Having first re-read and absorbed (as much as possible) the meaning of the written job description, the next port of call for the CSM to determine a greater understanding of their role is their manager. In theory, your manager will have had a considerable input into the written job description. However, people come and go and so it may not have been your current manager who originally wrote the job description. Additionally and as we have already stated, circumstances change and in the world of customer success management they commonly change very rapidly, so even if your manager did originally write your job description they may well have other or additional requirements of you that do not feature in the written documentation. The only way to find out is to ask. If you have not yet done so, then one of your very first tasks after reading this chapter should be to sit down with your line manager to discuss your role with them. This may seem like a statement of the completely obvious; however, it is my experience that people very often miss what is completely obvious in favor of working on the abstract and difficult stuff. If that describes you then you know what to do!

What the CSM (and indeed anyone else) needs above all else is clarity. When you next get the chance to sit down and discuss your job role with your line manager whether formally or informally, here is what you ideally need to find out (or work out with them) (Table 2.1):

Table 2.1   Understanding Your Specific Job Role

Information	Explanation
Overall description	What is the overall description for the role? This should be in the form of a short paragraph that describes the job as if in conversation to a third party so that this third party "gets it" without needing to ask further clarifying questions
Specific, prioritized duties	Any task, duty or activity that will encompass more than say 10% of your time needs to be defined and explained separately, since it is critical that you understand these duties adequately and pay sufficient attention to them. Ideally they should be provided in priority order, or better still a rough percentage of overall time should be allocated to each one
Targets	A very important consideration is to know how you will be measured. What will your manager and/or your company as a whole use as indicators to rate your performance? These should ideally be listed as clearly and unambiguously as possible, since it is far easier to aim for a clearly revealed target than for a partially hidden or fuzzily described one
Documentation and reporting	This should include not just who you report to but also what types of digital or other information you will be expected to create and how much time you should anticipate will be spent in completing this information
Support	It is important to understand what support you will be given in order to perform your role adequately. The support you are interested in should include access to assets and resources such as software systems and templated forms, as well as formal and informal training, coaching and consulting where necessary
Career development	As a final point, it may be interesting to understand what opportunities lie in front of you for developing your career. It's great to have aspirations for personal improvement and advancement and if that describes you then it makes sense to know what the possibilities are and to have some sort of idea as to how you might go about making these career advances

Of course, there are other things in a job description aside from duties and responsibilities that are also well worth reading carefully whether it relates to your existing job or a potential new job you are thinking of applying for, which might, for example, include required or desired skills, experience and qualifications. But this book is not about *applying* for a CSM job, it's about *doing* the job so we will leave our discussion there and move on.

2.2.3 Teamwork Is an Essential Element

Regardless of the particular information that relates to your specific job in your specific company, there is one thing that we can emphasize in general about the CSM's role in fulfilling their company's customer success strategy, which is the crucial role of team work. Achieving customer success generally takes a team effort. At the very least it will take the efforts of both the CSM and a range of customer stakeholders, but more than likely it will also take team work within the CSM's own company. Depending upon circumstances this may include the intradepartmental team efforts of multiple CSMs but more commonly will involve interdepartmental efforts from a variety of personnel including (but not limited to) people from R&D, Marketing, Sales, Engineering, Professional Services, Support Services and Service Management as well as additional subject matter experts in particular products and services that may be called in from time to time to provide their expertise.

Aside from the above, the actual list of typical tasks that CSMs perform will be explained in Chapter 4 when we review the Practical CSM Framework, which breaks a typical customer engagement into a number of key phases or steps, with each phase containing a list of activities that need to be completed. Following this, Chapters 4–11 will then take you through the performance of these activities in greater detail, one phase at a time. In effect pretty much all of the rest of this book is dedicated to helping you know what to do and how best to do it!

2.3 What Assets and Resources Are Available to Help You?

2.3.1 The Problem of a Still-Maturing Profession

I wanted to include a discussion about assets and resources because over the course of delivering customer success management training to delegates across Europe, North and South America and the Far and Middle East it has been my experience that many CSMs get very little practical help from their companies in terms of assets and resources to help them perform their job. This is because the majority of customer success departments are either brand new or still relatively immature and have not yet created those assets and resources. The above of course is assuming a department even exists at all, since an appreciable percentage of my delegates have been tasked with creating (or just simply being) the department themselves, or with performing customer success-related activities alongside their "day job" in some other role such as Sales, Marketing or Customer Services.

Perhaps the above description fits your own situation, at least to some extent. If so then I hope this section will help by describing the types of assets and resources a CSM might find useful. Once you are aware of what you might find of help to have access to, it becomes a lot easier for you to deal with the process of creating or securing those assets and resources. On a practical note, throughout Chapters 4–12 we will be exploring the Practical CSM Framework and in those chapters I will be introducing some templates that you can download and either start to use exactly as they are or modify to suit your own specific requirements. For now though we will limit ourselves to a discussion about what assets and resources might be useful to a CSM as they perform the various tasks that they are likely to encounter.

2.3.2 Using Assets and Resources

(Note that an asset is something that you own and can use over and again to perform a particular task or set of tasks that you encounter multiple times, and a resource is something you use up in the process of creating an output. Let's use a furniture manufacturer as an example. The lathes in the factory would be examples of assets that are used over and again each time a chair or table leg needs to be created. The energy used to drive a lathe and the wood that is turned on a lathe to create the leg would be examples of resources since they are used up in the process of creating the output. As can be seen, the wood turner who is employed to create chair and table legs needs access to both the right assets and the right resources if they are going to be able to perform their role.)

What types of assets and resources do CSMs need? In truth the answer is "not that many" since the most important asset is the knowledge and experience of the CSM him or herself; however, just like the wood turner in the above example, having access to the right assets and resources will make life significantly easier for the CSM and make the results significantly better for both the customer and for the CSM's own company.

2.3.3 Customer Success Management Software Systems

We will first discuss one core asset that in my opinion all CSMs need—customer management software. Some sort of system for managing customers is the most obvious asset that every CSM needs as a mechanism for documenting and viewing information about customers and activities. The CSM needs this system in order to store and review customer information and to organize and record their work and to report on the results of this work. This might include information about the customer's business, the stakeholders, the specific engagement, what has been sold, progress through the adoption process, targets for customer success, progress toward those targets, what work the CSM has done and so on.

There are three options here. The first and potentially the simplest option is to use an existing software tool such as the CRM (customer relationship management) system that might be already used by Sales. The principal benefit of this approach is a reduction in costs and time to get it up and running and available for use. The problems with this approach are that it may be difficult to modify the system to meet the specific needs of CSMs, and it may be expensive from a per-user licensing perspective if the CRM tool includes many features and functions that CSMs do not require but would be paying for anyway.

The second option is to use a dedicated tool for CSMs. These are often referred to as "health score systems" and several software vendors have sprung up in the last few years, who specialize in providing such systems. The main advantage of this option is that the tool will provide all of the functionality that CSMs need to perform their duties, and will likely do so in a way that makes them more efficient and effective in their role. The problems with this approach are that it will either be necessary to integrate it with existing systems, which may be difficult or expensive, or to store duplicate information on the new system, which is time-consuming to create and maintain and produces problems of data consistency and accuracy as well as requiring additional storage space.

The third option is not to use a software system at all and instead to ask CSMs to create their own manual records for customer information and their own activities and the results from those activities. The advantage of choosing this direction is that it doesn't require any upfront invest-ment and is available instantly. The downside however is that CSMs will have to work out for themselves what information to store and how to store it and then they will need to create some way of doing this and only then will they be able to actually perform their role as a CSM. All of this takes time and effort and thereby reduces the CSMs effectiveness in their role. This option also gives rise to further potential problems. CSMs may not store all the information they need or may make mistakes in storing it that lead to problems further down the line. Additionally, the information stored is likely to be inconsistent between the CSMs in a team and even with the same CSM over time (since they are not following any guidelines for data creation and management). Worse still, this methodology leaves the company open to litigation from customers for both storing the wrong information about them and storing that information without the necessary security protections in place.

Needless to say, this third option is not recommended (though I have seen it in use in more than one company, some of whom have publically recognizable brand names and all of whom have reputations to lose). Of the first two options, companies with a good quality CRM tool, which offers functionality specifically for customer success management, may find the first option to be more effective. In either case my recommendation for new or relatively immature customer success teams is to keep your software for CSMs simple at first. Complexity breeds inefficiency, especially at first, which is precisely when what is needed most is results to prove the value of customer success to the rest of your business and to start generating increased revenues from customers in order to pay for the costs associated with the new department.

2.3.4 The Problem with Too Much Data Entry

Do not get your CSMs too wrapped up in data entry and complex reporting—especially when they are also learning their role and gaining important experience in the field. Instead, use the simplest possible system you can get away with, and choose something which enables you to grow its sophistication over time as your team's needs grow. Another advantage of the "keep it simple at first" approach is that you will likely find that as your customer success department matures so you will learn more about your true data storage and reporting needs. With this approach you leave the door open to adapting your system to meet your as yet unknown future requirements, rather than getting locked into a more expensive system that you may ultimately find either provides functionality you do not require or does not provide the functionality you do require.

Further discussion on this topic can be found in Chapter 10.

2.3.5 Other Resources for CSMs

Having discussed one key asset—the customer management system—let's turn our attention to resources. Many job roles are about repetitive performance of fairly simple tasks or functions and workers in those roles usually follow prescribed processes to create the outputs they are tasked with producing. An example of such a role would be a production line worker in a factory or a picker and packer in a warehouse. Other jobs require a greater or lesser element of creative think-ing and/or autonomous decision-making on the part of the worker, yet still the methodology used to create the outputs will remain fixed and prescribed. Examples of this sort of role might be software development or share trading. By necessity customer success management is a lot more variable in terms both of *what* outputs will be created and *how* those outputs will be produced, and as such it is very much harder to be prescriptive about the role. This is one reason why it is difficult for first jobbers (typically young people fresh out of college and with no previous work experience) to perform well as CSMs until they have spent time gaining experience (especially customer-facing experience) in other more prescriptive roles first. In essence, the CSM has to figure out both what to do and how to do it for themselves, and in each customer engagement the rules will change and the CSM will need to at least some extent to go back to the drawing board and reinvent their role.

This is simply the nature of customer success management and is not necessarily a bad thing, so long as you employ people who have the creative problem-solving skills needed to work out what they should do and the self-discipline required to get on and do those things. However, what is not desirable is that the poor old CSM has to start from scratch and reinvent the wheel every time they kick off a new customer engagement. The fact that there is much variation in what CSMs need to do between different customers and even between different engagements with the same customer does not mean that everything that needs to be done is unique. In fact, there are patterns of similar tasks to fulfill similar needs that can be templated so that the CSM can then draw upon and use these templates as a resource whenever such a task is encountered.

2.3.6 Using Pre-Created Templates

What should be templated? The value of a template lies in its quality of reusability, allowing an activity to be performed multiple times, each time maintaining a consistent methodology, ensuring a consistent level of quality and providing maximum efficiency in terms of time and effort involved in completing the activity.

Questionnaires and tools perform slightly different (though often overlapping) tasks. A questionnaire is used in research tasks to uncover and document the necessary information needed for a particular purpose. The use of a questionnaire helps to ensure that all of the right questions get asked and all of the necessary information gets discovered and recorded, with minimal wasted time in pursuing unnecessary information. Once completed, the questionnaire also serves as a way of recording the information and making it available to others within the team. It can also be reviewed and updated at any time to keep it fresh and relevant. Information from previous questionnaires can serve as great starting points for information analysis exercises and for planning activities.

2.3.7 Using Tools for Analyzing Information

Tools are more specifically used to analyze information. When you use a tool, the information might already be known, in which case no new information is uncovered. However, the tool is an aid to creative thinking and to problem-solving. The tool is a visual aid that presents information in a different way to just simply a list. It is this presentation of information that makes the tools so powerful, as it enables the CSM to spot patterns and pattern disruptions and to find similarities and differences. In short, the power of the questionnaire is in the way which information is *ordered* and the power of the tool is the way in which information is *presented*. That said, questionnaires do also present information and tools do also order information, hence the overlap.

In terms of resources then, what the CSM ideally needs is a range of templated questionnaires and tools that enables them to repeatedly perform the types of information research and analysis tasks that they commonly come across, to maintain standards of consistency, quality and efficiency both as an individual CSM and across the entire customer success team. The specific templates that I recommend CSMs use are shown and discussed in detail from Chapter 5 onwards which deal with the recommended activities that CSMs perform within each phase of the Practical CSM Framework. These tools can be accessed from the Downloads section at www. practicalcsm.com.

2.4 How Will You Plan and Manage Your Time?

2.4.1 Managing Time Is a Critical Skill

Time management is critical in any job role. In many roles time management is performed simply by clocking in and out of the office, factory or other place of work and getting on with the allotted tasks. The CSM however cannot just "get on with it." First, they have to work out what to do and how to do it. This in turn requires a consideration of all the options and then a prioritization of those tasks that are found to be desirable or necessary to have performed. Then time to perform each task needs to be allocated into the CSM's schedule based upon its priority and needs, not forgetting of course to leave plenty of unallocated time for all those things that are as yet not known about but which will inevitably need to be dealt with when they do become known about.

2.4.2 General Rules for Time Management

Here are some general rules about planning and managing time for CSMs. These rules could also be considered to be a series of filters, which you apply one after the other:

Rule 1: Prioritize Activity Based Upon Your Company's Customer Success Strategy

This first rule is what ensures that the CSM remains relevant to their own company's success. Needless to say, this rule can only be followed if the CSM actually knows what their company's customer success strategy is. If you do not know your company's customer success strategy then please make it your number one priority to find out what it is. Applying the rule is very straightforward. Simply ask the question "*which activities that it is in my power to take will contribute the most toward the fulfillment of my company's customer success strategy?*" Once you have filtered out those things that do not contribute toward the fulfillment of your company's customer success strategy, you can then prioritize the rest by placing those that contribute the greatest higher up in your list than others.

The result of applying Rule 1 should be a list of activities in priority order, where the activities that contribute the most toward the fulfillment of your company's customer success strategy are at the top of the list, the activities that contribute the least toward the fulfillment of your company's customer success strategy are at the bottom of the list and anything which does not contribute at all toward the fulfillment of your company's customer success strategy has been removed from the list.

Rule 2: Prioritize Activity Based Upon Practical Considerations

Some activities (or the resultant outputs from those activities) have best before…or must be completed by…dates attached to them. Obvious examples are meetings—you cannot turn up to a meeting 2 days late, you have to turn up to it at the date and time the meeting is scheduled to take place on. Another example might be a report which you need to complete in order to hand it in to a manager by an agreed deadline. Other activities may produce outputs that are necessary for other things to happen and these are referred to as dependencies. An example might be the research on a product you might need to do before your initial customer meeting. Another example might be the completion and approval of an adoption roadmap before the adoption activities themselves can occur. Where there are practical considerations of time or dependency this needs to be taken into consideration.

To apply this rule the CSM should re-prioritize their activity list to allow for these considerations, so that items that must be done by a certain date or that enable other things to happen are moved up the list as necessary. The result of applying this rule is a revised list with new priorities based upon this additional information.

Rule 3: Keep Your Customers Satisfied

Customer satisfaction is not the number one concern for CSMs and hence this features as Rule 3 rather than Rule 1. But nevertheless customer satisfaction is important to CSMs, just as it is to any other customer-facing role, and as such it needs due consideration. Customers are not concerned about your company's customer success strategy, nor are they concerned about whether or not you are successfully balancing your time between their needs and the needs of other customers you might also be the CSM for. All they are focused on is their own needs for their purchases to be successful, and we need to make sure that we are able to reassure them at all times that we are working with them toward the fulfillment of their company's outcome requirements. This may well include routine meetings to communicate progress and discuss next steps, or it may include the generation of reports to be sent to key stakeholders. It might also from time to time include the kicking off of certain activities so that progress is being seen to be made, even if you may be planning to actually complete those activities at a later date.

While I most definitely do not advocate ever lying to a customer in any circumstances, sometimes perception is just as important as reality in keeping customers satisfied and the fact that they can see you have kicked off an activity may be all that it takes to reassure them that you are on the case and looking after their interests.

To apply this rule the CSM should again re-prioritize their activity list to allow for customer concerns and add any further activities into the list as necessary, so that customer's concerns and requirements are satisfied as best as possible. The result of applying this rule is another revised list with new priorities based upon this further additional information.

Rule 4: Determine Your Unscheduled Time Needs

The next consideration should be the amount of time you need to set aside for unplanned activity that will need to be dealt with on an as-it-happens basis. This might include dealing with requests for information from the customer, your manager or your colleagues, taking on new tasks that were not previously known about, attending meetings that were arranged at the last minute, responding to emergencies and generally dealing with whatever occurs in a timely fashion. Of course just because someone requests your time, doesn't mean you have to give it. So, for example, you might be invited to a meeting but you may decide that attending that meeting is not the best use of your time. Discernment as to what really is important (based upon Rules 1–3) is very important if you want to manage your time wisely. Personally, I like to calculate a percentage of my time to allocate to unplanned tasks. How much that percentage might be will depend upon your specific role. It might be as much as 50% or more or it might be as low as 10%. If you're not sure, choose something in-between such as 20%–30% and then adjust the number over time as you learn from your experiences.

The result of applying Rule 4 is simply an amount (or percentage) of time to allocate to unplanned tasks when you are filling your diary.

Rule 5: Determine Your Routine Activity Requirements

The final consideration for calls upon your time is the routine stuff. This includes such mundane but essential activity as filling in expense forms, reading and dealing with emails, answering the phone, attending weekly team meetings, documenting activity on corporate systems and so on. This is the type of stuff that can easily overwhelm your diary if you allow it to, so you need to be careful about what activities you engage in, always asking the question "is this really essential, or is it a distraction from what I should really be doing?." You might also want to consider career development activities such as training and coaching activities within this rule. Taking time to read this book, for example, could be incorporated as a Rule 5 activity.

Once you have completed Rule 5 you should know the amount of time to allocate to planned routine tasks when you are filling your diary.

Now that you have applied all five rules you can go to your diary or scheduling system and start filling it in, starting with the prioritized Rule 1 and 2 stuff and then working other activities from Rules 3 to 5 in as appropriate. The secret of this system is that you must review it to learn where your diary management is working well and where you need to make proactive changes to it in order to address any issues. A good idea is to color code activities so that you have a very immediate visual aid to see how much of your day, week, month or quarter is devoted to your prioritized core success strategy activity, how much to maintaining customer satisfaction levels, how much to unplanned activities and how much to routine activities. This makes it a lot easier to review your time management and where necessary address any scheduling issues that are causing problems.

2.5 Internal Evangelization of Customer Success Management

2.5.1 Explaining Customer Success Management to Your Colleagues

An important point to bear in is that if customer success is still relatively new in your company you may well find some confusion, misunderstanding, ignorance or even hostility toward you as a CSM from some of your own colleagues in other roles—particularly customer-facing ones. This is only to be expected and the best CSMs recognize it and are prepared for it. It may be necessary for you to explain your role and where you fit within the wider picture in a way that is nonthreatening and that makes sense to the person who you are talking to. This internal evangelization of the role and purpose of customer success management is an important task for CSMs to get good at, and practicing and honing your skills in front of your own colleagues is not such a bad preparation for doing the same thing with customer stakeholders.

Chapter 3

Customer Success Management Tasks, Tools and Techniques

3.1 The RAPAE Task Model—A Way to Categorize CSM Activities

3.1.1 Getting to the Important Stuff Quickly

In Chapter 2, we discussed how CSMs can manage their time by applying a series of rules as filters to enable prioritization of more essential tasks over less important ones. Of course, regardless of how important they are, all tasks need to be performed eventually, so another useful way of thinking about task management is by thinking about each customer engagement as an overall project and categorizing the activities within that engagement by *type*. This can be helpful for the CSM because in customer success management it can be easy to get caught up in one or two *types* of activity which then dominate the CSM's schedule, leaving insufficient time for other activity types which may be just as essential or even more important for making the engagement successful.

3.1.2 Categorizing Activity by Type

There are many different tasks that CSMs need to complete over the course of an engagement with a customer, but they can all be classified into just five *task categories* using the RAPAE model. The RAPAE model categories are Research, Analysis, Planning, Action and Evaluation. By considering how they are dividing their time between these five aspects of their work, CSMs can calculate which types of tasks they or others who they are working with on the engagement may be spending too much or too little time on. This insight enables CSMs to adjust activity to improve productivity within the engagement. Thinking about tasks in this way and proactively adjusting the focus of activity based upon the RAPAE task model can bring substantial productivity benefits to you as a CSM. The RAPAE task categories are simple to understand and are described in Table 3.1.

Table 3.1   RAPAE Task Categories

Task	Description
Research	Finding out (and where necessary validating) information relevant to the engagement
Analysis	Classifying and studying the information to both understand and contextualize it
Planning	Determining what actions need to take place, in what order and with what qualities
Action	Executing the plan by carrying out the planned activities in the right order and to the right quality
Evaluation	Measuring results to track and report on progress and to determine further needs

3.1.3 The Benefit of Using the RAPAE Model

The point of a model is to simplify the complexities of reality into something that is easy to understand and follow, which in turn then helps us to make good quality decisions—in this case around management of activity. Note that in this model the use of the term *Action* specifically refers just to those activities that have been included in the plan, rather than to *all* activities.

As you will see from the table, there is a logical order to the tasks within the model based upon the concept of dependencies:

1. You cannot evaluate the success of an activity until after the actions have been taken
2. It makes sense to formulate a plan to ensure that time is spent performing the right actions
3. Before a good quality plan can be formulated it is necessary to analyze the situation to determine what needs to be done
4. Finally, one cannot analyze information that is not yet known or has not been validated as accurate.

3.1.4 Iteration throughout the Engagement Lifecycle

Despite this logical order or flow of tasks from *Research* through to *Evaluation*, this does not mean that the RAPAE model should be seen in a purely linear sense. The model should be considered less as a linear progression (or a simple list of tasks to perform once in sequence), but rather as a continuum of tasks that the CSM will iterate around and between many times throughout the lifecycle of any one customer engagement. For example, it is often the case that once sufficient research has been conducted the CSM will move on to the analysis of that information as a natural and logical sequence of tasks. However, it is not uncommon for the CSM to realize during the analysis of that information that some of the information that they need to know is not yet known in sufficient detail or perhaps some other information is also required in order to build up a complete picture of the situation. In this case, the CSM may need to go back to the research stage to uncover and/or validate further information before proceeding again to the analysis stage.

This concept of uncovering more tasks to perform in preceding (or indeed later) stages of the model works equally at all stages of the model. So, for example, the CSM might sometimes move forwards from *Planning* to *Action*, but at other times might need to move back to *Analysis* or even go all the way back to *Research* again, before jumping forward again to *Planning* and ultimately to *Action*.

In addition, once the CSM has reached the evaluation stage, the results from this evaluation may well indicate shortfalls (expected or otherwise) that now need to be addressed through further cycles through the RAPAE model—either in its entirety from *Research* through to *Evaluation* or by jumping directly to those stages that the CSM recognizes as needing more attention. A not uncommon result of iterating through the RAPAE model is therefore an understanding of the need to iterate through the model *again*, each time getting closer to the ultimate desired outcomes.

3.1.5 Spending Time Where It Is Most Needed

An important consideration with the RAPAE model is the division of a CSM's time between these five different task categories. Although all five task areas are equally essential for CSMs to accomplish, the performance of only one of the five categories actually leads to any real-world change for the customer, and that category of course is *Action*. CSMs should therefore attempt to reduce their time spent performing tasks from within the other categories to the bear minimum in order to maximize the time they have available to perform tasks within the Action category. Figure 3.1 illustrates how this might look from the perspective of the percentage of time a CSM might spend performing tasks within each category, although the actual time spent will of course vary (sometimes wildly) between different customer engagements and between different stages within any single customer engagement.

Again, it is up to the CSM to determine what needs to be done and to allocate their time accordingly. However, the purpose of the RAPAE model is to focus the CSM onto the most impactful tasks—the *actions*—while helping them to make good quality decisions around what

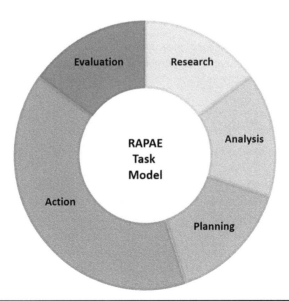

Figure 3.1   The RAPAE task model.

other tasks from research, analysis, planning and evaluation categories also need to be accomplished in order to support those actions. To do this, CSMs need to proactively monitor their activity and determine how much time they are spending on each task category and then make adjustments where necessary.

3.2 Research, Analysis and Planning as Enablers of Action

3.2.1 The Secret Is in the Preparation

Research, analysis and planning are essential tasks for the CSM to perform throughout the entire ongoing customer engagement. This is because it is only through performing sufficient research, analysis and planning that the CSM will be positioned to take the right actions—the right actions are those that will bring the greatest benefits to both the customer and the CSM's own company in the shortest space of time.

The following is a good maxim to bear in mind:

> The deeper your understanding of the customer, their initiative and your solution, the better you can perform your role as a CSM.

Deepening our understanding of the customer provides us with the context that we need to help that customer make high-quality decisions around how they can generate value from our solution. Increasing our understanding about the specific initiative that our solution has been purchased to support will enable us to help the customer decide what the focus of time, energy and precious resources should be and in what order activities should occur. A high level of understanding of our own solution enables us to provide the customer with the information they will need to make high-quality decisions around how that solution should be adopted and consumed.

CSMs need to ensure they spend time in gaining a sufficient level of understanding in all three of these areas, in order to be useful to their customers. When performing research and analysis, it is sometimes difficult to know what types or areas of information needs to be researched and analyzed and to what depth the CSM should go for each area. Time could easily be wasted researching and analyzing unimportant information, but conversely a sufficiently broad and deep understanding of the situation could be prevented by *not* researching and analyzing the *right* information.

3.2.2 Cutting through the Complexity

Performing research, analysis and planning activities can be very time consuming, and it is safe to say that few if any CSMs have the luxury of too much time on their hands and not enough things to do. Generally speaking, the CSM will be expected to deal simultaneously with multiple customer engagements and will be under a fair amount of pressure to get all their tasks completed within the necessary timeframes. As well as workload pressure from within their own organization, the CSM also needs to recognize that from each customer's perspective, time is also a precious commodity. Customers need to realize a return on their investment in our solution, and the sooner they begin to experience that ROI, the less risk they will experience and the greater the total ROI is likely to be. *CSMs therefore need to carefully balance the trade-off between utilization of time for research, analysis and planning activities versus taking action as quickly as possible in order to bring results forwards.*

Research, analysis and planning are key tasks that CSMs will regularly perform, so it is important that we hit the right balance between not enough and too much. A key concept and general rule of customer success management are this:

> Perform enough research to gather the information you need to analyze…in order to create a plan that enables you to take the actions you need to take…in order to generate value as soon as possible.

That's quite a long sentence, so let's break it down.

The first part of the sentence states that we should: "Only perform enough research to gather the information you need to analyze…". In other words, instead of researching anything or even everything about a customer organization, CSMs need to be more selective about the use of their precious time. Before starting to do research, CSMs should already have a good idea as to what it is they need to know about the customer.

So how do we work out what we need to know? This comes in the second part of the sentence: "…in order to create a plan that enables you to take the actions you need to take…". We need to keep in mind the purpose of our research, which is to formulate a high-quality plan of action. In other words, the tasks of both research and analysis are performed purely in order to support the task of planning. Knowing what activities you intend to plan for will therefore help you to determine what information you need to research.

Planning is the task that enables the CSM and others to perform the right actions in the right order to the right quality and within the right timeframe. But what actions are the "right actions" to perform? This is explained in the final part of the sentence: "…in order to generate value as soon as possible." This last part of the sentence describes what enables us as CSMs to maintain a laser-like focus on value creation at all times throughout our engagement. Understanding what needs to be done in order to generate value *as soon as possible* is a core aspect of becoming a successful CSM.

3.3 Understanding the Critical Path

3.3.1 *What Is the Critical Path?*

As stated above, as a general rule, CSMs who spend too much time performing research, analysis and planning tasks will underperform in their CSM role because they will not be spending sufficient time on performing action-related tasks that lead to real-world change. On the other hand, CSMs who spend too little time performing research, analysis and planning tasks will also underperform in their CSM role because they will not be performing the right action-related tasks, at least not in the right way, in the right order or to the right quality standard.

Customers need to generate value from our solutions, and they quite understandably want to see this value being generated as soon as possible. Our job as CSMs, therefore, is to help our customers to get to this value creation as soon as it is practicable to do so. What we are looking for in order to do this is to follow the critical path to customer value creation, which comprises just those tasks that need to be completed in order for value to begin to be generated and nothing else.

The concept behind your research at this stage then is to uncover all of the information you will need to know about the customer to get them successfully onboarded, but no more. What might that include? Of course, it will depend entirely upon what you already know. So if, for example, this is your first engagement with this particular customer and it is also the first time you have been involved with the adoption of and value creation from the particular solution they have purchased then it is likely that you will have a lot more research to do than if this was an existing customer whom you have known and worked with for multiple years that has purchased a solution that you are already very familiar with and which you have helped many other customers to generate value from in the past.

Even if the latter situation is true, you are advised to still go through the research process, albeit at a more superficial or summarized level. This is because things change. Customers change in terms of their vision, their strategies, their initiatives and their personnel, and our own solutions change as new versions or editions with new or amended features and functionality are created and released to replace the old ones.

3.3.2 Widening Out the Concept

Please note that in the RAPAE model tasks within each task type are not limited to those undertaken by the CSM. It may well—indeed, it generally should be—the case that the customer's stakeholders or the CSM's own colleagues will also be responsible for some of the research, analysis, planning and action taking as well as evaluation afterwards. The CSM in their functions as an informal leader and project managers should consider *all* tasks relating to the engagement, not just their own and do their best to help everyone through the balancing act of performing sufficient research, analysis and planning to enable effective action taking as soon as possible.

3.4 Introducing the Practical CSM Framework

3.4.1 A Step-By-Step, Repeatable Process

In Chapter 2, we discussed ways for CSMs to think about and manage their time in general based upon applying a series of rules that enable the CSM to prioritize more essential activities over less important ones. In the first section of this chapter, we reviewed the RAPAE model which gives us a mechanism for keeping the focus on getting to the Action tasks within a customer engagement as soon as possible in order to make a real-world difference. Hopefully, you now feel that have some useful rules and concepts which you can apply to manage and prioritize your own and others' time, so for the remainder of this book we are going to focus on understanding and performing the tasks themselves.

In this section, we will overview the Practical CSM Framework (PCSMF) and in later chapters we will review the tasks within each phase contained inside the framework in detail. The PCSMF will serve as an entire structure within which all activity relating to a customer engagement can be found. The advantage of using a framework is that all of the work of calculating what tasks need to be performed, how they should be accomplished and in what order they should be carried out has already been done. This provides several distinct benefits. Firstly, it increases productivity, since the CSM can now get on and perform the tasks without having to do any of the above thinking and working out beforehand. Secondly, it increases quality, since it ensures that best practice is followed at all times. Thirdly, it increases consistency both from the perspective of one CSM over the span of multiple customer engagements and of multiple CSMs within a team. In essence, by using the PCSMF you can get to work more quickly, while simultaneously being assured that you are doing the right things in the right way to get the best possible results.

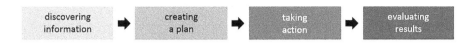

Figure 3.2   The customer engagement journey.

Figure 3.3   The Practical CSM Framework.

3.4.2 Practical Guidance

The purpose of the PCSMF is to provide the CSM with practical guidance through the lifecycle of a typical customer engagement. A typical customer engagement follows a predictable pattern or journey which starts with activities relating to discovering and validating information, moves into decision-making and planning, proceeds from there into taking the actions that were set out in the plan and ends with evaluating and reporting on results (Figure 3.2).

The PCSMF simply takes this typical journey and expands upon it to enable a more sophisticated approach to customer success management that yields higher quality results.

Figure 3.3 shows the PCSMF. The framework contains seven phases, starting with Preparation and ending with Engagement Evaluation. Each phase has its own chapter within this book. Each phase contains a series of tasks that need to be completed, and a description for each task together with an explanation for how to perform it will be provided in the chapter for that phase.

3.4.3 Practical CSM Framework Components

Let's, first of all, describe each of the components and explain their purpose. The table below divides the PCSMF into stages of a typical initiative and provides both an overview for each stage and a specific description for each individual Phase contained within that stage, plus it also explains an additional component called the Central Repository (Table 3.2):

Table 3.2   Components of the Practical CSM Framework

Phase	Description
Initial Stage: The early stages of an engagement are about getting things ready—primarily getting oneself ready as the CSM to be useful and relevant in the context of the customer's needs and desires and getting to know the customer's key stakeholders, as well as reaching an agreement on the types of ways the CSM will be able to help the customer with their journey toward value realization.	
Preparation	Before meeting the customer and indeed before performing *any* activity related to a new customer engagement, the CSM should engage in some basic preparation to get themselves ready for the engagement and to ensure they hit the ground running in terms of their usefulness to the customer. The preparation phase deals with what the CSM should do at this initial stage.
Commitment	It's essential that both the CSM and the customer share the same understanding about what needs to be done in order for the customer to realize the value they need to see from the initiative and what role the CSM will play in helping that value realization to occur. It is also important for the CSM to meet key customer stakeholders and to start to develop meaningful and trustful relationships with them. Additionally, it is useful for the CSM to validate some of the information that was learned during Preparation that was an assumption rather than a known fact, and to agree on timings for and pace of engagement to best suit the customer's needs.
Onboarding Stage: The first job that CSMs might be called upon to assist a customer with is to make sure the customer understands what they've bought, why they've bought it and how to use it. In some instances, this may be a very straightforward and simple task. In other (especially multi-user) environments this may be more complicated and require careful planning and a good knowledge of both customer and product/service.	
Onboarding	Onboarding is the process of getting the customer started with a new product, service or solution, with the idea being to help customers start attaining measurable value from their purchase as quickly as possible and to reduce customer frustration around lack of information and/or support to get them going. The Onboarding phase explains what the CSM needs to do to manage this onboarding process as effectively as possible.
Adoption Stage: The majority of a CSM's energies will generally lie in helping the customer to generate maximum value from the products, services and solutions they have purchased. There are two key aspects of this and the first and most labor-intensive from the CSM's perspective is adoption. Adoption means the process of getting the product, solution or service into use so that it is able to generate value for the customer.	
Adoption Planning	This is the process of researching and analyzing customer information relating to who will be using the solution and how they will be using it. This phase explains how to create a high-level adoption roadmap for sign-off from senior sponsors and a detailed adoption project plan to be followed during the Adoption Implementation phase.

(Continued)

Table 3.2 (*Continued*)   Components of the Practical CSM Framework

Phase	Description
Adoption Implementation	The Adoption Implementation phase explains the role of the CSM in helping the customer to carry out the planned adoption in a smooth and orderly fashion.
Ongoing Stage: *The final aspect of generating maximum value from the products, services and solutions they have purchased is Value Realization. This takes over as soon as adoption is completed and pertains to ensuring that the maximum value is generated and continues to be measured and reported on into the future for as long as the customer continues to use the product/service. At some point during this stage the CSM also needs to take stock of the engagement and determine what went well, what could have gone better and what lessons have been learned for future engagements.*	
Value Realization	The Value Realization phase takes over directly after adoption has been completed. Once users are using the new functionality they have been provided with, the value being created needs to be measured and tracked and adjustments may need to be made from time to time to ensure progress toward outcomes continues to be made.
Engagement Evaluation	Every time a CSM engages with a customer the CSM gains in experience. This experience together with any resources that were created for the customer that could be templated and re-used in future customer engagements need to be evaluated and recorded. Lessons can be learned from every engagement to help become better CSMs in the future.
Storage: *It's handy to have everything stored (or at least referenced) in one place so that it can be managed more easily and to make sure it is available when needed.*	
Central Repository	The concept behind the Central Repository is to provide a place to store all information from each of the phases in a central location so that anyone who needs to access the information at any stage within the engagement can do so. Ultimately, new content created and stored within this Central Repository can also be templated for re-use in future engagements if this seems like a good idea.

3.5 How Should the Practical CSM Framework Be Used?

3.5.1 The PCSMF and Cycles of Iteration

The PCSMF is depicted as a wheel or *cycle* rather than as a linear progression. This has been done deliberately in order to illustrate the concept of cyclical work, although in fact there are both linear and cyclical patterns that occur in most customer engagements. In a typical customer engagement there is a linear progression from initial meetings through to reporting on end results, as described earlier in this chapter. This is a fairly obvious progression since most things have a beginning, middle and end to them. However, in addition to this progress from beginning to end it is important for CSMs to recognize that the reality of their progression is likely to be more complicated than that. Typically the CSM will have to revisit previous phases (or even stages) and/or jump ahead to future phases/stages in order to get the job done. Sometimes this is due to outside pressures such as deadlines or budgets. At other times it's simply a product of learning on the job and uncovering new needs or requirements that need to be dealt with but which were not known about at the start. The Practical CSM cycle is therefore illustrative of the need for the CSM to be flexible in their approach and willing to jump forwards and backwards through the phases as necessary while at all times maintaining an overall progression forwards in order to ensure the engagement's desired outcomes are attained.

3.5.2 Tasks, Templates and Outputs

In broad terms however, it is simply a case of starting at the beginning with the Preparation Phase and moving forwards through each Phase, one at a time. Within each PCSMF phase the CSM will encounter *Tasks*, *Templates* and *Outputs* as follows (Table 3.3).

In just the same way as the CSM should work through the phases within the framework, the CSM should also work through the tasks within the phase, moving cyclically forwards and backwards between tasks where necessary but always with the idea in mind of ending up with all tasks achieved. Note that it is perfectly OK for the CSM to decide for practical reasons to temporarily

Table 3.3   Components of a PCSMF Phase

Item	Description
Task	A task is an activity that the CSM (or someone they delegate to) needs to complete. Tasks are displayed in a logical sequence so that the CSM can complete them in the order shown in the Framework. However, it may sometimes be necessary to miss out a task and come back to it, or to jump ahead to a later task, or to partially complete a task with the intention of completing it at a later stage—perhaps when further information becomes available for instance.
Template	A template is an aid that the CSM can use in the execution of the task for which it was designed. The concept of a template is to make it faster and easier for the CSM to complete the task, while also ensuring the task is completed to the right quality and covered to the appropriate depth. Not all tasks have templates associated with them. There are two types of templates: Questionnaires provide a means to research and record information, and Tools provide a way to analyze and make sense of information. Wherever there is a template, the book will provide the template's name and describe how it should be used. Templates can be downloaded from www. practicalcsm.com. It is entirely up to the individual CSM to decide if they wish to use the template or perform the task some other way.
Output	An output is simply the result gained from performing the task. Sometimes this could be no more than the ability to tick the box to say that the task has been completed, while at other times it might be a completed Template. Other examples of outputs would be a commitment from a specific stakeholder or the minutes from a particular meeting. Outputs should be stored in the Central Repository so that they are always available for future reference by the CSM and anyone else who needs access to them.

omit one or more tasks within a phase and jump to the next phase, returning at some later stage to complete the missing tasks. It may also sometimes be best simply to omit a particular task altogether on the basis that it is not required for the particular engagement the CSM is working on. Of course, the CSM might also find additional tasks that need completing at any stage—only the tasks that are commonly found in all or at least most engagements are included in the framework but that is not to say that other work will not need to be completed from time to time.

The framework serves as a guide only. The CSM is still responsible for determining precisely what tasks need to be done, how those tasks should be completed, in what order the work should be carried out, to what quality it needs to accomplished and how long it should take. The framework acts as a reference and start point for the CSM's journey, but it is still just a framework with the details still to be filled in by the CSM.

3.5.3 Gaining Experience Enables Greater Autonomy

Over the course of time CSMs should find that they gain more familiarity and experience both with the framework and indeed with the nature of their work. It may well be that the more experienced CSM starting out with the framework or the CSM who gains experience over time through using the framework might decide that the generic PCSMF as it stands could be modified to suit their specific circumstances and needs better. The author encourages CSMs to go right ahead and adapt the framework as much or as little as necessary in order to make it as useful and relevant to the CSM's role as possible.

Similarly, the CSM might also find that one or more of the generic templates needs to be customized to suit their specific needs and again the author recommends that CSMs who decide this to be the case should go ahead and do so. There is one proviso about adaptation of the framework itself and the templates within it which is to do with working as a team. If the CSM works on their own then there is no issue. However, if the CSM works within a team it may make sense to develop a unified approach to the work that all team members follow. If this is the case it is recommended that adaptations to framework and templates are made at the team level and disseminated to all team members to use, rather than leaving it to individual CSMs within the team to make their own adaptations.

3.6 Getting in Front of Senior Management and "C" Level Customer Stakeholders

3.6.1 The Need to Meet Senior Leaders

As with all customer-facing roles, the CSM needs to get in front of and communicate with the customer's key stakeholders, which oftentimes will include senior managers such as heads of department and even "C" level executives. This is because these are the people who understand the customer's business from a strategic perspective and they are also the people whose sponsorship and involvement will go a long way to ensuring the success of any specific customer initiative that the CSM is engaged in supporting.

The problem that CSMs face is the same problem as that faced earlier on in the overall engagement by their pre-sales colleagues such as account managers and other pre-sales consultants, which is how to get to meet these senior people, when there is no existing relationship with them? Pretty much every course I run for customer-facing professionals of all kinds I get asked this question:

> How do I get to meet more of my customers' senior business managers and/or 'C' level executives?

My answer is always the same, and I have summarized it below because I think it is an excellent question to ask and one that it is worth spending a little time on responding to.

3.6.2 Who Do You Really Want to Meet?

When I was in my early twenties and just starting out in my career, one of the "big bosses" came down from Head Office to give us all a talking to, and a talking to we certainly got. He told us in no uncertain terms that we were not meeting enough senior managers, and that this was why our sales figures were too low. He got quite animated about it—banging the table and exhorting us to "Get out there, pick up the phone and start getting yourselves in front of your customers' 'C' level execs."

Being very young and inexperienced, this encouragement had a profound impact on me. So when I got back to my desk I did exactly as I had been asked. I picked up the phone, called one of my customers (a medium-sized company) and asked to speak to the CEO. I was immediately put through to him, at which I didn't even blink an eyelid, since I was so new to all this that I did not fully realize that this sort of thing just doesn't "happen," even though I had been told as much by my older and wiser colleagues. I explained who I was (we'd never met before) and asked if I could meet him, and he said yes and we agreed a date and time. Again according to all the received wisdom from colleagues this doesn't just "happen," but for me it obviously did—this was easy in fact! Why all this fuss? Feeling very pleased with myself I told my immediate manager about the upcoming appointment, and she also was pleased, and since this was my first appointment with such a senior stakeholder, she offered to come along with me, to which I readily agreed.

When we got there everything initially went very well. We were welcomed by the receptionist, and after a very short wait we were ushered into the CEO's office where he greeted us very warmly and sat us down. Then he turned to me and asked me a question. It was a very simple question and indeed a very reasonable question—one which in hindsight I should have prepared myself for, but which regrettably I had not. "So" he said in a pleasant tone of voice. "What's the purpose of this meeting?"

Looking back at this meeting now always brings a smile to my face, though at the time it was a very awkward 10 min or so of red-faced mumbling between myself and my manager (who was equally unprepared since she had assumed quite wrongly that I knew what I was doing) about wanting to explain what we did and the value we offered, etc.—all the sorts of things that one might say in such circumstances when one is completely and utterly unprepared with anything "real" to say.

Although it turned out to be a short and unproductive (at best) meeting, it did teach me two very valuable lessons which I will never, ever forget. The first lesson is that despite rumors to the contrary it really *is* possible to get to meet "C" level executives and other senior managers of customer organizations—though I am not for one moment suggesting it is always as easy as it was for me on that occasion. The second lesson of course is never to have a meeting unless you are absolutely clear on the value of that meeting—both to yourself and to the person/s you are meeting with. Throughout my career, I have always applied these lessons to the situations I have found myself in, and I believe they have been a small but important part of what has brought me those successes that I have managed to achieve.

3.6.3 Identifying the Right Customer Stakeholder/s to Meet With

Turning now to how the above can be applied, in this part of the chapter we will consider *who the right customer stakeholder really is*, and let's do so by applying that second lesson which I learned, namely:

> Never have a meeting unless you are absolutely clear on the value of that meeting – both to yourself and to the person/s you are meeting with.

The key word here is of course "value." To get at this value, I recommend applying a few rules:

Rule 1: Before arranging any meeting ask yourself "what am I trying to achieve from this meeting?" or you could word it as "what outcome or outcomes do I need to attain from this meeting?"

The point of Rule 1 is of course to focus our thinking on the end result from the meeting rather than on the meeting itself. It's a good idea to write down what you want, perhaps as a sentence or two, or even perhaps as a bulleted list if you have multiple objectives that you wish to attain. Either way, having things written down is helpful. Firstly in considering what you have written you may find you have not completely covered all the angles and there is more that you need to achieve from your meeting, which you can then of course add to the list of required outcomes you have already written. Secondly, it provides the information you need for Rule 2…

Rule 2: Based solely upon your outcome requirements, who needs to attend the meeting in order for the outcomes to be attained?

The point of Rule 2 is also to focus our thinking on the end result from the meeting rather than on the meeting itself, but this time when determining who should attend. This "outcomes first, attendees second" approach is the rational way to do it. It helps us think logically about who really needs to be there and who does not. And it leads us nicely into Rule 3…

Rule 3: For each attendee, you have decided to invite to your meeting, what outcome or outcomes will *they* attain from attending?

Rule 3 is there to consider the needs and desires of more than just ourselves. This may be particularly important where we are going to invite senior managers to attend a meeting, but there is really no reason whatsoever why this third rule cannot be applied to everyone whom you invite. Not only does thinking in advance about the needs and objectives of others help to make your meeting more valuable for those others, it also has the long-term benefit of building stronger bonds of empathy with those others.

Rule 4: Never try to meet with someone (especially anyone from senior management) who you *do not really need to meet*.

Rule 4 is very important. We are often so bound up in the desire to "meet senior managers" and indeed many of us find ourselves under a certain amount of pressure from our own managers to do so, that we can forget this important rule. Always try to think of the meeting from the perspective of the senior exec with whom you are meeting. What will *they* think about this meeting? What impression will they come away with about you and the organization that you represent? Will they resent the time they spent with you, or at best feel neutral about it, or will they consider it as being time well invested on their behalf and from which they gained one or more outcomes? In short, was your reason for meeting with them *real* or could you in fact have gotten the same information from your existing contacts, or indeed did you really need the information at all?

At the end of the process I have outlined above you should be clear both on *who* needs to attend your meeting and *what outcomes* will be attained from the meeting for all attendees—both you and them. You should also be clear that there really *is* a need to meet the person you are trying to meet and you should therefore be confident in moving to the second part of this section, which is where we discuss how you get the senior executive's consent for the meeting.

3.6.4 Getting Senior Managers to Agree to Attend Your Meetings

For the majority of people (sales people, solution architects, customer success managers, service managers and other professionals) who are commonly tasked with organizing meetings with customer stakeholders, the major issue they face is not *who* to invite but *how* to invite them. Or to put it another way:

> How do I get to have a meeting with a senior manager whom I currently do not have an existing relationship with?

This was certainly the problem that I was faced with on numerous occasions throughout my own career. Because of this, I did a lot of research on executives' behavior especially as related to sales meetings, which was my focus at the time. What I learned is that it is relatively rare for a senior manager to agree to meet a salesperson when the proposal is made by cold calling (regardless of whether that is by phone, letter, email or in person). In fact, it is highly likely that they will not even see the communication at all and instead it will be fielded and dealt with on their behalf by a gatekeeper.

However, there is a way which has a far, far higher chance of success—indeed somewhere around a 75% chance of success, based upon my own experiences and those of others with whom I have shared this knowledge. The way to do it is very simple:

> Get the person you *can* meet within the customer organization to arrange the meeting with the person you *want* to meet for you.

How this works is very simple. It moves the problem from being one which you cannot resolve (since you have no way to influence the mind of the senior exec whom you wish to meet) to become a problem which you *can* resolve (since you *do* have the ability to influence the mind of the person whom you can meet).

Now all you need to do is to convince the person you can meet that it is in their interests to arrange the meeting you are looking for. How is this done? In a nutshell this is done as follows:

> Speak the language of the person you *want* to meet when talking to the person you *can* meet.

What this means is that you will discuss issues and ask questions about challenges that the person you *want* to meet faces, even though you are talking to your existing contact or contacts for whom these issues and challenges may be less relevant. In doing so you are showing your existing contact that you understand the role of the senior manager and also revealing their relevancy to the initiative or project that you are involved with right now. What is more, you are also reassuring your contact that if you *did* meet that senior executive you would be comfortable talking to them in that exec's own language and about things that interest and concern them. In other words, you would represent both yourself and your contact well in front of the senior stakeholder and would not be wasting their time. This is important.

3.6.5 Working through a Real-World Scenario

Let's use an example here. Let's say your company has sold a high-tech IT solution to your customer and you are the CSM assigned to help that customer realize the value from their purchase. Your colleagues in the sales team already have a great relationship with the leadership team within your customer's IT department and have introduced you to this team and you have now started to formulate a relationship with them yourself. You are aware that the VP Sales & Marketing (EMEA) is a highly influential rising star within the customer's organization and has big ideas about how they want to grow the company and expand its revenues over the next few years. You are also aware of a highly ambitious target your customer has recently announced, which is to double revenues from their EMEA region within 3 years. You are fairly sure that you could really help this person *if only you could get to meet them*. The problem is you never *have* met them, and your conversations to date with the IT team have been technical in nature rather than business orientated and relevant to the IT department rather than the Sales & Marketing department. In short, you are not at all sure that your existing contacts in the IT team will understand *why* you should speak to the regional VP for Sales & Marketing, nor have any confidence in you doing anything but making a fool of yourself in front of them if you *did* meet them.

The above scenario illustrates a very common situation that many CSMs find themselves facing time and time again. It's certainly one that I get asked about all of the time when training CSMs and indeed other customer-facing professionals from beginners right through to highly seasoned and very experienced old timers. So here's what you do: You request a meeting (or a series of meetings) with whichever of your existing contact/s you think are best placed to arrange a meeting with the person you want to meet, and you use that meeting to influence them over time and ultimately to gain their commitment to arranging the *real* meeting, i.e., the one you really want to have with the exec you really want to meet.

In this initial meeting with your existing contact/s, you need to start talking the language of the senior manager or "C" level person whom you want to meet, and making sure that the relevance of that person's issues and challenges are clear to your existing contact/s. What you are aiming for is to help your existing contact/s see the importance and value of you having a meeting with this exec. Ideally, you want to make it so unambiguously obvious that you need to meet this person that your contacts themselves will end up suggesting the meeting. This has happened to me, and of course it's great when it does, but it's not important either way. What is important is for you to make sure they "get" the point of you meeting this senior exec. This is where the previous work you had already put into following the three rules outlined above comes into play. In particular, Rule 3 focused on the outcomes of others who will attend the meeting, so in considering Rule 3 you will have worked out what value both your existing contact and the senior exec will get from the meeting as well as yourself. You can now use this information about outcomes within the discussion with your existing contact to reinforce the value of having the meeting.

Let's return to our example above. In the previous scenario, we said had a good relationship with the IT managers, so we will leverage that relationship now. We will arrange to meet the Chief Technology Officer (CTO) with whom we have a very good (though always to date technically focused) relationship. In the meeting, we mention the recently announced and very aggressive target of 100% revenue growth within 3 years for the EMEA region and ask our contact how the IT team will be supporting this initiative and what impact that will have on their IT. Notice that you have now moved the conversation from general technology to the area of interest to your "target" exec—the VP SM for EMEA. Maybe the CTO has some thoughts on the matter which are very interesting and worthwhile listening to, but in any case at some stage you will ask further questions such as "What will the EMEA sales organization be relying upon your team to deliver for them to support this revenue growth?," or "What plans for using technology innovations does the VP SM for EMEA have?," or "How will technology be used as an enabler for this revenue growth?," or "Who within the Sales & Marketing department will be impacted by change, and in what ways?." Try if you can to get some quantitative questions in as well as qualitative ones, such as "How many more product sales per sales person does this target equate to?" or "What level of increase in productivity will the regional sales team need to achieve in order to hit this target?" These types of questions are usually unknown or harder to guess at from outside of the specific department or organization. Generally, the answer will be "I don't know," but of course we know who *does* (or should) know, right? Yes…the VP SM for EMEA should know. And that of course is the whole point of asking the questions. We want to position it so that it becomes an obvious next step for you to ask to meet this person.

These of course are just examples of questions; it may be that more questions than these will need to be asked and it might not all take place in just one meeting. Over time as you focus away from discussing the technology itself and toward technology *as it relates to the issues and challenges faced by the exec you wish to meet* you show two things: Firstly, you show the *relevance* for you having a meeting with the exec you wish to meet. Secondly, you show your *ability to handle* such a meeting without making a fool of yourself or (more importantly) of your existing contact. Ultimately what you want to prove to your existing contact/s is that there is a need to have a meeting with this senior manager and that you are absolutely the right person to have that meeting.

At this point of course you need to propose exactly what you want. For example, you might say something like "Given that this will have a significant impact on the types of discussions around implementing and adopting the technology that you and I are having right now, can I suggest that you arrange a meeting with your VP SM for EMEA so that the two of us can ask them exactly what their plans are for this growth and what ideas they have for how they wish to see your IT organization support those plans?" Once you feel you have proved both the value of a meeting and your ability to hold your own in front of the stakeholder *do not wait any further*—it's time to ask for the meeting.

You have now asked the person you *can* meet to arrange a meeting on your behalf (and indeed their own behalf as well) with the person you *wish* to meet. And here's the thing; unlike other routes such as cold calling which have a very small chance of success, 75% of the time on average, senior executives *will agree* to have a meeting with a salesperson when that meeting is requested by a colleague.

3.6.6 In Summary

Does this system work? Yes it does. I have used it myself many hundreds of times, and so have many others. What is the system?

1. Only attempt to hold meetings with senior executives whom you know actually need to see you because you have already worked out what the outcomes from the meeting will be for both you and for them too. Use the three rules about meetings that I explained above to work this out.
2. As a starting point, rather than trying to contact the person you wish to meet directly, instead, you firstly hold a meeting with the person you *can* meet (i.e., your existing contact or contacts)
3. In this meeting you will *speak the language of the person you **wish** to meet to the person you **can** meet* in order to show them that arranging a meeting between yourself and your target exec

would be both practical and beneficial. This may take more than one meeting or conversation to do, depending upon your starting point in terms of existing relationships and the level of obviousness of the need for you to meet your target senior exec.

4. Rather than relying upon your contact to propose it, take the plunge at what you judge to be the right moment and proactively ask your contact to set up a meeting between you, the exec you wish to meet and themselves.

If this tactic doesn't work the first time, do not give up. It simply means you asked too early and you have not yet shown sufficient value in the meeting taking place. Carry on subtly working on your existing contacts and when you judge the moment to be ripe try again.

Chapter 4

Practical CSM Framework Phase 1: Preparation

4.1 What Is Phase 1: Preparation All About?

4.1.1 The Purpose of Preparation

In this chapter, we are going to take a thorough look at what the CSM needs to do in order to prepare for a new customer engagement. Of course, every customer and each customer engagement will be somewhat different, but while there will be variation in detail between customers and engagements, the *process* of engaging with customers is likely to remain the same or similar each time. Because of this, the way to prepare for this process of engagement can be reasonably well defined and documented ahead of time (Figure 4.1).

It is true to say that good preparation will make a big difference to both the quality of the outcomes obtained from the engagement and the efficient use of time and other resources in getting to those outcomes. In this sense, a customer engagement is no different from any other project which has at least some level of complexity. Whether you are redecorating the living room, launching a new product, performing heart surgery or helping a customer obtain value from the products, services and solutions they have purchased from you, the secret to a great result lies in good preparation. I would suggest that for every hour you spend in good quality preparation activities you may well save 3–5 h of your own and your customer's efforts further down the line.

4.1.2 Types of Preparation

What types of preparation activities might a CSM look to accomplish when readying themselves for a new customer engagement? The focus of their efforts should be on getting a profound enough understanding of what is going on to become immediately useful to the customer *before* they start meeting with the customer. To do this, they need to spend some time in conversation with those colleagues (and with partners if applicable) who have already been involved in the customer engagement to date, and in reviewing information recorded on corporate systems and tools, and possibly in uncovering additional information from elsewhere as well. They then need to assemble and compile this information into some sort of logical order so they can review and make sense of it.

Figure 4.1   PCSMF Phase 1: Preparation.

Finally, they need to make themselves a plan of action for the, based upon the level of understanding about the engagement that they now have.

4.1.3 A Reminder about Managing Time

One point that is important to emphasize is that the CSM needs to keep in mind the concept of the RAPAE model here. What is needed is for the CSM to get ready for engaging with the customer as quickly as possible, so they can begin to add value immediately, although it is also important to make sure that the Customer is ready to begin their adoption journey and to be prepared to start when the customer *is* ready and to move forwards at a pace which the customer is comfortable with. This concept of readiness is especially important in the early stages of an engagement, where the customer is usually very keen to commence adopting and gaining value from their newly acquired products and services as soon as possible. In terms therefore of customer experience, the CSM who is ready to start helping the customer to adopt their products and services immediately upon those products and services becoming ready for the customer's company to use is likely to be a CSM who is perceived in a more positive light by customer stakeholders. My advice as always is that the CSM needs to carefully tread the line between doing enough preparation to become useful while ensuring they do actually start *being* helpful as soon as possible. Enough preparation then, but not too much. Remember that the best CSMs take an iterative approach to their research, analysis and planning work. Once you have sufficient understanding and have developed a good enough plan of action it's time to start taking that action. Further research, analysis and planning can still take place in parallel alongside this action as necessary.

4.2 Defining the Engagement

4.2.1 Defining the Term "Engagement"

A reasonable question to ask at this point might be "what exactly are we preparing *for*?". Or to put it another way, what do we mean by the term "customer engagement"? In a sense the answer to this question goes back to our earlier discussion about customer experience.

Let's take a look at the entire end-to-end process through the eyes of the customer for a moment. From the customer's perspective, their engagement with the vendor (or other technology seller) starts at pre-sales with selecting potential vendors, undertaking initial discussions and scoping their requirements. It then proceeds through the process of requirements analysis and solution formulation, then moves through to the proposal stage. In this stage, a proposal is formulated and negotiated and possibly a trial of some kind occurs, and ultimately the final contract is agreed. The engagement then moves into a delivery stage where products and services are configured and/or customized as necessary and shipped, installed, integrated and otherwise made ready for use. Now the customer either has the product or has access to the service and needs to make adjustments internally in terms of changing their business processes and training their workforce to prepare them for any changes that will occur. Then they can go live and start using the new products and/or services and supporting their workforce while also taking measurements to determine value creation is occurring as desired and where necessary making adjustments to ensure this happens.

4.2.2 The Customer's Perspective

Figure 4.2 shows the stages in the complete end-to-end customer engagement. Note that there may be some small variations in this engagement between industries, vendors and customers but the concept is always the same. Looked at from the customer's perspective they have to make the right purchasing decision, then they have to get the selected solution up and running and finally they have to drive value out of it by using it. For the customer steps 1–5 are purely a means to an end, that end being step 6 (hence, it is marked with a big asterisk) because this is where all the value creation takes place. Think of it this way: Step 6 is really the only step that matters to customers. If they could get to a satisfactory step 6 without the intervening steps 1–5 they would of course very happily do so.

4.2.3 The Seller's Perspective

From the seller's perspective however, the traditional (i.e., not X-as-a-service) way of viewing an engagement would look different. For the seller, it is steps 1–3 which are a means to an end, that

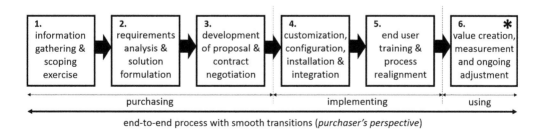

Figure 4.2   Stages in the overall engagement.

end being the closing of the sale which is made at the end of step 3 and the "delivering of the goods" in step 4. All that adopting and using stuff that happens in steps 5 and 6 is an irrelevance since their job is done and now they can move on to helping the next customer. Of course, that is not exactly what happens or how the seller thinks, but it can be how it *feels* for the customer when they get to the end of step 4 and experience a distinct falling away of energy and interest from the vendor (or other sales company).

4.2.4 The Value of Post-Sales Customer Engagement

This of course is precisely why customer success management teams are growing in popularity. The customer success team typically gets involved at the beginning of step 5 and will work closely and intensively with the customer's stakeholders through step 5 to make sure that the step is completed satisfactorily. They then keep in touch throughout step 6 on a less intensive basis, during which they help with measuring, reporting and making any changes necessary to keep the customer on track in terms of value creation. Steps 1–5 will typically take place over a period of weeks and/ or months. Step 6 will typically take place over a much longer period of months or years during which the customer is putting the new products and services to use in order to generate outputs which over the course of time will combine to create the desire final outcome.

4.2.5 The Importance of Smooth Transitions

From the customer's standpoint what they ideally want is an elegant and transparent transition between each step in order to maximize the quality of the end result and reduce the effort involved in getting there. What they do not want to experience is a lack of communication between different teams or worse still any friction between them as they "hand the customer over" between each step. Neither do they wish to be left hanging without any support and wasting precious time and money while the vendor or other sales company gets their act together to provide the relevant people and resources for the next stage. The customer wants a smooth and joined up transition between stages so that they do not experience any frustration through unnecessary waiting or having to re-explain their requirements to a new set of people before those people become useful.

The CSM needs to be aware of this and should do their best to ensure they are apprised of any customer engagements that are currently in step 4 and which they will be the CSM for when the customer is transitioned to step 5. If the CSM knows which customers are in step 4, then they can utilize the time that the customer is in this step to prepare themselves for their engagement with the customer in step 5. In this way, when step 5 finally happens the CSM is already well prepared and able to hit the ground running. No time is wasted, the customer's frustration level is reduced, their satisfaction level is increased and value is realized that much sooner for all concerned. Figure 4.3 focuses on the parts of the overall customer engagement that the CSM is involved with and shows how the phases within the PCSMF fit to the steps in this engagement.

4.2.6 Engagement Pace and Cadence

As we stated earlier, from the customer's standpoint what they ideally want is an elegant transition between each step. Additionally, as the customer moves from pre-sales decision-making into post-sales implementation and adoption, they may well have very clear ideas about the pace at which they wish the engagement to move forwards. Some customers may be in a hurry to get to value realization as soon as possible, but others may have various practical considerations around timing such as

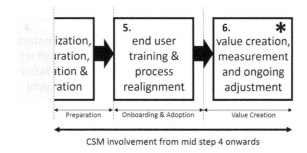

Figure 4.3   Phases of the PCSMF within the overall engagement.

workforce productivity, availability of key stakeholders, cash flow, requirements of parallel projects, dependencies upon completion of one or more additional initiatives and other concerns that may give rise to the customer's need to move faster or slower with this initiative at any time. While the CSM can make the general assumption that the sooner value realization occurs the better it will be for all concerned, it is important to understand that this *is* just an assumption. The CSM should therefore make it their business to discuss engagement timings with the customer to get a feel for what pace the customer needs to move at, and the type of cadence or rhythm of engagement in terms of regularity of reporting, of face-to-face and of telephone or virtual meetings is going to best suit their needs.

4.2.7 You Are in It for the Long Haul

Do not forget that for the most part, the journey will be a long one. It may take many years (certainly many months) for customers to even get as far as breaking even on the investment they have made in your products and/or services let alone to realize the types of overall returns on their investment that they would ideally like to see. As CSM, you will be accompanying them on this journey. What is more, the destination is likely to move further away as you approach it, since the customer will very probably need to adjust their outcome requirements to suit new situational requirements over time, based on additional information learned en route that was not known upfront.

4.3 Accessing Information

4.3.1 Where to Find Information

At this early stage in preparing for the customer engagement you may well not yet have had the opportunity meet the SPL (senior project lead) or other customer stakeholders and to introduce yourself and explain the role of customer success management in helping achieve their outcomes from their initiative. This will not always be the case—sometimes, for example, you may already know the stakeholders intimately because of your involvement in other engagements with the same customer. Other times you may have been invited by the account manager (AM) to come in to meet and introduce yourself to customer stakeholders during a pre-sales meeting. Incidentally, if this latter situation is the case then what you have there is a forward-thinking AM whom it would definitely pay to remain in touch with. Commonly however, you will be working toward your first customer meeting, and indeed part of the purpose of the research you are doing is to ensure you are well prepared for that initial meeting when it does occur.

For now we will assume that you will not be meeting the customer stakeholders until after this initial research has taken place. So if we leave out the route of asking customer stakeholders for the information we want, where should we look for it? The answer is in three principle locations: your company's pre-adoption team (and most importantly the AM), your company's data systems (and most importantly the CRM (customer relationship management)) system and the Internet. Let's examine each of these locations in more detail.

4.3.2 Talking to the Pre-Adoption Team

The first port of call for most CSMs who are looking for information about the customer, the initiative, the solution that was purchased, and the progress that has been made to date should be their colleagues who have already been involved in the engagement. This includes but is not necessarily limited to those people who were involved in the sales process. In addition to the sales process it might also involve people who were involved in design, custom development or other customization, installation, integration, configuration, and the provision of professional and managed services.

The AM is the obvious start point in talking to the pre-adoption team. This is because the AM for a particular customer is generally easy to identify and because the account management role requires this person to have a good overall understanding of all aspects of the engagement. The AM can usually therefore both provide the CSM with a thorough briefing about most aspects of the customer engagement and serve as an excellent source of information as to who else the CSM should go to in order to collect any additional information that may be required.

Whenever you meet other people it is important to recognize they are indeed people, not automatons. This means they come with emotions and feelings, and with preconceived opinions and judgments. They may, for example, be suffering under the stress of a particularly heavy workload right now, or struggling to meet important role-based targets that direct impact their remuneration. Additionally, they may not understand the role of the CSM or recognize the value that customer success management can deliver to the customer and potentially to themselves. In fact, for some of your colleagues they may even see the CSM as a threat to their own success.

Many AMs, sales specialists, design architects, service managers, consultants and other members of the pre-adoption team are likely to be well educated in the value the customer success management brings and are very happy to work closely with CSMs in their customer engagements. However, you need to be aware of potential issues within your own organization where colleagues may not understand the purpose and value of customer success management and may even perceive it as a threat to their own personal success. Where problems do exist, you won't necessarily be able to fix these problems—and certainly not overnight—but by making yourself aware of them you can plan to deal with them as best you can by engaging the necessary resources for problem resolution.

Sometimes it may be lack of education about customer success management that is causing the problem. Other times it may simply be a lack of time available or an unwillingness to share information. Whatever the case, the CSM needs to think about how they can present their role and the benefits it brings to both customer and your own company to those colleagues who are not yet familiar with this information, so that they understand both that it is of value to them and to the customer and that it does not threaten their own position. Most importantly you need to make sure you show the value of working with the CSM to that person in the role they occupy. Where a difficult relationship exists, try to make it easy for them to do what you want them to do. If that means you traveling out to meet them where they happen to be, or you fitting in an awkward meeting time when they happen to be free then so be it. Remember that at this stage in the proceedings it is you who wants something from them, not the other way around. Of course as your customer success organization matures and becomes a valued fixture within your company's overall structure, your colleagues from other parts of the business will start to see customer success in its true light, and treat it accordingly. So if this issue does arise for you, consider it as a temporary problem—one that will only occur during the initial "bedding in" process that is perhaps an inevitable concomitant of the newness of the customer success role.

A final thought on this important topic. Managing people is a critical skill for all CSMs to have. We often think of people management (or stakeholder management) as being all about managing the relationships we have with the customer, but *the management of relationships with others within our own company is equally if not even more important,* since we will potentially need to work with those people on many different customer engagements on into the future.

4.3.3 Interrogating Corporate Data Systems

Much of the information you need may be stored in your company's data systems. This is likely to include systems that store records about customers such as your CRM system. It is also likely to include information systems that store data on and that manage your company's products and services. This might include, for example, customer support systems and in the case of Software-as-a-Service (SaaS) organizations it might also include systems that host the products and services themselves and that make them available for customers to log in and use.

4.3.4 Researching on the Internet

Another obvious port of call for information is the Internet. The Internet holds a fantastic amount of information, not all of which is accurate or up-to-date. It is an excellent source of information for CSMs—especially about customers who are in the public eye such as brand name organizations, government-funded entities and business whose shares are publically traded. For these types of organizations there will generally be substantial amounts of data for the CSM to review. A good starting point is generally of course the customer's own corporate website, but there may well be other sites that contain equally interesting information. These may include websites relating to the customer's industry, websites relating to the financial industry, websites from the news media sector and websites from relevant government agencies.

It is generally a good idea to try to get information from more than one source, as information gathered from multiple locations tends to provide a more rounded and insightful view of the customer than information gathered from just one location. Remember that even if particular information is trustable, they may still have a bias or an "angle" that paints a less three-dimensional picture of your customer's business than exists in reality. In addition to checking the quality of the source of any information you uncover via the Internet do also make sure you know how up-to-date it is. Sometimes information can remain relevant for a long time, but other information becomes rapidly out of date. Be aware of this as you conduct any Internet research.

4.3.5 Validation of Information

One final point about researching in preparation for the onboarding process is about the process of validation. Validation is the act of checking information to ensure its accuracy and completeness. Having information is one thing, but knowing that the information you have is accurate and complete is another. Whenever you research information relating to your customer success management role, you need to be aware of the level of trustworthiness you can place on the sources of information you are going to. This applies to all information from all sources whether internal to your own company, from the customer stakeholders or (of course) from the Internet more widely. We will talk more about the concept of forming and validating assumptions in later chapters of this book.

4.4 Internal Handover

4.4.1 Types of Handover

A great starting point for CSMs to prepare themselves for an upcoming customer engagement is to obtain some sort of handover from colleagues who have already been involved with this customer engagement. Typically this handover should come from the AM or other sales executive who has been actively leading the sales process, but others such as solution architects, service managers and implementation/configuration engineers may also be important to talk to. It really all depends on what your company sells and who is involved pre-customer adoption. If you're new to your company you will definitely need to find out who is typically involved in customer engagements prior to your own involvement as the CSM. You should also find out whether there is an existing handover process or methodology and if so how it works.

4.4.2 Working with Colleagues

Remember that if the concept of customer success management is new or relatively new to your company the individuals you will be getting the handover from may have a limited or even no understanding of what customer success management is or what CSMs do. If this is the case you will need to do some internal evangelization and education as discussed in the previous section above to help them understand your role and to help them to feel comfortable working with you and sharing information.

There is no need to make your description of the CSM's role complicated. An initial "elevator pitch" of one or two sentences in duration might be a good starting point to get the basic concepts of the role across. This can then be followed up by responding to specific questions. The elevator pitch might say something like:

> The idea of the customer success manager is to continue the support and assistance to the customer that the salesperson provided during the pre-sales phase on into the post-sales phase. This support and assistance focuses on helping the customer with their onboarding, adoption and value realization processes. The benefit for the customer is greater levels of value being realized more quickly and efficiently from the solutions they have purchased from us. The value for us is a deeper relationship with the customer, higher renewal rates for annual contracts and more upselling and crosselling opportunities.

The one person who can sometimes feel most uncomfortable is the AM (or equivalent) and this tends to be because they are concerned about protecting what they perceive as "their" account from negative interference. This is understandable since salespeople either thrive or die based upon their sales performance and so of course they will want to protect their livelihood by making sure that the existing trust relationships that they have built up with their customers over the years are not trashed by having someone else coming in and making a fool of themselves in front of those customers. It's a natural concern and one that the CSM should be aware of and be prepared to deal with should it occur.

Just as for ourselves as CSMs your colleagues in other departments will also have busy schedules, so help them to help you by not waiting until the last minute to arrange a handover from them. Instead, give them plenty of advance notice and get something organized into you own and their diaries well ahead of time. That way if the meeting has to be re-arranged you will have time left to make that re-arrangement and will still not miss your own deadline of being available and ready to hit the ground running with the customer as soon as they are ready to commence with their step 5.

4.4.3 Conducting a Handover

If a formal handover process or methodology already exists then make sure you have familiarized yourself with it prior to this meeting. If no formal process or methodology exists then you will need to give a little more thought to how to conduct the meeting. It is important that you get as much out of the handover as possible, so you will need to make sure that you cover everything you need to know. This might include information on the following topics (Table 4.1):

Table 4.1   Handover Topics

Topic	Description
Customer information	Basic customer information including name, contact details and some background on what they do, where and how they operate, who their customers are, what type of relationship we have with them, etc.
Solution and contract information	A description of the products and services that were sold together with any customization, configuration or other professional services sold alongside them and any important contract terms including deadlines, qualities, duration, etc.
Customer outcome requirements	The required or anticipated outcomes from the solution that were specified by the customer or assumed by us, and a breakdown of any outcome commitments that were made by us. Information about any agreed measurements, milestones and deadlines
Our outcome requirements	An understanding of the deal value, both immediate and predicted over the lifecycle term. An understanding of any other anticipated or desired outcomes such as contract size increases, additional sales, and/or advocacy
Stakeholder information	A breakdown of the people who have been, are and will be involved in the engagement on both sides (us and customer)
Third parties	Information about any third-party organizations who are also involved in the project and a summary of their involvement

(Continued)

Table 4.1 (*Continued*)   Handover Topics

Topic	Description
Project status	A summary of the current situation together with any agreed activities and deadlines moving forward. An understanding of how well the project has gone thus far and any known problems
Key supplier contact information	A list of essential contacts relating to each product and service that is contained within the solution that the customer has purchased, including those from third parties
Existing meeting and reporting arrangements	An understanding of how often customer meetings have taken place and their style and format. An understanding of what information is already being reported to the customer and how thus information is formatted and presented
Processes for handling problem resolution	An understanding of how technical support and problem resolution services are provided, together with relevant contact details and authorization information

The order that these are shown in is the recommended order in which to discuss the project during your handover, since there are occasions when information from earlier topics may serve as context that makes it easier to understand information from later topics. However, in reality the important thing is to get as good a briefing as possible and you can always review the information again in your own time later. With this in mind, the CSM should have a plan but should maintain flexibility around the order in which these items are discussed, since sometimes certain information may be incomplete or unknown and may need to be circled back to at a later stage.

We will now take a separate section to discuss each of these topics in more detail, with a particular focus on *why* and *how* to get the information on each topic, as well as *what* information to obtain.

4.5 Customer Information

4.5.1 Understanding the Customer

Understanding the customer as an overall entity could arguably be described as the most general and least directly related to the specific solution that has been sold of all the recommended topics contained within a handover. However, a good understanding of the customer provides a strong context from which other information such as outcome requirements can be understood far better. This is why it is first on the list of topics and it is also why my own belief is that a profound understanding of the customer as a whole is actually paramount for CSMs who wish to work consultatively with their customers and generate some real business value for their customers. Time spent understanding the customer as a whole will help the CSM to appreciate the reasons behind the outcomes that were determined, the decisions that were made around the solution details and the types of challenges that might be faced in getting the solution adopted.

4.5.2 Researching Information about the Customer

Information about the customer should be fairly readily available. The AM is likely to be able to provide you with a sufficiently thorough briefing about who the customer is, what they do and also what type of relationship exists between the customer and your own organization. However, you may need just to take a moment to explain why you need this information and prompt them with a few well-chosen questions to help them understand what information you require from them. Any information gaps can generally be discovered either by referencing your own company's CRM system or a more general search on the Internet, although of course the Internet will not be able to tell you much if anything about your own company's relationship with the customer. If getting hold of the AM or other colleagues to perform the handover is difficult and perhaps if they have indicated that they have limited time available to brief you it may be worthwhile doing this sort of research before your handover so that you can reduce the burden on them. However, it is always worth getting some sort of overview from your colleague if at all possible, since this will include *opinion* as well as *facts* and will therefore provide you with a richer and more three-dimensional understanding than just the facts alone.

There is really no end to the amount of research one could do on a customer organization—especially a larger or more complex one. The CSM needs to bear the RAPAE Model in mind and gather enough information for their purposes. As has previously been stated this may also mean taking an iterative approach and gaining enough of the picture to kick off the engagement, filling in more details later as the need arises. This approach might save some time and is particularly important if the CSM had little or no prior notice about the engagement and the customer is waiting for the CSM to start. Of course ideally the CSM will have made sure they had plenty of notice and therefore plenty of time in which to conduct whatever research is necessary prior to the engagement start.

4.5.3 Types of Customer Information to Research

What we need as a CSM to make sure we know about the company is their basic information—name, location, industry, size, etc.—plus a basic understanding of their position and standing within their industry (i.e., are they an industry leader, are they very specialist or quite generalist in what they sell, etc.) and a basic understanding of what they sell and who their customers are. It's useful to understand the customer's business model in terms of what departments or organizational units exist (such as the company's org chart) and how they interrelate with each other, including how the customer produces its products and/or services and how it goes about reaching and selling to its customers. We will discuss the concept of business models in more depth in later chapters, but for now a basic understanding of the corporate structure and any key partners or suppliers will suffice.

As well as this it is important to understand the current status of the business and the company vision and core strategies. This gives the CSM a picture of both where the company is now and where they desire to end up in the mid to long term. This information in terms helps the CSM to understand at least the general direction in which the customer is headed and perhaps even some of the more specific qualities of the journey that they will be undergoing.

If the CSM is not familiar with the customer's industry it will pay the CSM to spend a little time familiarizing themselves with it, as this is the context for the customer's business—the sea in which the fish swims as it were. Information such as market size and maturity, key players and current opportunities and challenges is very useful as it helps the CSM to be relevant when talking to customer stakeholders. Also, knowing which KPIs (key performance indicators) are important to this customer's industry can be extremely useful. This sort of information is readily available on the Internet for most if not all industries. For example, if the customer is retail bank with branches across South America the CSM might type "retail banking opportunities and challenges in South America" into a search engine. A little bit of exploration along these lines can uncover all sorts of interesting contextual information. Of course if the customer is a larger organization with an established brand name then a similar but more specific search using the customer name may well also yield interesting information about them that you may not get from the customer organization itself.

4.6 Solution Information

4.6.1 What Have We Sold Them?

Perhaps the most obvious information to discover is information about what has been sold. It certainly pays for the CSM to ensure they have a thorough understanding of this topic since they will be responsible for helping the customer to make sense of what they've bought and to get it up and running and creating value for them. A bill of materials or similar list that details on a line-by-line basis what precisely the customer has purchased is a very good start point. However, sometimes the bill of materials is quite technical and it may require some interpretation and explanation by the AM or solution architect who put the list together. In any case, it will only give you a very basic understanding since it only explains what they have purchased and not why or how.

Alongside the (interpreted and explained as necessary) bill of materials, and assuming that the solution is a complex one with multiple components to it, the CSM should enquire about the architecture of the solution. What I mean by the architecture is how the different components of the solution fit together to deliver a particular output or result for the customer. In other words, as well as understanding what each line item is, it is equally important to understand what role that particular item plays within the overall solution. This will give the CSM a more holistic (or architectural) understanding of what has been sold and how it all fits together to generate value. Of course, there will potentially be many highly technical decisions made by a solution engineer in determining solution components that will be beyond the technical understanding of a CSM. This is fine however, since regardless of our level of technical understanding, CSMs are principally focused on business outcomes not technical ones. We need enough of a technical understanding to appreciate the concepts and to follow the conversation, but our role is not to replace the engineer but to work with the customer to get value delivered. Remember that the CSM is not expected or required to always be the "smart" one in the room nor to have an answer for every question that is asked. The CSM's role is to provide access to others' knowledge and expertise as much as or more than their own.

4.6.2 Additional Components

As well as the solution itself there may be additional professional services items that have been sold alongside the solution to enhance its effectiveness. These might include consultancy around requirements, customization or one or more of the products or services, installation and configuration services, and ongoing management and maintenance contracts. Of course, there is likely to be some kind of technical support contract in place and possibly user support as well. All of this needs to be uncovered and understood by the CSM.

4.6.3 Revenue Information

Finally, the CSM should make sure they are aware of how revenues will be generated from the deal. In particular, the CSM needs to be aware of any renewable contracts for services, and expectations as to the lifecycle for these contracts. A significant part of the CSM's duties is to ensure as best as possible that customers renew their contracts. Of course not *every* contract is anticipated to be continued each period (monthly, quarterly or yearly) since some services may be deliberately planned to be temporary; hence, it is essential to understand lifecycle expectations for each renewable service. An understanding of overall revenue amounts from the deal (both immediate and planned) can also be useful as it provides a basis for determining how much of the CSM's time and effort should be allocated to this customer engagement.

4.7 Initiative Information and Customer Outcome Requirements

4.7.1 Understanding the Customer's Initiative

The next aspect of the engagement to research is the reason behind the customer's decision to purchase your solution—the customer's initiative. Make sure you know what the initiative that you are supporting is called and the purpose of the initiative, i.e., what it will achieve. It is also useful to understand how the initiative fits within and supports the wider vision, mission and corporate strategies of your customer's business.

Of course, the most essential initiative information to understand about the customer's initiative is their outcome requirements, since these will be what you will be working with them to help them attain. However, it is also important to understand any significant milestones along the way to attaining those outcomes that are also important to the customer. In addition, there may be other considerations about the initiative that are worth the CSM knowing about, such as technical or business challenges, installation, configuration or customization work, security concerns and business continuity implications. All information of this sort should be understood and documented by the CSM so that when they meet the customer they will understand the landscape of the initiative sufficiently well to be useful in helping the customer's stakeholders formulate meaningful plans for adoption and utilization.

4.7.2 Outcomes

Now let's turn to a more in-depth discussion about outcomes. Customers require outcomes from their purchases. This is only reasonable since they have invested their time and other resources and of course they have invested (and will continue to invest) their money in determining the business case and making the purchase. Now they need to work hard to gain a return on this investment in time, money and effort for their shareholders, their owners and/or their customers or clients as appropriate. This generation of value is very much the central focus of a CSM's efforts, so it is critical to the CSM that they ensure they have as full and detailed an understanding of the customer's outcome requirements as possible.

4.7.3 Capabilities, Inputs, Outputs and Outcomes

In order to understand how outcomes are attained, it is important to grasp the relationship between outcomes, inputs, outputs and capabilities. The word *capability* simply means "the ability to perform a function or task" and it includes the *people*, the *process* and the *tools* that are needed to perform that task, together with the inputs and outputs for it. Inputs are things like raw materials

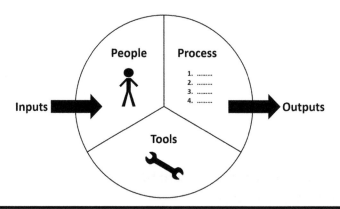

Figure 4.4 Business capability.

or data from a person or previous task, and outputs are the end results from the performance of the task or function such as the creation of a product or the processing of information into a report. The basic concept of a capability is simple: *the people involved in the capability follow the processes and use the tools to turn the inputs into outputs.* Outputs can be defined therefore as the direct results of the actions taken within each capability. All the outputs from all relevant capabilities combine over time to create the *outcome* or *outcomes* that the customer has defined as its target or goal. Outcomes therefore describe the end result that is ultimately attained by performing all the relevant capabilities over time (Figure 4.4).

It is customary to define business capabilities in three levels from the most macroscopic to the most detailed. An example of a high-level business capability would be "Sales," which could be defined as the capability to engage with clients, negotiate contracts and win new business. An example of a mid-level capability within Sales is "Taking New Orders" which could be defined as the ability to take a new order for a product or service from a customer. This is not the only thing that happens within the overall Sales capability, but it's certainly an important part of it. An example of a detailed level capability would be "Taking New Orders for Product X" which of course is the ability to take a new order for a specific product from a customer. Taking an order for Product X might be significantly different from taking orders for other products and services. For example, perhaps there are a range of options for the customer to select from, a range of financing or payment choices to be made, customization work to be documented, a delivery date to negotiate and so on.

The concept of capabilities is often used in both the technical and business consulting worlds to break down an entity such as company into its constituent parts in order to see how those parts fit together. From there decisions can also be made as to which parts (i.e., capabilities) are no longer required, which can be kept as they are, which need improving and which are needed but do not yet exist. This is called *capability analysis* and of course it leads to *capability improvement* that in turn leads to better outcomes for the company.

Capabilities are very powerful since they define everything that needs to be done at all levels within the business and can therefore serve as a simplified model of either the business as a whole, or a department, or even a specific function. Once we know what the business's capabilities are and how they work it becomes easy for consultants and senior decision-makers to determine what changes need to occur and at what level within their business in order for that business to successfully adapt to change, whether that change is due to external drivers such as new customer requirements or updated legislation, or internal drivers such as a low productivity or high costs.

We will discuss how CSMs use their understanding of their customer's business capabilities in later chapters of this book when we deal with adoption research and planning. For now the important thing to grasp is that because capabilities comprise people, process and tools, an understanding of which capabilities are being modified by our solution will also tell us which people may be impacted, which processes are likely to change and which tools might be replaced, adapted or used differently.

Finally, this understanding of how the customer's capabilities will change helps CSMs to understand the differences in outputs between the existing capabilities as they are now and the new capabilities as they will be post-solution adoption. From this information, the CSM can determine how those outputs might be measured in order to calculate and report on value creation and (since outputs combine over time to generate business outcomes) how to track and prove progress toward customer outcome attainment.

4.7.4 Documenting Outcome Requirements

With all of the above in mind, the CSM should make sure they have documented all of the known customer outcome requirements for the initiative in as much detail as possible. At a minimum it should include a description of what the outcome is together with a quantity (either relative or absolute) and a deadline (either relative or absolute) for achieving the outcome. Ideally, the way in which the outcome will be measured should also be included if known. Examples of outcomes documented with this information are given in Table 4.2.

Hopefully what you can see from this is the level of clarity this information brings to the CM (and often to the customer as well) around the targets the customer has for the engagement, and therefore what the CSM needs to ensure happens in order to ensure (as much as possible) that the customer renews their service contracts and/or makes further purchases and/or provides some great advocacy for marketing to other prospective customers.

4.7.5 Validating Customer Outcome Requirements

Sometimes customer outcomes are known for certain (generally because the customer has stated them during the sales process) but sometimes either the outcome itself or some of the data pertaining to an outcome such as the quantity, deadline or method of measurement are not known for certain but have been assumed or estimated. It is important that the CSM is clear what is definitely an outcome requirement as stated by the customer and what is an assumed outcome requirement that needs validating with the customer.

Table 4.2   Outcome Examples

Description	Quantity	Deadline	Measurement
Quality of service experienced by customers after they have purchased our products	15% uplift	24 months from now	Annual customer survey
Reduction in raw materials wastage in the manufacturing process for Product X	20% reduction	By end December 2020	Materials used divided by number of products made
Faster speed to market for new releases of Software Y	Max 6 months between releases	Immediate	Date of release of Software Y upgrades

4.7.6 Primary and Secondary Outcomes

A final point on customer outcomes. Sometimes one or more outcomes are the most important ones and attaining just these outcomes alone might be the driving force behind the purchasing decision. In other words, if those outcomes are attained then the customer will be at least satisfied with their investment. However, in the course of delivering these outcomes, other outcomes may also be attained which were not necessarily the reason for the customer's initiative going ahead, but are still of value to the customer. These could be described as primary and secondary outcomes. Examples of this might be where the primary (i.e., the required) outcome is increased productivity in the Manufacturing department and a secondary outcome from the initiative put in place to support this outcome might be increased customer satisfaction due to reduced waiting times between ordering and receiving their products. It pays therefore for the CSM to always be asking themselves "how else might this initiative impact my customer's business?" when they are researching and uncovering customer outcome requirements.

4.8 CSM Outcome Requirements

4.8.1 Internal Outcomes

As well as the customer's outcome requirements your own company will (or should) have its own agenda for this engagement, and these could be defined as the "internal outcomes." This might be as simple as "make sure as best you can that they renew their contract each year" but it might sometimes be more complicated than that. For example, this might be the first time that your company has sold this particular solution type to a customer in their industry. If this is the case then assuming it all goes well, your colleagues in Marketing might be particularly keen to utilize the engagement as a case study and get a testimonial from a senior executive that they can use as marketing collateral. Maybe this is the first time that this particular customer has bought anything from your company, and perhaps Sales has been working on winning this customer's business for a very long time. Perhaps if this goes well, the customer has promised to consider making further high-value purchases in the near to mid-term and so there is a lot more revenue riding on the success of this engagement than just the value of this one purchase. Alternatively, maybe a product within your solution is brand new and your R&D team is very keen to gain real-world feedback from users as to the product's usability, quality or functionality. Conversely, maybe this is not a very important engagement for your company compared to what else is going on and your team manager has requested that you do not spend too much of your previous time on it but instead focus your energies on some of the other, more important customer engagements that you are also looking after.

These are some examples, but whatever the situation it is valuable knowledge for the CSM to be aware of, since it might well impact your decision-making in terms of prioritizing your time and other resources with this customer over other customer engagements and perhaps even in some of the details of what you do within the customer engagement and how you go about doing it. Some of this information (for example, whether or not this is an important new customer making their first purchase from your company) may be known by the AM or other colleagues who have already been involved in the engagement. However other aspects (such as whether this engagement is perceived as more or less important than other engagements by your manager) will not be known to them and may therefore require further follow up and discussions with other from within your own department or from other parts of your organization as necessary.

4.9 Stakeholder Information

4.9.1 The Importance of Understanding Stakeholders

Stakeholder management is a very important aspect of customer success management, and so it is very important for the CSM to receive a thorough briefing on the people who are involved in any customer engagement.

4.9.2 Key Stakeholders

From the perspective of the CSM a *key stakeholder* is someone with an important role to play in funding, planning and/or implementing the necessary change management activities that will enable adoption of the new solution to occur. This should include (but not necessarily be limited to) those people who are involved in all decision-making related to the customer's initiative, especially the budget holder or holders themselves and may also include those people who advise and influence these decision-makers. The people who will play a role in managing or overseeing the adoption and utilization of the solution should be considered as key stakeholders, and particularly the SPL who will be your primary liaison within the customer organization and whom it will therefore be very important to form a good working relationship with. Another group who might be considered to be key stakeholder are managers of teams or departments whose staff will be significantly impacted by the initiative, since these people may be need to give their consent to make their staff available for training and other activities, and may also be partially responsible for managing processes. The final group to think about as key stakeholders are those people who may be involved in the change management process. This may include people from HR with regard to determining job roles changes and communicating change to employees, from Operations regarding determining process changes, from the Training department regarding any training activities and finally any Adoption/Change Management specialists if any will be involved (Table 4.3).

4.9.3 Other Stakeholders

Aside from key stakeholders, other stakeholders would include anyone who is not a key stakeholder but who nevertheless will be impacted by any change which occurs because of the initiative. This would definitely include staff whose job roles are directly impacted by the change, since they will at a minimum need to be communicated to so they are aware of the change and may also need

Table 4.3 Key Stakeholders

Key Stakeholder	Description
Senior decision makers	Budget holders and other senior-level authorities who are involved in overall strategic decision-making for this initiative
Managers and overseers	The senior project lead (SPL) and anyone else who will play a role in managing or overseeing the adoption process
Department/Team managers	Managers of staff whose job roles will be impacted by the initiative
Change managers	Operations, HR, training and adoption/change management specialists who are involved in the initiative

additional activity such as training or even professionally qualifying to operate new equipment. The directly impacted stakeholders' activities and outputs may also need to be measured in order to help ascertain progress toward the customer's desired outcomes.

4.9.4 Directly and Indirectly Impacted Stakeholders

In more complex situations the CSM may also need to consider those who are *indirectly* impacted. These might include members of the workforce who will not use the new solution themselves but who work alongside and collaborate in some way with those who will be using the new solution. Perhaps, for example, they will receive different outputs from those directly impacted workers which in turn becomes their own inputs for the work they are involved with. You could also argue that people from outside of the customer organization such as customers/ clients or suppliers might be indirectly impacted since they may, for example, receive a changed level or quality of service, a different product, or a new type of request for materials or other supplies. It may be important to know about indirectly impacted stakeholders because these people may also need to be communicated to in some way to make them aware of the changes ahead of time, and also because they also may need to be measured to help build up a complete picture of progress toward outcomes. For example, if our customer wants an outcome of increased customer satisfaction levels, our customers' customers might need to be surveyed both before and after the change has occurred in order to measure the impact of the change on these satisfaction levels (Table 4.4).

4.9.5 Researching Stakeholder Information

The types of information that CSMs ideally need to know about each stakeholder includes name, job role, department, who they report to, who and what they manage, their role in the initiative, their specific needs or requirements from the initiative, any concerns they have expressed about it and their overall level of positive or negative support for it. It is also a good idea to try to understand where there is consensus between the stakeholders that comprise a management or decision-making team and where there could be disagreements that may need to be resolved, and what level of support toward the CSM's own company each stakeholder has expressed. As well as the "hard facts" it would be good to get an understanding of their personality as well, and to be made aware of any particular problems or challenges around relationship management with them that may be useful for the CSM to be made aware of. If they are a key decision-maker then the AM may also be able to brief you on their decision-making style and on who influences their thought processes and decisions.

Table 4.4 Other Stakeholders

Key Stakeholder	Description
Directly impacted stakeholders	Anyone whose role will change due to the initiative, perhaps through changes to tools and/or processes that they are involved in following and/or using in their job role
Indirectly impacted stakeholders	Anyone whose role does not change but who may still have some level of impact such as receiving different outputs or experiencing different service levels

4.9.6 *Managing Your Time*

Just as with the customer's company as an overall entity, there is no limit to the amount of information that CSMs could spend their time learning about stakeholders. It is important to get enough information to be able to start interacting with the customer effectively, but it may well be the case that the CSM can kick off their activities with only partial stakeholder information—though obviously they need to know who the SPL is so they can reach out to that person. Again, the CSM needs to be realistic with their time and bear in mind the RAPAE model when conducting research, analysis and planning activities.

4.10 Third Parties and Project Status

4.10.1 *Who Else Is Involved?*

As well as the customer itself both as an organization and in consideration of its workforce as stakeholders, the CSM also needs to be made aware of any other organizations who are involved in the initiative in any way. This might, for example, include other vendors or resellers/systems integrators who are supplying other products and services that also support the customer initiative alongside the CSM's own products and services. It might also include any third parties who are involved in the change management process such as third-party training companies and change management specialists. It may also include any third parties that are working with the senior decision-makers such as management consultants. In each case, the CSM needs to make sure they are aware of the role of the third party and what level of influence that third party has over any aspects of decision-making. It is also a good idea to understand if there is any competitiveness between the CSM's own company and each third party, as this may impact strategy around communicating with them.

4.10.2 *What Progress Has Already Been Made?*

One additional and very important piece of information for the CSM to gather at this early, preparation stage is information on current status. It's important for the customer to know how far through the overall initiative the customer is. This may include several different aspects, for example, the CSM might need to know that the customization work is now completed, the installation and configuration is completed, but there was an issue with integration of the new service with one particular existing IT system which is holding everything up is expected to be resolved by Date X. Or maybe everything is good to go, but the customer's Legal department has decided they are not happy with a particular clause within the contract, so everything is held up while the two legal teams negotiate the clause so that the contract can be signed. The CSM needs to be aware of the impact of the current status on their own work. In the first example, it may well be perfectly fine for the CSM to get going on the initiative. In the second example maybe they need to hold fire until the issue is ironed out and the contract has been signed. The current status information that the CSM collects should include the facts as described above but should also include stakeholder emotions. For example, are the stakeholders frustrated and angry about what they perceive to be an unnecessary hold up caused by the CSM's company's incompetence? Or are they keen eager and excited to get going and feeling positive about the customer experience they have encountered so far? This stuff is always good to know as again it may influence when and how the CSM communicates with these stakeholders.

4.11 Managing Information Gaps

4.11.1 What Do We Mean by "Information Gap"?

Once you have gone through the process of information gathering it is highly likely that you will have discovered "information gaps." An information gap is simply a piece of information that you need but do not (yet) have. This can happen for all sorts of reasons. For example, maybe the person who knows the information you need has not yet become available for you to talk to them. Or maybe it turned out that the person who should have known this information in fact did not know it, and now has to go and find out. Or maybe this information hasn't even been created yet, and you have to wait until a report has been filed or data has been published. These are just some common examples, but there are many more reasons why it may not be possible for the CSM to complete their research in one go.

4.11.2 Planned and Unplanned Information Gaps

Of course, on top of this there is also the question of the level of need for the as yet missing information, which we have already discussed in Chapter 3.3: Understanding the Critical Path. This was where we discussed the concept of a critical path and the preferred approach of only performing a sufficient amount of research, analysis and planning to enable the required actions to take place. So as well as information gaps that do need filling right now, there may also be information gaps that you do not intend to fill until later on. It is important that you can easily identify the difference between these different gaps. One suggestion for dealing with this is to color code the gaps according to whether they are planned (for example, in green) or unplanned (for example, in red).

4.11.3 Identifying Information Gaps

Identifying one or more information gaps is a very straightforward process if you use the tool I have provided for you, since it collates all research information together in one checklist. To identify information gaps, all you will need to do is review the checklist to spot the gaps, and perhaps color code those gaps as suggested above. If you are using a different system, or if your information is stored in a variety of places then you might need to do a little more work to calculate and document all the gaps, but in any case it is an important task which the CSM needs to make sure they have accomplished thoroughly.

4.11.4 Taking a Realistic Approach to Information Gaps

At the end of the day, the CSM will almost certainly experience what might be described as the law of diminishing returns when it comes to information gaps. Some as yet unknown but necessary information will be relatively straightforward to find, whereas other information may either less critical to know, or less easy to identify or both. In these circumstances, the CSM may decide not to bother attempting to plus those particular gaps—at least not at this stage. As with most things, it will come down to your own judgment as to what information is essential and worthwhile to invest further time and effort in uncovering and what information can be left unknown either for the time being or even entirely.

4.11.5 Filling Information Gaps

Once you have determined what information is as yet unknown but needed to be uncovered, you need to go ahead and "plug the gaps" by discovering/uncovering the as yet unknown information. To do this may require some effort—even allowing for a certain amount of paring down of the list to include just the information that is essential to research at this stage in the customer engagement.

4.11.6 Dealing with "Unknown Unknowns"

Those of us with longer memories and an interest in politics may recall US Secretary of Defence Donald Rumsfeld discussing information gaps during one of his press briefings. In his parlance what we have discussed so far is the process of turning "known unknowns" (i.e., information that we know we need to know but which we do not yet already know) into "known knowns" (i.e., information that we know we need to know and which we do indeed know). However, there is a third category of information which is that of "unknown unknowns" (i.e., information that we do need to know but which we did not know we needed to know).

As you work through the customer engagement you will naturally progress in our understanding of the customer's business, the initiative they are engaged in and your own solution and how it can help the customer to fulfill its stated objectives. In doing so you may well uncover an "unknown unknown"—a piece of new information that you hadn't realized you would need to research but which you now find is necessary to uncover and learn about. This is natural and to be expected. By employing best practice techniques such as the use of the tools provided along with this book you can reduce the number of these unexpected additions, but inevitably they will still occur from time to time. Do not be alarmed by this; instead, simply add them to the checklist and research them the same as any other information.

As your own CSM practice and that of your colleagues within the customer success team matures, so will your understanding of both your customers and your solutions. You will find that after multiple similar engagements you will have refined and improved what started off as generic tools and templates such as the ones accompanying this book into a highly polished set of tools that deal efficiently and effectively with the types of engagements you encounter in your role. Over time you will therefore be likely to encounter fewer such "unknown unknowns" than at first, though it is unlikely that the issue will ever go away entirely.

4.12 Formulating an Engagement Strategy and Roadmap

4.12.1 What Is an Engagement Strategy and Why Do I Need One?

This whole section is a slight aside from the topic of onboarding, as it discusses the concept and uses of an engagement strategy and how to formulate and engagement strategy roadmap. An engagement strategy is simply a high-level plan of action that you have created for yourself to help you manage your activity within a particular customer engagement and to keep you on track with getting the results from that engagement that you and your company (and the customer) desire. This engagement strategy is part of the CSM's leadership role in that it will help to set direction not just for the CSM but for others who the CSM will work with and whom the CSM may need to bring on board in order to gain their assistance in working toward a common goal.

For very simple and low priority customer engagements that do not have a lot of different tasks to consider and do not take place over any extended time period, an engagement strategy might be kept to a very simple to-do list, or not created at all. But for customer engagements with any level of importance and/or complexity and/or any duration over a week or so, it's good practice to get an engagement strategy written down. It means that not only can you follow the strategy yourself, but also if necessary (for example, if you become ill, or take leave, or if you are seconded onto an important project and need to divest yourself of some of your other work) your colleagues can pick up the reins for you more easily should that be needed at any time, since the strategy is documented and the roadmap is there for them to review progress to date and understand what needs to be done next.

4.12.2 Components of an Engagement Strategy

An engagement strategy should be derived equally from an understanding of the customer engagement to date (gleaned from the handover and other research activities as documented in Chapter 4 of this book) and the corporate customer success strategy which details the vision and targets for your company's customer success team. It will not typically be shared with customer stakeholders, but it might be shared internally with other colleagues both within and outside of the customer success team.

The last thing that any CSM needs is more paper work—whether virtual or actual—or more administrative tasks that divert their time and attention away from the all-important customer-facing activities they need to be spending their time doing. With this in mind, my recommendation is to keep your success strategies simple and formulaic so that they are easily created from a template.

Using the PCSMF to indicate stages within the engagement makes things easy. Assuming you go that route, your engagement strategy components might include the following (Table 4.5):

Table 4.5 Engagement Strategy Components

Component	Description
Priority level	Rate from 1 to 5. Understanding what level of priority this customer engagement is compared with all others helps the CSM to allocate their time appropriately
Complexity level	Rate from 1 to 5. Knowing how complicated the customer engagement is will give CSMs an idea of the amount of time the engagement might require
Customer maturity level	Rate from 1 to 5. Knowing how experienced and competent the customer is at adopting the type of solution your company has provided will give CSMs an idea of the amount of time the engagement might require
Customer outcomes	The customer's outcome requirements with a description, a quantity and a deadline for each one
Our outcomes	Your company's outcome requirements with a description, a quantity and a deadline for each one

(Continued)

Table 4.5 (*Continued*)   **Engagement Strategy Components**

Component	Description
Milestones and measurements	Note any important milestones that have been stated by or agreed with the customer (or indeed that your own organization requires). Provide a description, a quantity and a deadline for each one
Preparation activities	Brief overview of preparation needs and estimate of time requirements
Onboarding activities	Brief overview of onboarding needs and estimate of time requirements
Adoption discovery activities	Brief overview of adoption discovery needs and estimate of time requirements
Adoption planning activities	Brief overview of adoption planning needs and estimate of time requirements
Adoption implementation activities	Brief overview of adoption implementation needs and estimate of time requirements
Value creation activities	Brief overview of value creation needs and estimate of time requirements
Engagement evaluation activities	Brief overview of engagement evaluation needs and estimate of time requirements

4.12.3 Roadmap Components

A roadmap is simply a high-level timeline that makes it easy for both you as the CSM and for others that you share your roadmap with to track engagement progress and the completion of key milestones over time. The concept of a roadmap is that it enables you to break the entire journey into a series of shorter and therefore more manageable segments or phases. This makes the management of the journey more easily since at any one time you need only worry about carrying out the activities of the current phase and preparing for the activities in the upcoming phase (Figure 4.5).

For each phase of your customer engagement strategy roadmap you should establish its start criteria, activities, methodologies, completion criteria and outputs (Table 4.6).

4.12.4 Creating a Roadmap

Just to reiterate that the purpose of the roadmap is not to overburden the CSM with more admin and planning, but rather to simplify the task of project management. The recommendation is not to write volumes of information but instead to keep the roadmap as short and simple as possible while of course ensuring sufficient information is provided to make sense of it. Again if the customer engagement is very simple (for example, if all you are doing for a customer is the onboarding of a relatively straightforward service and there's no adoption or ongoing value creation work planned for this engagement) the CSM may elect not to bother with completing a roadmap since it is probably not required. It's up to the CSM to make this decision and also to decide how much or how little time to spend creating the roadmap if they have determined that one is desired.

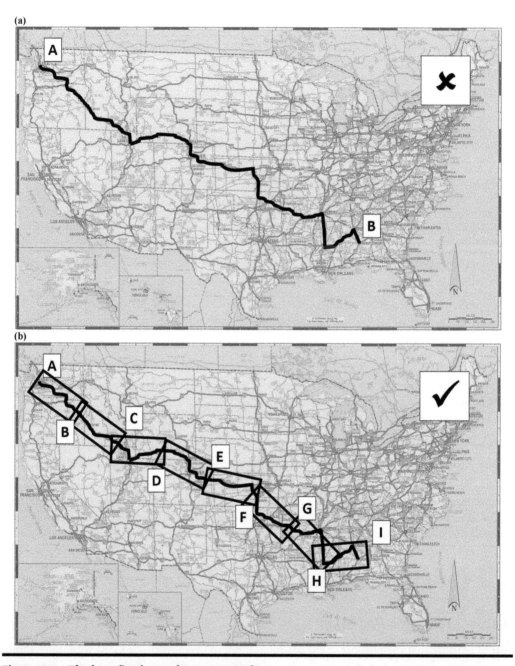

Figure 4.5   The benefit of a roadmap approach.

A good strategy to use when creating the roadmap for a more complex or long-term customer engagement is to create the bare bones or skeleton of the entire journey, but just to focus on fleshing out in detail the upcoming phases—perhaps just the next one or two—and to iterate back to complete more detail on future phases as you move forward through the engagement. This reduces the admin and planning burden at the start and also caters for situations where not all information is known or decided at the beginning about the later stages of work.

Table 4.6 Components of a Customer Engagement Roadmap

Item	Description
Start criteria	The start criteria may often be as simple as the completion of the previous phase; however, sometimes it may include things like a contract signature, approval from the SPL to move forwards, payment from the customer, or completion of some other work upon which this phase of the journey has a dependency
Activities	Activities are those tasks which must be done in order to be able to state that the phase has been completed to a satisfactory standard. If one or more of the activities will be worked on but not completed in this phase then a note to this effect and where possible explaining criteria to determine sufficient progress has been made within this phase should be provided
Methodologies	As well as defining an activity itself the CSM should also explain the methodology for performing the activity. This doesn't have to be detailed, but sufficient to remind yourself (or explain to others) how the activity will be done.
Completion criteria	Generally speaking, phase completion occurs when all activities within the phase have been completed, although as stated above sometimes an activity might be commenced in a phase and continued through other phases. The CSM should make a simple note of the criteria for phase completion, sufficient to remind themselves or explain to others
Outputs	A list of outputs should be provided. There may sometimes not be any outputs as such, in which case the output could be described simply as the satisfactory completion of all activities within the phase. Often there will be something more solid than this. It could be as simple as approval from the SPL that a certain task has been completed, but may also involve measurements taken or ratings given to an activity. It might also include a physical output such as a report completed, a meeting held or a decision reached
External impactors	Anything from outside of the project or initiative itself that may have an impact on the running of that initiative and therefore needs to be managed within the roadmap. For example, no network changes might be allowed during the holiday season, which may lead to a number of weeks where project activity ceases during the summer months

The good news is that you will almost certainly find a strong pattern between each customer engagement in terms of activity to be documented in each phase of the engagement. This means that once you have created your first customer engagement strategy roadmap, you can copy and paste much of the information created in it to other roadmaps for future engagements.

4.12.5 Using the Roadmap

Once the roadmap is in place, the CSM can use it as a guide to current and upcoming activity and can also share it with colleagues in discussions around work that needs to be completed and with their line manager to show progress and agree any details about how upcoming work should be completed and/or prioritized.

As with the customer engagement strategy itself, the CSM should think carefully before sharing the roadmap with customer stakeholders since it may contain activities or criteria relating to the CSM's own company's outcomes (for example, getting advocacy, or getting the customer to be more self-reliant or simply ensuring a renewal takes place) as well as to the customer's outcomes. Of course, there's nothing to stop the CSM from creating a "customer friendly" version for sharing with customer stakeholders if this seems like a good idea.

4.13 Tools for PCSMF Phase 1: Preparation

4.13.1 Preparation Styles

There are many ways to go about completing your initial preparation for a new customer engagement. These range from the very brief and informal, such as a casual conversation with the AM and a few notes about what they have purchased through to the very detailed and formal where a corporate handover process is performed and where the CSM then follows up with further research of their own to validate the information gleaned from the handover and expand that information further. What you actually do as a CSM in preparing for a customer engagement will largely be down to your needs in terms of the complexity and importance of the engagement and the time you (and your colleagues) have available. Maybe to some extent your own personal style of working will also impact your preparation. Whatever the case it is down to you as the CSM to make sure that you are prepared sufficiently for the upcoming engagement.

4.13.2 Capturing Research Information

To assist with your engagement preparation work, I have created a Microsoft® Excel™ workbook called *Customer_Research_Checklist* which contains separate worksheets for each of the research areas described in the sections above. You can download this workbook from www.practicalcsm. com and either use it as-is or modify it in whatever way you wish in order to make it more specifically suited to your own customer success management needs. This might include adding further information you need to research or removing information you do not require, or modifying names to meet your own company's naming conventions.

Each worksheet lists the essential information to gather for that aspect of the handover and provides space to record your findings. Of course, the worksheet format has its limitations so you may need to be a little creative at times in the way in which you organize and record the information you gather. You might also find that in the process of gathering this essential information you also uncover other useful information. My recommendation is to create additional rows with appropriate headings and record this information alongside the essential information as well, so that everything is in one place.

The worksheets within the workbook have been placed into what I consider to be the most logical order for a handover; however, you should feel free to research the information in any order that suits either you or others from whom you are gaining the information. Also, you may find that information from other aspects of the engagement gets discussed in the course of discussing one particular topic, and so of course if this occurs the CSM should simply flip between the workbooks to record the relevant information in the right place.

Another point about using the workbook is that sometimes the information you are researching is already in a digital format, or is in some other format that makes it difficult to include in the workbook (for example, a flow diagram of the customer's reporting structure). In these instances you should instead either summarize the information in the workbook and reference the existing information, or simply reference the existing information if a summary is not practical. The reference might be to a location on another system such as your customer success health score system or sales CRM tool, or a file name and location.

4.13.3 Formulating the Customer Engagement Strategy

I have again used Microsoft Excel to create a simple template to help you develop your engagement strategy. The template is in the form of a workbook called *Customer_Engagement_Strategy* and as before you can download this workbook from www.practicalcsm.com and either use it as-is or modify it in whatever way you wish in order to make it more specifically suited to your own customer success management needs. This might include adding further information you need to research or removing information you do not require, or modifying names to meet your own company's naming conventions. The first worksheet within the workbook can be used to document the engagement strategy details.

4.13.4 Creating the Customer Engagement Strategy Roadmap

To create the roadmap, use the remaining worksheets within the same *Customer_Engagement_ Strategy* workbook that you used to formulate the strategy. There is one worksheet for each PCSMF phase for your use. As noted above, you will almost certainly find a strong pattern between each customer engagement in terms of activity to be documented in each phase of the engagement. This means that once you have created your first customer engagement strategy roadmap, you can copy and paste much of the information created in it to other roadmaps for future engagements.

You will see that for each activity within each phase there is a space for a description and another space for notes. Use the description field to describe the activity itself and any resources needed for it. Use the notes field to remind yourself and others about any special concerns or considerations about the activity that you or they need to be aware of, and to note the name of the person who will carry out the activity if that person is not you.

Remember to keep the roadmap up-to-date by adding more details for upcoming phases as these details come into view. Remember also to check off activities and phases by marking them as completed as you go along.

4.13.5 The Central Repository

Once you have started working on the workbook, make sure to save it (or a copy of it) to the Central Repository. The Central Repository is simply a corporate storage location that is appropriate for saving customer-related information to and which anyone who needs access to it can get hold of it when necessary. Other documents that you create can also be added to the Central Repository so that they are available alongside the workbook. How you organize the Central Depository and what (if any) tools for data management you use are of course entirely up to you.

The CSM should consider carefully who does need access to the Central Repository. Certainly, the CSM themselves and their colleagues and managers within the Customer Success team require access to it. It might also be useful to consider extending full or limited access to others within the CSM's own organization such as colleagues in Sales, Service Delivery, R&D, marketing and other functions that may find a use for some of the information which the repository will contain, as may partners such as third-party service or product providers. Customer stakeholders may also need access to some of the information contained within the Central Repository. Customer and partner access however does need to be carefully limited to just the relevant information they require.

Essentially, a customer success team needs to develop a proper strategy around information management and information sharing which is beyond the scope of this book to define in more detail than this brief discussion. Please note that CSMs should of course make sure they are aware of any legal and corporate requirements in their region regarding storing corporate or personal data and ensure that they follow these requirements. If necessary take advice from your line manager and/or your legal team.

4.14 Summary of Activities and Outputs for PCSMF Phase 1: Preparation

4.14.1 Activities for Phase 1: Preparation

The Activities for Phase 1: Preparation include:

1. Make sure you are aware of upcoming customer engagements and schedule engagement handovers for these engagements well ahead of time
2. Review the *Customer_Research_Checklist* (or other tool you use in handovers) and determine what you need to discuss ahead of the handover meeting
3. Complete the handover from colleagues
4. Perform further research on corporate systems as necessary
5. Conduct wider research on the Internet as necessary
6. Complete the *Customer_Research_Checklist* (or other tool you use to record research efforts) to the level required at this stage
7. Review the information documented within the *Customer_Research_Checklist* and elsewhere to get a sense of the customer engagement requirements
8. Formulate the customer engagement strategy using the *Customer_Engagement_Strategy* workbook
9. Create the customer engagement strategy roadmap using the *Customer_Engagement_Strategy* workbook
10. Store the *Customer_Research_Checklist* and the *Customer_Engagement_Strategy* together with any other documents that have been created in the Central Repository.

4.14.2 Outputs for Phase 1: Preparation

The Output for Phase 1: Preparation is the completed or partially completed Engagement Questionnaire itself plus any other documents you have created. By the end of your preparations, you must make sure that you have sufficient information to move forward to Phase 2: Onboarding.

Chapter 5

Practical CSM Framework Phase 2: Commitment

5.1 What Is "Commitment" All About?

5.1.1 You Cannot Help the Customer Who Does not Want Your Help

The initial task of the CSM when engaging for the first time with the customer is to gain that customer's agreement to allow the CSM to help them with onboarding, adoption and ultimate value realization for the products and services they have purchased. This may be very straightforward for the majority of customers—after all, the service that the CSM is offering does not (generally speaking) cost any additional money and most customers can therefore say "yes" to working with the CSM without too much deliberation. At other times it might require a little more effort to break through any barriers that might exist, perhaps due to a misunderstanding from customer stakeholders about what customer success management is all about, or a mistrust of the CSM's company's motivations for providing this service (Figure 5.1).

It is also possible that the customer organization has a role or function or even an entire team dedicated to fulfilling the same objectives as the CSM—i.e., the adoption and onboarding of solutions and the realization and measurement of value from those solutions. If this is the case, then the CSM might need to explain the specific value that they bring to the table as an expert in the solution rather than in the customer's company.

Better still than a general acceptance of help from the CSM is the customer's specific agreement on what forms this help will come in as well as agreement on the outcomes, timelines and major milestones that will be involved. Ideally, the customer needs to give their commitment not just to passively allow the CSM to help them but to assist the CSM to do so by working together in a proactive partnership.

5.1.2 The Help You Give Must Be Clearly and Explicitly Explained and Agreed

Even when the customer is happy to agree to have the CSM work with them, it's important to make sure that the CSM and the customer understand what they are actually agreeing to. If this

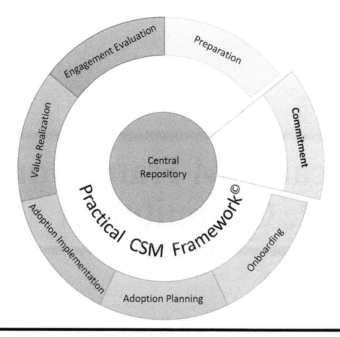

Figure 5.1 PCSMF Phase 2: Commitment.

is not clear from the outset, then problems can rapidly arise when CSMs in their efforts to help the customer either mistakenly overstep any comfort zone boundaries that the customer thinks are in place, or fail to deliver on expectations that the customer has for the types of help that the CSM will be giving.

CSMs therefore need to ensure that their customers understand what types of help are available and why they might be useful. Following this, it is important for the CSM and customer to agree on a few basic principles around what the CSM will be doing for the customer, what the timelines for and outcomes from this help might look like and how the CSM and customer will communicate with each other.

5.2 The Customer Commitment Process

5.2.1 Commitment to What?

Before asking the customer if they'd like to make use of their company's customer success management services, it would help if the CSM was clear in their own mind about exactly what they are offering and how they will explain it to their customers. If you work within a mature customer success team then the likelihood is that your customer success offerings have been formalized and documented, including documentation that can be shared with customers to explain the service offerings to them. If this is not the case then a strong recommendation for any CSM team is to go through the processes necessary to clarify what the customer success service offerings are and to document them for both internal and external use. If you do not have the luxury of working within a formal customer success management team then it will be a good idea to create these types of assets for your own use.

Types of customer-facing documentation might include a short digital or printed brochure to leave with customers that explain the customer success service to them and provides details for how to contact either the customer success team or any assigned CSM directly. It might also include a brief presentation on the company's customer success management services that can either be presented by the CSM themselves and/or by the account manager during the sales process to help differentiate from competitors by showing the level of post-sales customer service that is available.

Another great type of document to be able to share with the customer is one or more case studies that act as success stories for the customer to see how the provision of customer success services in previous similar engagements has led to measurable and provable value realization for the customers involved. (Naturally, these case studies/success stories must either be anonymized or authority given by the requisite customer for their name to be used.)

One final document that can be very powerful is a case study or other customer testimonies that prove the potential value gained by other customers through utilization of the customer success management service. This might be in the form of a leaflet but could also be a video or indeed be in any other format that helps to get the message across clearly yet succinctly. This documentation can be stored in the Central Repository for use by all CSMs and of course will need to be reviewed and updated from time to time—perhaps on an annual basis plus whenever there is a significant change to the services that are being offered.

5.2.2 The What, Why and How of Customer Success Management

Remember that not all customers will necessarily understand the role of customer success management, so the CSM must be prepared to explain that role and how it works. Again, having documentation can assist greatly with this. The explanation does not need to be long or technical, it just needs to put across the concepts of who, *what, why, how and when* as follows (Table 5.1):

Table 5.1 Who, What, Why, How and When of Customer Success Management

Item	Concepts
Who?	Explanation on who benefits from using customer success management services. This should explain which stakeholders CSMs tend to engage with and what value those stakeholders gain from this engagement.
What?	Explanation of what customer success management is. This should briefly describe the service overall and each of its main components. The description should be non-technical and use business language.
Why?	Explanation of the value the customer success management can generate for the customer. This should include both financial and other benefits that customers typically experience from using the service.
How?	Explanation of how customer success management works. This should (again briefly) explain the process and likely timelines involved in a typical customer success management engagement.
When?	Explanation on when to customer success management engagements should occur. This should overview the timings involved in providing CSM assistance with onboarding, adoption and value realization.

5.2.3 The Explicit Offer of Help and Assistance

Alongside the important and necessary general descriptions and explanation around what customer success is, why it can be useful and how it works, the CSM should also be prepared to explain in explicit terms precisely what help and assistance they are offering to their customer. The CSM should review the Engagement Strategy and Roadmap documents they created during PCSMF Phase 1: Preparation to remind themselves of the customer's outcome requirements from their initiative (as understood by the CSM at this stage, prior to actually meeting the customer) and their own company's outcome requirements from the engagement with this customer. This information should help the CSM determine both what types of help and assistance this customer might need and also how much time and effort they can afford to devote to this customer.

5.2.4 The Customer Success Proposal

The CSM might decide to keep their offer purely informal, but customer success management best practice includes the creation of a written proposal that documents the overall purpose of the customer success services being offered and explicitly lists the types of help that will be given, together with information on roles and responsibilities (both CSM and customer), timelines, milestones, outcomes, measurements, communication mechanisms and reporting on progress. It is entirely fitting that this proposal is first discussed and negotiated with the customer before being documented and sent to them for their validation and approval. A copy of the approved customer success proposal can then be stored in the Central Repository for future reference—for example, at quarterly progress review meetings. Needless to say, it is best practice for the proposal to go through the usual legal and financial channels to ensure it is accurate and complies with any administrative requirements, especially if there are any paid for professional services included.

The purpose of the proposal document is to serve as an ongoing reference to both parties. It clarifies what will be done, how it will be done, who will be doing it and how long it will take as well as what the results should look like. Having something that documents these details upfront enables much greater clarity through the engagement on progress being made and value being realized, and of course also serves at the end to show and prove the overall level of success engendered by the engagement. A template customer success proposal titled *customer_success_proposal* is provided for you in the downloads available from www.practicalcsm.com.

5.3 Communicating with the Customer

5.3.1 Meetings as Enablers of Customer Success Outcomes

Without a doubt, the role of the CSM entails communication with many people. Principally of course the CSM must engage successfully with customer stakeholders, particularly the SPL and other key stakeholders who are involved in planning and decision-making, but also with departmental and team leaders whose teams will be impacted by any change. Additionally, the CSM will need to communicate with colleagues including of course the customer's account manager and other salespeople who have been involved with the pre-sales process and other professionals such as solution architects and service managers who may have met and worked with the customer and therefore have useful information to impart to the CSM.

The ability to engage well with a wide variety of people and to form high-quality working relationships with them is a very important skill for CSMs to have and to cultivate. While the CSM may be tasked with the direct responsibility of maximizing the level of success each customer attains from the products and services they have purchased, they cannot perform this role in isolation. The CSM will need to be able to rely upon both their own colleagues and a variety of stakeholders from within the customer organization as well potentially as from third-party organizations to help to achieve this goal.

Communication with others can take place in real time (such as telephone calls, live chat facilities and face-to-face or virtual meetings) or can be conducted non-real time, primarily using emails but potentially also incorporating messages on social media forums, for example, LinkedIn. What is important to understand is that every single communication a CSM has with another person contributes to that person's understanding of and also to their beliefs about that CSM's personal and professional character. I think it is true to say that the CSM will be judged as much by the way in which they communicate as by the results which they achieve. CSMs should therefore take care to ensure as best they can that all communication via any medium is courteous, friendly and professional.

5.3.2 Maximizing the Value from Meetings

Meetings are of course one of the most obvious forms of engagement, whether that is with customer stakeholders or with others. Meetings can take many forms and be conducted using a variety of formats. It would potentially be possible for the CSM to arrange a meeting with the customer (whether telephone, online or face to face) and then just turn up to that meeting and hope for the best. This is certainly one way to get the job done, but it's unlikely that this approach will generate the best value for either the customer or the CSM's own company. Wherever possible, every engagement with the customer should be planned in advance, and certainly the most important meetings (which most definitely includes the initial meeting) need some careful consideration and possibly some specific preparation prior to conducting them. Of course there may be times when unplanned customer meetings need to occur straight away without any prior warning and therefore without any planning or preparation, but that's fine—rules are often designed to be broken when necessary and this is just such a rule.

With this simple rule in mind, it would be worthwhile to know what types of planning and preparation before a meeting might be worthwhile completing. It could also be useful to have some guidance around how to conduct the meeting itself, and finally it may be interesting to think about whether there is anything that should be done post-meeting that the CSM should make sure they are aware of.

The steps in planning for a customer meeting (or indeed any other important meeting) should include the following (Table 5.2).

5.3.3 Is All This Meeting Preparation Really Necessary?

The above steps will most definitely help CSMs to deliver effective meetings that produce great outcomes. Of course different meetings will require different approaches and different levels of preparatory effort. It is not the intention here to burden the CSM with unnecessary tasks that do not lead to much reward in the way of results. A decision should be made on the appropriate course and level of preparatory activity for the CSM to complete for any given specific engagement, and this should be based upon its importance and complexity. This decision is of course for you as the CSM to take, in consultation with any of your colleagues if necessary.

Table 5.2 Steps in Planning for a Customer Meeting

Step	Title	Description
1	Outcomes	The CSM should ensure they are clear as to what the desired outcomes are for the engagement. The more clearly defined these outcomes are the easier it will be to guide the engagement through to successfully accomplishing them. Outcomes for both long (strategic) and short (tactical) term should be considered. For example, a tactical or short-term outcome might be to agree next steps in an upcoming process, and a strategic or long-term outcome might be to start to develop a trust relationship with a particular customer stakeholder whom you have not met before. Outcomes for all attendees should also be defined where relevant (i.e., what value does the customer get out of this meeting?). It is also reasonable to have thought of both required (must be attained) and desired (nice to attain if possible) outcomes, since this potentially expands the value returned from the engagement and enables a certain amount of flexibility in time management.
2	Attendees	Once the outcomes have been defined the CSM can determine who will be needed in the engagement in order to contribute to the attainment of those outcomes. Outcomes *must* be defined first, since it should be the outcome requirements that determine who will attend the engagement. Anyone who does not contribute to the attainment of the outcomes should not be an attendee. If you find a need for an attendee that does not contribute to attainment of any of the outcomes you have defined this is telling you that you need to go back and redefine your outcomes, perhaps including additional ones.
3	Agenda	Step 3 is to create an agenda. This should include both activities and timings. An activity is more than a topic for discussion, it does indeed define *what* will be discussed but it should also define *how* the discussion will be performed. For example, it may just be a simple conversation, but it may be a more structured survey of pre-created questions, or it may be a whiteboard exercise, or a short video followed by a round-table discussion, etc. Timings (including breaks if it is a longer engagement) are also critical to get right. It is essential that sufficient time is given to enable all outcomes to be attained. At the same time, it is unprofessional to waste people's time by asking them to attend meetings that are unnecessarily long. Having a few non-essential outcomes placed toward the end of the agenda can be a good way of providing some flexibility in time keeping. This is especially useful where it is difficult to calculate how much time one or more activities will need to be completed.

(Continued)

Table 5.2 (*Continued*) Steps in Planning for a Customer Meeting

Step	Title	Description
4	Assets and resources	Consideration should be given to any assets and resources that may be required for the engagement. This may include basic assets such as a room, a projector and screen, a microphone and speakers (for larger rooms), etc. It may also include catering for refreshments on arrival or at break times and if appropriate pens, note pads and name cards for attendees. It may also include more specific assets such as a case study presentation prepared on Microsoft PowerPoint slides. It could also include people—subject matter experts who are not attendees themselves but who are invited in to (for example) provide their expertise for attendees to take on board and consider. This might also include people to help you facilitate the engagement, perhaps, for example, by helping you to supervise attendees, manage time or record outcomes.
5	Outputs, measurements and next steps	Consideration should be given to engagement outputs. The engagement outputs are the results from the engagement. For some engagements a simple, verbal acknowledgment from each attendee that a consensus has been reached may be all that is required. Often however it may be necessary to create written documentation of discussions and agreements, or even to record the entire engagement for future reference. In addition, thought should be given to how the engagement will be reported on and who should receive this report. It may be necessary to create minutes for dissemination to all attendees and/or a summarized report on outcomes attained that can be sent to one or more particular stakeholders or simply stored in the Central Repository for the CSM's own reference. A final consideration might be around measuring or otherwise evaluating the relative success of the meeting and using those measurements or evaluations to help determine next steps. Measurement or evaluation of the meeting's success is usually based upon the level of attainment of the stated outcomes for the engagement.

5.3.4 Verbal Communication—Consultative Questioning

This book is not primarily about enhancing your communication skills, but these skills are so critically important for CSMs that a brief discussion about them is probably worthwhile. Consultative questioning is the process of gaining the necessary understanding to be able to help the customer through the use of good quality questions. A good quality question is quite simply the question which enables the stakeholder being questioned to understand what the CSM wants to know so that they can provide them with that answer. As simple as this sounds, to be good at consultative questioning takes practice and experience, and also requires the right trust relationship to have been developed so that the person being questioned feels comfortable with providing the answer. Below are some general rules for verbal communication that can help CSMs to refine and improve upon their existing consultative questioning skills (Table 5.3):

Table 5.3 Rules for Consultative Questioning

Rule	Description
Know your outcome requirements	Whenever you know ahead of time that you will be conducting a meeting where you need to gain information from one or more people you should ensure you are clear on what your outcome requirements are for this meeting, and this should include whatever information you need to collect.
Plan and document your questions	Rather than just hoping to remember everything that needs to be asked, or hoping you will be able to think of a way to ask for the information you need, plan your questions in advance and document them so that you can have them in front of you during the meeting.
Brief the attendees ahead of time	It helps attendees to know ahead of time what information you need from them. This enables them to prepare their responses and gather any information they might wish to bring with them to reference in their answers. Doing this also helps to prevent the possibility of humiliating attendees by asking them questions that they do not know the answers to.
Provide the right environment	If it is within your power to do so, try to create an environment that is appropriate to the meeting. Concerns relating to comfort, noise and other distractions and particularly to confidentiality if sensitive information will be discussed should be addressed. If the meeting will be a long one you may want to consider breaks and refreshments to keep attendees energized.
Build the trust first	Even if you already know and have a good relationship with the stakeholders, do not start the meeting with asking about sensitive or difficult topics. Instead start the meeting in a comfortable way and build empathy and rapport in the room first before touching upon delicate subjects.
Ask the same question many times	Do not always accept that the answer you have received is the complete answer or that it contains everything you need to know. Try asking the same or similar questions several times (for example, "what else…") to help the stakeholder think more deeply about the topic and provide further information about it.
Break down complicated topics	Use the concept of "chunking" to break down any large or complicated subject into a series of smaller and more digestible topics that can be discussed and dealt with more easily one-by-one.
Use open questions to explore topics	When a topic needs further exploration use open questions to enable this exploration to take place. Open questions are questions that require a sentence or two or even a paragraph or two in response, for example, "what do you think about…". Use multiple open questions to continue this exploration as long as necessary.
Use closed questions to gain consensus or commitment	When you need consensus (such as from multiple stakeholders) or a commitment from one or more stakeholders use closed questions. Closed questions require a short, definitive response (for example, "are we all agreed on…").

(Continued)

Table 5.3 (*Continued*)   Rules for Consultative Questioning

Rule	Description
Use active listening techniques	When you want to either check you have understood something or reassure the stakeholder that you understood what they have said you should employ active listening. This entails paraphrasing back to the stakeholder what they have just told you and asking for them to validate the accuracy of your words (for example, "so what you are saying is…").
Ensure all stakeholders are able to have their say	If there are multiple stakeholders in the meeting you may find that some stakeholders are more dominant of the conversation and others more reticent to share their views or knowledge. Try to provide a supportive environment that enables all stakeholders to feel comfortable about contributing, and proactively ask quieter stakeholders for their contributions if you can do so without making them uncomfortable.
Summarize progress as you go along	Do not wait until the end to make sure that everything has been discussed and (if necessary) agreed. Instead, break the conversation down into a series of sections and summarize progress at the end of each section. Try to gain consensus from stakeholders that the section has been fully discussed before moving on.
Note any information that is missing	Even though you might ask all the right questions, that doesn't mean that the stakeholders will know all the answers. You may well uncover areas that require further research to determine the required information. If this occurs note what information is missing together with who will be responsible for researching this information, by when the research will be accomplished and what they will do with the information once uncovered.
Create an agenda and manage time	As with any meeting, it is important to manage the meeting so that as far as possible all topics are given adequate time for discussion debate and (where necessary) negotiation and consensus forming. An agenda with timings can be a useful help in managing the progress through a meeting.
Document the meeting outcomes	Make sure that information gained from the meeting is adequately documented in whatever format is necessary. If required, make sure that this information is circulated to meeting attendees and/or other interested parties.
Follow up!	Where further activities were agreed during the meeting (such as further research to uncover missing information), the CSM needs to ensure these activities actually take place and results are documented. Next steps should be considered after every meeting and again the CSM should ensure that progress forwards continues to be made.

5.4 The Initial Customer Meeting

5.4.1 The Importance of the First Meeting

The expression "you never get a second chance of creating a first impression" is a little clichéd, but no less true for being so. When meeting the customer for the first time the CSM will want to make sure that both they themselves and the role of customer success management are seen in a positive light by the customer's stakeholders. The first meeting is hopefully the start of what could be a long relationship—certainly weeks, often months and many times even years—so it's worth investing some time in doing whatever can be done to ensure the meeting goes well.

All the usual pre-meeting considerations for any customer-facing meeting should be properly addressed by the CSM prior to the meeting taking place. (If you're not sure what those pre-meeting considerations are then please review Section 5.3 of this chapter on the topic of communicating with the customer.) Whereas some meetings may be less essential and therefore warrant less effort to be expended in planning and preparation activities, the initial meeting with customer stakeholders is a very important one to get right, so my recommendation is to put extra effort into ensuring as best one can that it goes well.

For the initial customer meeting, it may also be important to have the Customer sponsor or someone representing the Customer to establish the importance and overall expectations of the engagement.

5.4.2 The Concept of Continuity

From the perspective of the customer, it is likely to be desirable for there to be continuity in style and approach between whoever the customer stakeholders were dealing with in the CSM's company beforehand and the way in which the CSM now engages with them. It is important that customers do not see the transfer of the relationship from pre-sales selling by the account manager to post-sales customer success management by the CSM as a negative thing.

Customers can sometimes express annoyance or anger if they feel that they are being handed off to a secondary, less important person now that the sales cycle is over. The account manager can easily deal with this by ensuring that the role of the CSM is explained in advance and that they introduce the CSM as an equal and as a person whom they perceive as being of great potential value to the customer.

Customers can also get irritated if they feel that they are having to "start again" as it were in building up the new person's knowledge and understanding of their business and its unique needs and challenges. Care should therefore be taken to prove to the customer's stakeholders as early on as possible that the CSM is fully briefed on the customer's situation and is well prepared to hit the ground running, rather than needing a lot of time and effort expended by the customer before they become useful.

5.4.3 The Concept of Timing

Customers want timely communications with the CSM's company. Leaving it until the last moment before introducing the CSM and kicking off the onboarding, adoption and value creation services may be irksome for the customer who wants to be able to plan in advance and allocate their own resources well ahead of time. Conversely however, customers do not wish to feel they are being pushed along at a greater pace than they are comfortable with in order to meet the CSM's company's own outcome requirements rather than their own. The CSM needs to be introduced at the right moment—preferably well in advance of the need for their onboarding, adoption and value creation activities—and from that point onwards the pace and style of customer success-related interactions with the customer should be dictated by the customer rather than the CSM.

5.4.4 The Concept of Demarcation and Liaising with the Account Manager

Of course the fact that the CSM has now started engaging with the customer does not prevent the account manager from continuing their own relationships and sales-related conversations with customer stakeholders. Indeed it should be seen more as man enabler and enhancer of this, since it takes the burden of post-sales onboarding, adoption and value creation off the shoulder of account managers, enabling them to focus more effectively on the types of conversations around opportunities and solutions that they want and need to have.

Prior to meeting the customer stakeholders, CSMs should liaise with the account manager to agree the best approach. Even if you have worked with the particular account manager for this customer many times before (but especially if you have not) it is worthwhile meeting up with them before your first customer meeting to discuss the customer together and agree how to work together with this particular engagement. The approach that is agreed should include agreement both around who will be responsible moving forwards for holding which types of conversations about what topics, and also how the two of you will communicate with each other to keep one-another informed on any progress or other necessary customer-related information. This need not be an onerous task and most times can be kept to just an informal conversation and friendly agreement.

5.4.5 Attending a Meeting Prior to the Initial Meeting

The best way for the CSM to start to form their own direct relationship with customer stakeholders is for them to assume control of the initial meeting, even if others with existing customer stakeholder relationships such as the account manager are present. This helps to establish and embed their authority with customer stakeholders and gives them the ability to conduct the meeting in a way which suits their own personal style and characteristics. However, it is also very powerful to have *already met* with key customer stakeholders prior to this initial meeting, so that first impressions have already been formed on both sides and a little bit of the social ice has already been broken and there is at least some degree of familiarity between the different parties.

A good way to do this is for the CSM to ask the account manager if they will invite them to one of the account manager's own customer meetings. The CSM can attend largely as a passive witness (on the basis of wishing to gain some familiarity with the customer and key stakeholders) but if the account manager is willing, could also perhaps spend 5 or 10 min introducing themselves and the role of customer success management at a very basic level. This gives the customer stakeholders a valid reason for the CSM's presence and also gives the CSM a great foundation for the relationship upon which to build in the actual initial meeting which will follow.

5.4.6 Topics for Discussion in the Initial Meeting

My opinion on the initial meeting is that it is generally good to keep it short and keep it simple. There are very many topics that could be broached, information that could be shared and discussions that could be had, but trying to do too much at once may be counter-productive. Better to focus on getting a few things right than trying to do it all at once and failing at everything, and further follow-up meetings can always be arranged.

Similarly, it might be good to keep the list of attendees to as small a number as possible, as this tends to enable stronger and more meaningful relationships to be forged because it gives more

Table 5.4 Example of an Initial Meeting Agenda

Duration (min)	Topic	Facilitator
5	Welcome and general introductions	Account Manager
2	Introduce and hand over to the CSM	Account Manager
3	Personal introduction and background	CSM
5	Presentation: An overview of customer success management at XYZ company	CSM
30–40	General discussion on the customer's onboarding, adoption and value creation needs and how the CSM can help	CSM
20–30	Proposed way forwards from the CSM, with discussion and consensus on how it will work	CSM
5	Review of next steps and thank attendees	CSM
70–90	TOTAL (depending upon complexity of needs)	

communication time to those who are there. It also helps with time management and enables a shorter initial meeting to be arranged without losing out on important discussions.

An agenda for an initial meeting might look something like this (Table 5.4).

Care must be taken to determine what outcomes are required for this initial meeting. Aside from kicking off the formation of trust relationships with key customer stakeholders, and assuming the customer is both interested in utilizing the services of the CSM, there are two outcomes that are particularly desirable to achieve if not from the very first meeting then certainly as soon as possible thereafter. They are:

- High-level agreement on what needs to be done regarding onboarding, adoption and value creation and the type of role and involvement the CSM will have
- Agreement on communication between CSM and customer organization, including type and frequency of communication, reporting formats and which stakeholder/s the CSM will primarily liaise with

5.4.7 Validating the Customer Journey

The initial part of the first of the two bullet points shown above, i.e., the high-level agreement on what needs to be done regarding onboarding, adoption and value creation can be seen as a validation exercise, in the sense that prior to meeting the customer and being given this information, the CSM has already performed a fair amount of background research and analysis relating to the customer organization in general and the specific initiative they are engaged to help with in particular.

The CSM now needs to ensure the information they have previously received during PCSMF Phase 1: Preparation is entirely accurate and where possible to fill in any blanks caused by unknown information at that stage in the proceedings. This validation should include the data itself but also how far through the adoption and value creation journey the customer already is (if at all).

5.4.8 Getting to Know Stakeholders as Individuals

One final point to consider about the initial meeting is that in an ideal world the CSM needs to meet and form high-quality relationships with as many stakeholders as possible. As with other meetings, the initial meeting is an opportunity to further this aim. One methodology to further this ambition within the initial meeting or indeed any other meeting is what a close friend of mine describes as "working a crowd one person at a time." The idea of this technique is to try as much as possible to share a few minutes of one-to-one time with each individual stakeholder. This is valuable time which can be used to get to know them better and find out about their likes and dislikes and their strengths and weaknesses. By doing this, the CSM can gain a deeper understanding of who each stakeholder is and what is important to them. Similarly, it gives the opportunity to the CSM of helping each stakeholder to understand the impact to themselves of the engagement the CSM will be involved in. By doing this, the CSM can then "quarterback" the team members more proactively to help complement their skills and to help resolve issues more effectively and more efficiently.

5.4.9 Informing the Wider User Community

It is also important to note that the Customer needs to make sure their user community is aware of this new product or service, especially if it is to replace an existing solution that this user community is already comfortable using. The buy-in of this wider user community is extremely important upfront and throughout the engagement journey. CSMs are advised to raise the topic of informing the wider user community with the customer either in the initial meeting itself or as soon afterwards as practicable.

5.5 Developing a Stakeholder Management Strategy

5.5.1 Why Develop a Stakeholder Management Strategy?

Managing stakeholders is perhaps both a skill and an art form combined. It certainly takes a great deal of effort and calls for a strong amount of emotional intelligence and patience at times. CSMs who either have or can develop strong stakeholder management skills will definitely have a great advantage over those who struggle in this area.

There will generally be considerably more stakeholders that need managing than there is time available in which to manage them. The CSM therefore needs to be careful about how they utilize their time to perform this task, as it is entirely possible either to allow it to absorb so much of the CSM's precious time that it negatively impacts other essential duties or to simply give up in the face of overwhelming odds. To avoid both of these extremes, the CSM is advised to break up the overall stakeholders into categories and to develop a different stakeholder management strategy for each category—one which meets the needs of the stakeholders within each category yet simultaneously manages the CSM's own time in a wise and frugal manner.

5.5.2 Using an RACI Matrix to Understand Stakeholder Involvement

The RACI matrix is a tool which the CSM might find useful to deploy when dealing with stakeholder management—especially where this a fair amount of complexity. This tool is aimed at understanding which stakeholders are involved in each specific task relating to a project or initiative and also what role each stakeholder plays in performing each task.

The tool provides a simple format for identifying stakeholder roles by using a matrix whereby the rows represent tasks within the project or initiative and the columns represent stakeholders. Intersections between each task and each stakeholder can then be used to identify the specific role (if any) for that task which each stakeholder has.

RACI stands for *responsible, accountable, consulted* and *informed*. The classic RACI matrix is used to identify the ownership of each of these roles for each task within the project or initiative. The definitions for these four terms are shown in Table 5.5.

A simple example of how a CSM might use an RACI matrix within a customer success engagement to understand the different roles of customer stakeholders at different stages within the overall engagement is shown below, and a template for this tool called *Stakeholder_RACI_Matrix* is provided in the downloads at www.practicalcsm.com (Figure 5.2).

5.5.3 The Stakeholder Management Matrix

Not every stakeholder needs (or even desires) the same level of time and attention from the CSM. A tool that CSMs can use to help classify stakeholders into categories and then to assign relevant strategies to each category is the *stakeholder management matrix*. This tool is commonly used in sales, in project management and wherever else there is a need to manage complex needs of multiple stakeholders. It is simple to understand and reasonably quick to use, making it an ideal tool for CSMs to use (Figure 5.3).

Figure 5.3 shows a stakeholder management matrix. As you can see, the matrix divides a canvas into four sections, and the CSM can plot positions for each individual stakeholder or stakeholder group onto the canvas based upon the relative strength or weakness of two factors X (on the horizontal axis) and Y (on the vertical axis).

Using the matrix will be described below within the recommended steps for managing stakeholder, and a template for the tool called *Stakeholder_Management_Matrix* is provided in the downloads at www.practicalcsm.com.

Table 5.5   RACI Matrix Definitions

Term	Definition
Responsible	The person or people who actually perform the task. This person or group of people is often though not always appointed by the Accountable person.
Accountable	The person who is ultimately answerable for ensuring the task is performed to the appropriate standards of quality, time, etc. (this should always be just one person)
Consulted	These are additional people whose opinions, expertise or other inputs are sought by the Responsible person or people in the process of performing the task
Informed	These are people who are not involved in either the performance or oversight of the task, but who need to know when the task has been completed (for example, in order to know when to start another task which they are responsible for)

	Chief Finance Officer	EMEA Director of Finance	EMEA Director of Operations (SPL)	VP for Global Operations	VP for Global Sales & Marketing	EMEA Director of Production	EMEA Director of R&D	EMEA Director of Distribution	Chief Information Officer	EMEA Director of IT Systems
R = Responsible A = Accountable C = Consulted I = Informed										
Determining scope of initiative	I	R	R	A	C	C	C	C	C	C
Creating the business case	I	I	R	A	C	C	C	C	C	C
Funding approval	R/A	R	I	I						
Providing information on impact to Sales workforce			R/A	I	C					
Providing information on impact to Marketing workforce			R/A	I	C					
Providing information on impact to Production workforce			R/A	I		C				
Providing information on impact to R&D workforce			R/A	I			C			
Providing information on impact to Distribution workforce			R/A	I				C		
Providing information on impact to IT workforce			R/A	I					C	C
Determining overall stakeholder impacts			R	A						
Creating onboarding plan			R	A	C	C	C	C	C	C
Approving onboarding plan	R/A	R	I	I						
Implementing onboarding plan			I	R	A	I	I	I	I	I	I
Creating adoption plan			R	A	C	C	C	C	C	C
Approving adoption plan	R/A	R	I	I						
Implementing adoption plan			I	R	A	I	I	I	I	I	I
Measuing and reporting (KPIs and milestones)			I	R	A					
Evaluating success and approving further phases	I	R/A	C	C						

Figure 5.2   Example of an RACI matrix.

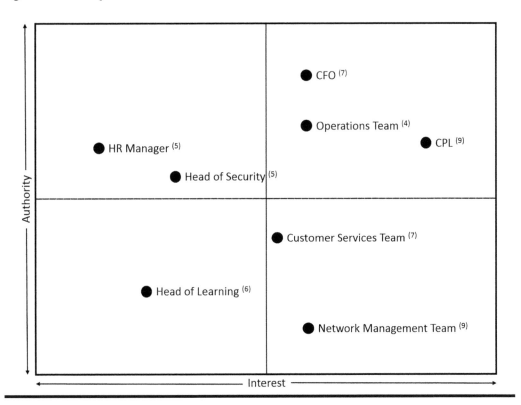

Figure 5.3   Stakeholder management matrix.

5.5.4 The Stakeholder Management Plan

As well as a tool for classifying stakeholders, the other asset that is useful for CSMs when developing a stakeholder management strategy is a stakeholder strategy plan. This does not have to be especially detailed or intricate; in fact, sometimes the simplest plan is the best one since there is a greater likelihood for a simple plan to be actioned.

All the plan needs to do is to provide a way of documenting the strategy for each stakeholder (or stakeholder group) that you have identified. I find that a basic spreadsheet that uses a row for each stakeholder or stakeholder group works well for me. Columns can be added for each piece of information to be included in the plan which will therefore contain data relating to each stakeholder or group. These might include (Table 5.6).

Naturally, the CSM will not know all of the data about stakeholders nor formed complete strategies for managing every stakeholder and stakeholder group at the very early stages of the engagement. In any case, stakeholders' desires and concerns and levels of authority, interest and

Table 5.6 Stakeholder Management Strategy Information

Data	Description
Name	The name of the stakeholder or a title for the stakeholder group
Job role	The job title of or other role-related description for the stakeholder or stakeholder group
Relevance	A description of the relevance that the stakeholder or stakeholder group's job role has to the initiative
Seniority level	The stakeholder or stakeholder group's level of seniority within the customer organization
Authority	The level of authority or influence they have over decision-making related to this initiative (from 0 to 10)
Interest	The level of interest or concern they have regarding the outcomes and/ or strategy for attaining those outcomes within this initiative (from 0 to 10)
Support	The level of support they have for the SPL and CSM in terms of their plans for this initiative (from 0 to 10)
Primary desires	The most important desires for what they want the initiative to include or deliver
Primary concerns	The most important concerns they have over the initiative
Notes	Any additional information about the stakeholder or stakeholder group which it is important to note
Category	The stakeholder category that you have classified this stakeholder or stakeholder group into
Current situation	A summary of the stakeholder's current opinion and related activities regarding the initiative

(Continued)

Table 5.6 (*Continued*)   Stakeholder Management Strategy Information

Data	Description
Desired situation	A summary of the CSM's desired stakeholder's opinion and related activities regarding the initiative
Specific Strategy	A brief explanation of any specific activities or interactions will occur with this stakeholder or stakeholder group
Assigned to	The name of the person responsible for carrying out the strategy
Deadlines	Any specific date or dates by which certain parts of the strategy must be completed (if relevant)
Measurement	A description for how the strategy's success will be measured (if relevant)

support can often fluctuate depending upon the current phase of the initiative and of course the results of activities to date. The recommendation therefore is to review and where necessary update the stakeholder strategy plan regularly—perhaps once per month, for example—plus whenever there is a significant change (for example, new personnel assigned to the initiative or a change to requirements). Rather than overwriting the original plan from the previous month, I use a Microsoft Excel workbook and create a separate worksheet for each month which I simply copy from the previous month and then amend as necessary. That way I can track and review my progress over time. A template for this tool called *Stakeholder_Management_Plan* is provided in the downloads at www.practicalcsm.com.

5.5.5 Recommended Steps for Managing Stakeholders

5.5.5.1 Step 1: Determine Who the Stakeholders Are

This should already have been partly completed in PCSMF Phase 1: Preparation where the CSM gained a handover from the account manager and/or other colleagues and performed their own additional research. CSMs can refresh their memories regarding this research by reviewing their findings in the documentation they have stored in the Central Repository and copy across relevant details into the stakeholder management plan as necessary.

At this stage the CSM may already have learned some additional information about stakeholders from the conversations they have had during initial customer meetings, and of course this information should also be documented both in the research documentation and the strategy plan. They can also use the RACI matrix to further analyze and investigate which stakeholders are involved in each task within the initiative and what roles they play.

5.5.5.2 Step 2: Create a Stakeholder Matrix

Create the stakeholder matrix by plotting each stakeholder/group onto the *X*- and *Y*-axis of the matrix grid by referencing their authority and interest levels from 0 to 10, and showing their support level from 0 to 10 as a numerical value next to their plot.

At this point I have sometimes found that since I am now viewing all stakeholders holistically together rather than considering them one by one (as I had been doing up to this point) I have been

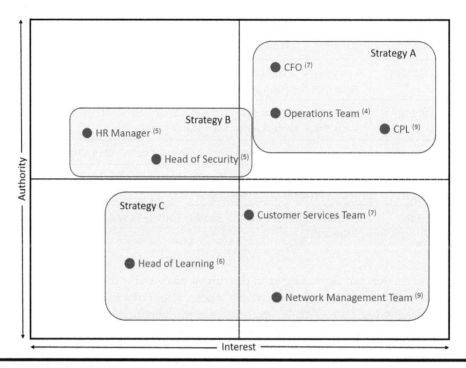

Figure 5.4   Categorizing stakeholders.

wrong in some assumptions around levels of authority, interest and/or support for one or more of the stakeholders/groups and the data needs adjusting. If you find this to be the case simply amend the values in the strategy plan and move the plots in the matrix according to the new position.

5.5.5.3 Step 3: Classify the Stakeholders into Categories

If you only have a handful of stakeholder/groups and can create separate stakeholder management strategies for each one without too much difficulty then you may elect to skip this step. On the other hand, if you have a lot of different stakeholders/groups with similar positions regarding the initiative it may be advisable to classify all similar stakeholders/groups into a category which you can give a relevant name to. You can then treat the entire category as one entity in terms of developing a stakeholder management strategy. An example of this is shown in Figure 5.4.

5.5.5.4 Step 4: Determine Your Management Strategy for Individual Stakeholders/Groups and/or Categories

Now you can create the strategy itself, either for an individual stakeholder/group or for the category you have classified them into (or both if you so desire). Make sure you assign a person to be responsible for enacting the strategy and provide any other relevant information such as deadlines and measurements. Most of the time it is likely to be the CSM who will be responsible for fulfilling the strategy, but sometimes actions might be given to others including the account manager or even customer stakeholders such as the SPL who may be better positioned to, for example, negotiate with or influence one of their colleagues than the CSM would be.

5.5.5.5 Step 5: Work the Plan

Once you have completed the strategy planning you are in a position to start executing those plans in the real world. Remember that if you are not performing all of the activities yourself you will need to communicate activity requirements to others and liaise regularly with them to ensure they are actually performing the activities you wish them to undertake.

5.5.5.6 Step 6: Review the Plan Regularly

Your stakeholder strategy plan will need regular updating in order to remain useful and relevant. Change occurs due to both your own activities in working the plan and external forces such as new personnel, strategic direction changes and so on. The recommended approach is to diarize a regular monthly review of the plan. Each month make a new copy of the plan, keeping the old plan for reference and amending the new version with any necessary changes to stakeholder information and to strategy for managing them.

5.6 Tools for PCSMF Phase 2: Commitment

- Customer success proposal
- Stakeholder management matrix
- Stakeholder management plan

5.6.1 Tools for Planning the Initial Meeting

To help with planning the initial meeting it may be a good idea to review the information you researched during PCSMF Phase 1: Preparation. The *Customer_Research_Checklist* which you created during that phase should contain the information you need. If there are information gaps that can be usefully filled before the initial meeting then do so now. If the checklist contains information that needs validation from the customer and/or gaps in essential information that only the customer can provide then make a note of what you need to ask during the meeting.

It might also be useful to review the *Customer_Engagement_Strategy* which you created in Phase 1 to refresh your memory regarding desired outcomes from the engagement.

It is a good idea to read the *Customer_Success_Proposal* template as a help for formulating your own ideas for what you wish to propose to the customer in terms of your ongoing help and assistance with their onboarding, adoption and value creation needs.

5.6.2 Capturing Results from the Initial Meeting and Developing the Proposal

After you have met the customer, presented the role of customer success management to them and secured their commitment to work with you, use the *Customer_Success_Proposal* template to create a proposal to send to the SPL for them to validate, sign and return to you.

Make sure to adjust the *Customer_Research_Checklist* which you created in Phase 1 to reflect any new information you have now gathered or assumptions you have now validated with the customer.

5.6.3 *Managing Stakeholders*

Use the *RACI_Matrix* to help determine which stakeholders are involved in the initiative and what roles they play in performing each task within it. Use the *Stakeholder_Management_Matrix* to analyze and categorize customer stakeholders and use the *Stakeholder_Management_Plan* to begin to formulate and document a stakeholder management strategy for this customer engagement. You may find at this early stage that more information about a wider range of key stakeholders is required before a full stakeholder management strategy can be determined, but it is good practice to kick off the stakeholder management journey at this stage by documenting what you do know. You can always come back to these documents to add more details at a later stage when more is known.

5.6.4 *Amending the Customer Engagement Strategy and Strategy Roadmap*

The customer engagement strategy and roadmap which you created in PCSMF Phase 1: Preparation may need adjusting in the light both of new information uncovered in conversation with the customer's key stakeholders and particularly now that your role in helping the customer with onboarding, adoption and ongoing value creation has been negotiated and agreed with the customer. Make sure you return to the *Customer_Engagement_Strategy* workbook that you created in Phase 1 to amend and update the strategy and roadmap as appropriate.

Remember to keep the roadmap up-to-date by adding more details for upcoming phases as these details come into view. Remember also to check off activities and phases by marking them as completed as you go along.

5.6.5 *The Central Repository*

As with Phase 1, make sure to save your outputs (or a copy of them) to the Central Repository. As a reminder, the Central Repository is a corporate storage location that is appropriate for saving customer-related information to and which anyone who needs access to it can get hold of it when necessary. Other documents that you create can also be added to the Central Repository so that they are available alongside the workbook. How you organize the Central Depository and what (if any) tools for data management you use are of course entirely up to you.

Please note that as was mentioned in the previous chapter, CSMs should make sure they are aware of any legal and corporate requirements in their region regarding storing corporate or personal data and ensure that they follow these requirements. If necessary take advice from your line manager and/or your legal team.

5.7 Summary of Activities and Outputs for PCSMF Phase 2: Commitment

5.7.1 *Activities for PCSMF Phase 2: Commitment*

The Activities for Phase 2: Commitment include:

1. Review the completed *Customer_Research_Checklist* for this customer (or other tool you use in handovers) which you created in Phase 1: Preparation.

2. If there are any information gaps that need to be filled or assumptions that need to be validated make a note of them and prepare questions for the customer
3. Review the completed *Customer_Engagement_Strategy* together with any other documents that have also already been created in the Central Repository for this customer to ensure you are up-to-date on requirements from the engagement
4. Plan the initial meeting including location, format and style, outcome requirements, agenda, duration, attendees and any collateral requirements such as presentations or case studies
5. Arrange the initial meeting and if necessary hold a pre-meeting conversation with internal colleagues such as the account manager to gain support and commitment from them to perform their part in the meeting as desired
6. If necessary practice your presentation about yourself and the role of customer success management and the types of help you can offer the customer so that you are confident and well prepared in the meeting itself
7. Try to learn as much as possible about any key customer stakeholders who will be attending the meeting but whom you have not met before so that you can focus on meeting their needs and managing the meeting successfully
8. Hold the initial meeting and present the SPL and other customer key stakeholders with your proposed offer of help and assistance with onboarding, adoption and value creation. In the meeting negotiate the help you will provide and agree how it will be provided and the way in which you and the customer will communicate with each other
9. After the meeting update the *Customer_Engagement_Strategy* and *Customer_Research_Checklist* as necessary and create the customer engagement proposal based upon the agreement made with the customer and using the *Customer_Engagement_Proposal* template
10. Use the *RACI_Matrix,* the *Stakeholder_Management_Matrix* and *Stakeholder_Management_Plan* to begin to formulate and document a stakeholder management strategy for this customer engagement, based upon the information about key stakeholders that you have learned so far
11. Send the completed *Customer_Engagement_Proposal* to the SPL for their validation and signature and store it together with any other documents that have been created in the Central Repository

5.7.2 Outputs for PCSMF Phase 2: Commitment

The Output for Phase 2: Commitment is the completed and signed *Customer_Engagement_Proposal* plus updated *Customer_Research_Checklist* and *Customer_Engagement_Strategy* together with the *RACI_Matrix, Stakeholder_Management_Matrix* and *Stakeholder_Management_Plan* (which may not yet be completed but which hopefully you can make a start on at this stage) and any other documents you have created. By the end of your preparations you must make sure that you have sufficient information to move forward to PCSMF Phase 3: Onboarding.

Chapter 6

Practical CSM Framework Phase 3: Onboarding

6.1 What Is PCSMF Phase 3: Onboarding All About?

In this chapter, we will look at the process of onboarding customers—in other words, the work conducted to get customers up and running and using our products and services in the days or weeks immediately following their purchase and implementation. The chapter will explain what is meant by onboarding and will review the differences and relative merits of both paid for (i.e., delivered for a fee as professional services) and not paid for (i.e., delivered as a value-added service at no additional charge) approaches to onboarding (Figure 6.1).

Whichever approach is taken the purpose of onboarding is to get the customer up and running as efficiently as possible with least amount of fuss and the most amount of productivity, and this chapter will explain how this is achieved. The chapter reviews onboarding from the customer's perspective and describes the needs of customers for timely and effective communication. It then considers the benefits of customer self-sufficiency and how this can be encouraged and promoted. It explains the differences between generic and customized onboarding approaches and discusses the potential for paid for professional services onboarding engagements. In my experience, onboarding is the most critical phase of an engagement because it:

- establishes expectations, roles and responsibilities for who does what to whom, when, how and why
- establishes processes and procedures that will be continued throughout the entirety of the engagement and if done correctly...
- gets an engagement off on the right track and headed in the right direction

In effect, if onboarding is done well then everybody wins. This chapter positions onboarding as an important part of customer success management which the CSM should take seriously and which should be measured as an aspect of the value they generate for their company.

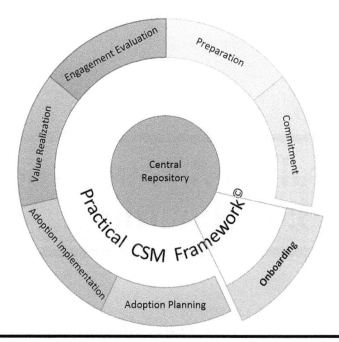

Figure 6.1   PCSMF Phase 3: Onboarding.

6.2 Understanding Onboarding

6.2.1 What Is Onboarding?

You may recall from our overview of each of the seven phases within the PCSMF in Chapter 3 that we defined onboarding as follows: Onboarding is the process of getting the customer started with a new product, service or solution, with the idea being to help customers start attaining measurable value from their purchase as soon as is practical (as quickly as possible, but always based upon the customer's own timeline) and to reduce customer frustration around lack of information and/or support in those early stages.

Onboarding therefore just covers the initial stage of what should ultimately become an ongoing relationship between CSM and customer that will last for many months or years as the customer engages with and utilizes the solution they have purchased over time to generate and realize the value returned from their investment. Because it is the first thing that the CSM will deliver to the customer it is also an opportunity for the CSM to introduce themselves and their services (if this has not been managed in earlier phases of the overall customer engagement that were not led by the CSM) and begin to form relationships with the SPL and other key customers stakeholders.

6.2.2 Why Is Onboarding Important?

For most if not all business customers time is money, and time wasted is therefore the equivalent of either money spent or money not earned or perhaps a combination of both. This makes sense if you think about it, since pretty much every possible customer initiative is ultimately going to come down to either increasing revenues or decreasing expenditures in order to maximize profits (or you could say to maximize value to the client if the organization is not for profit). The longer the delay between investing the money, time and energy into the initiative and starting to see positive outputs from the initiative, the less value may be returned in terms of how hard the investment is working for the company (usually measured as the time taken to break even on an investment, and referred to as the Payback period and is measured in years and months). To reduce the payback period for our customer not only have we got to make the return as big as possible but we also have to bring it forward as much as possible. From a financial perspective, reducing the payback period will almost certainly also reduce the TtV (time to value), which is the length of time it takes for the required value from an investment (i.e., the financial outcome targets for the initiative as defined by the customer) to be realized. A good quality onboarding service is therefore a contributor to the successful attainment of the customer's outcomes.

Although it may not be as sexy a topic as some of the deeper and more complex subjects relating to adoption and change management, the need for getting customers successfully under way at the earliest possible opportunity should not be overlooked by the CSM's company's senior decision-makers who are responsible for setting overall customer success strategy and targets or by CSMs themselves in fulfilling their customer success role. To my mind onboarding activities conducted by the CSM are important and should be tracked and recorded. Reducing the time taken to complete the onboarding process and reducing customer frustration by proving complete, accurate and understandable information about their purchase at the start of the post-sales stages should be one of the ways in which the customer success team is measured. Questions on the onboarding experience could also be usefully included when surveying customers regarding the overall customer experience.

6.3 Generic and Customized Onboarding Models

6.3.1 Selecting Generic or Customized Onboarding

There are two ways in which onboarding can be created and delivered to the customer—the generic way and the customized way. The simple way to complete onboarding is to provide a highly templated set of onboarding documentation to the customer. This information is rich in information relating to the generic products and services which the customer has purchased, but is poor in information relating specifically to the customer and their needs and requirements. This approach to onboarding is recommended where either of the following applies:

■ The products and services are themselves very generic in nature and are likely to have little or even no customization, configuration, integration or other manipulation beyond basic setup requirements that are the same for each instance of their use.
■ The products and services are of low revenue generation value and it is not financially viable to provide a customized onboarding service to every customer.

There is another possible use for generic onboarding, which is as the first component of a two-part onboarding process. This can be useful where there is a more complex requirement for onboarding but there is also pressure to get the customer up and running as soon as possible and/or a limited fund for providing non-chargeable onboarding to customers. In these circumstances the simple or generic onboarding packs can be created and delivered to the customer as a non-chargeable service to get them started and further more detailed and chargeable onboarding services can then be negotiated and agreed with the customer if required.

6.3.2 Generic Onboarding

If the simple route is chosen, then the CSM may be involved in the up-front process of creating an onboarding "pack" or "kit" for each product or service that this approach applies to. Once this generic onboarding pack is created it can be stored in the Central Repository and reutilized every time a customer purchases each of those products and services with very little or in some cases no requirement for editing.

Even the generic onboarding pack may require some simple customization for each instance of its use. This information can usually be highly templated though, so the CSM may need just to complete the blanks in a standard form for information such as customer name, CSM contact information, number of licenses sold, renewal date, customer support start date, etc., and then the form can update the changes to produce the unique pack for the specific customer. At the end of the process, an onboarding pack is created that is aimed at the SPL and/or other lead stakeholders which provides all of the basic information they need in order to understand what it is they have purchased and how to access and use it. It would then be up to that customer stakeholder to disseminate that information as necessary through their organization to the different stakeholder groups who will be impacted by the initiative.

Time invested by the CSM in the up-front activity of template creation is likely to be time well spent where products and services of this simple nature will be regularly sold, since it reduces the per-instance time needed by the CSM to prepare for each unique customer onboarding occurrence. This may be doubly useful in the sense that completing the onboarding faster is not only more efficient for the CSM's time but delivers a better customer experience and reduces the chances of any customer frustration occurring while waiting for the information they need to get started.

Although the creation of the generic onboarding pack is a one-off task, it is of course important to ensure that such packs remain up-to-date and so there I recommend the creation of a process that activates an onboarding pack refresh activity whenever a product, service or solution is updated.

6.3.3 Customized Onboarding

The other methodology is to do customized onboarding. In customized onboarding the concept is to provide an onboarding experience that uniquely matches each customer's specific onboarding needs. This of course entails first understanding those needs, and this in turn may require time spent consulting with the customer's stakeholders to gain this information.

Customized onboarding can range from the basic and simple in format through to the more complex and detailed in nature, it really is up to each company to determine what level of service they wish to deliver. At the more simple level, the customization may incorporate the customer's own branding and any specific configuration or customization of the products and services that the customer has purchased. The next level up in complexity may include customer-specific information about how the different products will be utilized (for example, in which processes and/or by which users and/or to generate what outputs).

The most complex level is where a series of onboarding packs are generated for the customer, with each pack aimed at providing the specific information required by each stakeholder group that has been identified as being impacted by the initiative. Each pack only describes the solution components that are relevant to the particular stakeholder group and the pack is both branded and written in the language of the customer. The information within the pack is tailored each time to provide the messages that need to be communicated to the particular stakeholder group that it is aimed at, and can therefore be much more pointed to the processes and uses of the solution that this particular group will experience.

For this more complex level of onboarding customization the CSM will need to engage with the SPL to understand which stakeholder groups will require an onboarding experience and to agree what that experience should be. The onboarding assets can then be created and (if necessary) approved by the SPL or other nominated customer stakeholder prior to being delivered to their intended audiences. Rather than containing information about what has been purchased, the focus of these packs would be on what has *changed* for those users. In addition to practical information about what the new process is and how to use the new products and services such as login URLs, support phone numbers and the like, there may also be wider contextual communication about why these changes are occurring and what the expectation is from senior management. These types of messages are likely to be crafted by the customer organization and sent to the CSM for inclusion within the packs.

As with any assets that have been created, my advice is that they should be stored in the Central Repository and where relevant should be templated so that future customized onboarding packs for other customers with similar needs will become easier to create.

6.3.4 Combining Onboarding Models

It is entirely possible to utilize both models for a customer. The CSM might start off by providing a basic, generic onboarding pack for the SPL and then the SPL might requests the development of a customized onboarding experience for each user group. This is most likely to be a requirement when multiple end-user groups will be impacted in a significant way by the initiative.

6.4 Onboarding as a Professional Service

6.4.1 Charging for Onboarding

While the simple or generic onboarding pack is usually provided without charge as part of the service surround for purchasing the solution, it is not uncommon to look upon the creation of a customized onboarding experience for each user group as a chargeable professional services activity.

How much information and/or customization it is determined will be provided without charge and at what stage to start charging for onboarding services is of course a decision that each organization needs to make, along with how much to charge for it and who will be involved. Criteria for determining whether the onboarding engagement should be a paid for professional service might include both the overall amount of work required and the percentage of specific customization of that work to meet the customer's unique situational requirements. In particular, if a customer requires onboarding not just as overall information for the SPL but customized for each impacted user group then charging a fee would seem reasonable in most circumstances.

In addition to the work that the CSM performs there may well be the need for others to be involved including specialists with product knowledge, marketing expertise, copywriters, artists, editors and people with training skills. In this type of situation the CSM takes on the roles of project manager and customer liaison, working externally with the customer to agree content, deadlines and costs and working internally with the project team to complete the work within the required timeframe and budget. All work that needs to be completed by anyone from the CSM's company will of course need to be considered when determining whether or not to charge a professional services fee and how much that fee should be.

In terms of spotting opportunities for chargeable onboarding services and negotiating with the customer, this may be something which will be completed with the customer at the pre-sales phase. It is also possible that a discussion around onboarding options and the pros and cons of these options versus the needs of the customer's organization has not yet occurred. In this circumstance, it may well be up the CSM to take the lead in discussing and negotiating the way forwards for onboarding with the SPL. If this is the case then winning professional services engagements may be seen as a formal part of the CSM's role and something that they are given a target for and possibly even remunerated for, although there is a strong argument not to remunerate CSMs directly for new business in order to keep them neutral in the eyes of customers. A better alternative may be a team target that either on its own or perhaps together with other targets when reached provides an overall team bonus.

6.4.2 When Onboarding Becomes Adoption

As you can probably see, the more complex and customized level of onboarding effectively becomes a solution adoption service since it starts to involve end users. Customized onboarding is a service that might be offered to customers by the CSM's own company (either for no charge or for an agreed professional services fee). Within this service the onboarding pack creation activities are performed by the CSM's company to the specified requirements of the customer. Of course, the customer may then use the assets that are created in a wider adoption service that they themselves deliver to their users (for example, this may include training and support).

A core difference between onboarding and full adoption that generally always does remain is that the focus of onboarding is on *getting started* whereas adoption goes further than onboarding and supports the customer through the entire process of getting to value realization. It is fair to say however that if there is a line between them at all it is a blurred one and could even be argued to be purely semantic in nature. What is important is that the CSM works with the SPL to determine both onboarding and adoption requirements and then agrees a way forwards to deliver appropriate services to fulfill those requirements in an efficient and effective manner. As with most things, a frank and open conversation and exchange of ideas around these needs and best ways of meeting them at an early stage is often the best way forwards.

6.5 Information for Onboarding

6.5.1 Determining Onboarding Requirements

The requirements for onboarding will be based upon an understanding of the generic complexity of each of the solution components, the level of unique customization required by this customer, the customer's needs for adoption and utilization of the solution (particularly where multiple end users or end-user groups are involved), and finally the customer's maturity and preparedness levels for adopting and utilizing the solution. Where one or more of these aspects of the initiative are rated as medium to high there may be a need to expend more effort in onboarding than where all of these aspects of the initiative are rated as medium to low (Figure 6.2).

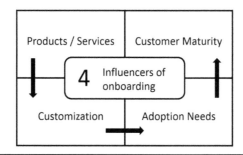

Figure 6.2   Four influencers of onboarding.

6.5.2 Generic or Custom?

Generic: Generic onboarding is relatively simple and straightforward and is (or should be) pre-templated and based mostly on the standard products and services themselves rather than any custom information about the specific needs of different users or user groups.

Custom: Customized information is customized to the specific requirements of a customer—usually one who has complex onboarding needs due to either

1. A wide and diverse range of users and user groups needing to be communicated to with different onboarding messages and/or in different ways during the onboarding process
2. The inclusion of one or more highly customized products or services within the solution that requires a customized approach to the onboarding due to the non-standard nature of the product/service

Some companies by the nature of what they sell and who they sell to may find that either all or the vast majority of their sales falls into the *generic* category. Other companies may find the exact opposite and they need to customize the onboarding experience for every customer. Still other companies may well experience a mixture of the two different approaches is needed depending upon which products or services have been sold and/or the level of complexity of the customer's utilization of those products or services.

6.5.3 Information for Generic Onboarding

Since generic onboarding is relatively simple and straightforward and is (or should be) pre-templated and based mostly on the products and services themselves rather than any custom information relating to the specific customer, the research for generic onboarding should be fairly straightforward. The hard work will already have been done in creating the templates and there should be little if anything left for the CSM to do except add some simple customer-specific information such as the customer's name, service start and renewal dates and any URLs or login information that have been created specifically for that customer. If a good quality template has been created then it should be immediately evident as to what information the CSM needs to complete for each instance of that template's use. Table 6.1 shows the types of information that CSMs may need to collect for a more generic onboarding engagement, although once completed the first time and templated, the idea would be that in future instances the solution-related information would already be in place and the CSM would only need to complete the customer engagement-specific information:

Table 6.1   Information for Generic Onboarding

Information	Description
Basic customer information	Who the customer is and who the SPL (senior project lead) is, together with their contact information
Products, services and solutions sold	Each solution and each solution component that has been sold to the customer and the quantities of each item. Any serial numbers, contract numbers or other identifying information (or login information and URLs to access this information) that the customer needs
Licensing and consumption models	For each item sold, whether it was sold as an outright purchase or as-a-service, numbers of licenses and whether there are any licensing issues that the customer needs to be made aware of, such as allocation of licenses to specific users
Configuration and/or customization included	Whether there is any configuration or customization work included within the deal which enhances or modifies the products and services in any way—particularly with regard to end-user training requirements
Configuration and/or customization needed	Whether there is any configuration or customization work not included within the deal which the customer needs to organize and complete prior to using the solution
Support services	What support services have been purchased or are included within the deal, or are otherwise needed by the customer and any specific access information (e.g., contract IDs, support URLs, login info, phone numbers, email addresses, etc.). This may include self-service support such as Help pages, FAQ pages, online reference information, etc.
Professional services	What professional services such as on-premises install and configure, integration, customization and management & maintenance have been purchased or are included within the deal
Current status and future deadlines	What the current position is (i.e., contract signed, ready for installation, installed and working, services in place, etc.) and the dates of any upcoming significant milestones
Training and certification requirements	What the training and certification requirements and recommendations are for each product or service, and whether any training is included within the deal
Training and certification plan	What (if any) discussion has taken place with the customer to date regarding training and certification and (if known) what the customer's training and certification plans are

(Continued)

Table 6.1 (*Continued*)   Information for Generic Onboarding

Information	Description
Training and certification availability	What training is available to the customer for free (or at no extra charge) and how to access it. What additional, chargeable training and certification resources and services are available either directly from the CSM's own company or from partners or other third parties
Onboarding assets	What assets such as brochures (hard and soft copy), welcome guides, user manuals, installation and configuration guides, and onboarding documentation templates are available for the CSM to utilize
Customer success management discussions	What discussions have already taken place with the customer regarding the ongoing assistance that can be offered to them for generating and measuring value from their purchase, and any agreements or other outcomes from those conversations

6.5.4 Information for Customized Onboarding

If further information needs have been identified due to a specific customer onboarding require-ment then this must be documented and researched. Quite simply, if the onboarding requirement is less complex then less information will need to be gathered. When there is a complex onboard-ing however, there will be more work for the CSM to perform.

In either case, assuming the CSM will be going on to work with the customer over the long term the more background information the CSM collects the better they will be able to perform their role. The downside of spending time collecting and considering information of course is that it may delay getting to the action component of the RAPAE model as quickly and efficiently as possible, so as always CSMs need to temper their research, analysis and planning with this goal in mind and may also need to negotiate and agree deadlines for completing onboarding preparations so that the customer remains in control and can organize their own schedules accordingly. During this early period, the CSM's primary focus needs to remain on the short term goal of getting the customer up and running with the solution as quickly and efficiently as possible, with a secondary goal of developing a wider understanding of what else may need to be done at a later juncture once this initial kick-off stage has been accomplished.

The exact details of what information is needed will depend upon the specific onboarding requirements of each customer, but the table below outlines the information that the CSM might need to know for a complex onboarding requirement in addition to the information needed for a generic onboarding requirement that was shown above in Table 6.1.

Do not be misled by the relatively small number of additional items within Table 6.2. There are fewer items to research but the amount and complexity of information returned for each item can be and likely will be much higher. This is due partly to the fact that for complex onboarding requirements much more information about which end users within the customer's organization will be using the solution components and in what way they will be using them is likely to be needed. The CSM needs to be clear about how this information will be uncovered and provided, since it may be beyond their own scope and capabilities to do so themselves. A lot of this sort of

Table 6.2 Additional Information for Complex Onboarding

Information	Description
Solution end-user adoption requirements	An understanding of what end-user adoption requirements or implications exist for each of the products and services within the solution. Note—this may be generic to the product or service or may vary based upon customer utilization
User groups	The name of and other relevant details for each user group that will be impacted by the initiative and which the customer wishes onboarding information to be provided for
User group onboarding requirements	For each user group identified above, the specific onboarding needs of that group which the customer has requested to be managed within the onboarding materials. This should include three aspects often abbreviated to KSA: *Knowledge* (the understanding required to perform each task), *Skills* (the ability required to perform each task) and *Attitude*: (the willingness of the user to perform each task)
Onboarding materials and inclusions	What format/s the onboarding information needs to be provided in for each user group and any information that the customer will be preparing that needs to be added to those materials
Onboard delivery and management mechanisms	What platforms will be used to deliver the information to each user group and who will be responsible for managing and maintain the process of delivering those materials and for measuring progress
Onboarding delivery plan	An understanding of how the onboarding will be rolled out to user groups (e.g., all at once, in phases, alone or together with other communications relating to other initiatives taking place simultaneously, etc.) plus agreement on which components of the plan the CSM's company will be assisting with and the form of that assistance

information is also a requirement for full adoption (see the section below on when onboarding becomes adoption) and more detailed information about gathering and making sense of information relating to end users is covered in later chapters that deal specifically with adoption.

6.6 Managing the Onboarding Process

6.6.1 Scoring the Customer

As a simple yet effective way of gaining an immediate understanding of the likely level of complexity of your customer's onboarding needs, use the customer onboarding scoring tool that is provided for you in the Downloads section of www.practicalcsm.com. This simply gets you to rate the customer's onboarding needs according to the four influencers of onboarding we have discussed above, namely: *product/service complexity, customization work, adoption requirements* and *customer maturity levels.*

For each influencer, you will be asked to provide a score from 0 to 5, where 0 means no complexity due to this influencer and 5 means a very high level of complexity due to this influencer. In this way, you will come up with an overall score between 0 and 20, which you can then use to help understand the overall onboarding complexity for that customer. The larger the total number the more complex the customer's onboarding needs. It's only a broad indicator, but it's a good starting point to prepare the CSM for more detailed discussions about onboarding needs with the customer's stakeholders.

6.6.2 Initial Conversations with the Customer

For all but the most simple and generic of onboarding requirements it will be necessary to sit down and talk to the SPL and/or other customer stakeholders beforehand about the onboarding process itself. You may already have a good idea as to what type of onboarding work is necessary for the customer even before you discuss it with them. Regardless of this, generally speaking the best approach is to have an open conversation about the onboarding options your company offers and the specific needs of the customer as seen through their own eyes. The simplest way to do this is to conduct a discussion that follows the order of the four influencers of onboarding, starting with a conversation about the products/services themselves, then moving to a review of any customization work that has been or will be carried out which might influence the onboarding requirement. After this you can ask the SPL to fill you in on their onboarding needs relating to the specific adoption needs of their users. Finally, touch on their level of maturity in terms of how much they are able or desire to take a DIY approach and how much and what type of help and assistance they are looking for from the CSM's company.

In addition to these four influencers of onboarding you should also ask for any specific outcome requirements that the customer is looking to achieve from their onboarding process. For each outcome try to get the customer to commit to three aspects for each outcome:

1. Quality (what is it?)
2. Quantity (how much of it is required?)
3. Deadline (when is it needed by?)

For example, the customer might say they want to make sure all staff who will be impacted by the initiative are made aware of it. To turn this desire into a properly defined outcome you might need to ask a few questions about this requirement. Ultimately you may end up with an understanding that the customer has 525 workers in three different locations and across four departments who will need to be made aware of exactly how the initiative will impact their role, and who will need to have the ability to ask follow-up questions of their managers to ensure they understand and are comfortable with the proposed changes. This needs to occur at least 1 month ahead of when the initiative itself will commence. With all three of these aspects defined for each outcome the CSM will be much better positioned to understand the relative ease or difficulty of attaining these outcomes and be able to start thinking about methodologies for doing so.

Once these four aspects of onboarding plus the customer's specific onboarding outcome requirements have been discussed you should have a good idea as to whether or not the customer requires a customized onboarding experience, and if so whether this is likely to require a professional services fee. You may of course need to take the information away to discuss with others within your company in order to determine any fees. Of course there may be some negotiations to conduct at this stage and perhaps some different potential routes to take that you can present as options for the customer to select from. Do not forget to discuss timing for the delivery of onboarding, especially any critical deadlines that the customer may have which the onboarding process will need to meet.

6.6.3 Onboarding Management and Communication

Once the approach and any additional fees (if any such exist) have been agreed with the customer, you should seek to agree on management and communication. You need to make sure that both the customer and you are 100% clear as to what tasks are included in the engagement, to what quality and/or quantity each task will be done, and when each task will be completed by as well as who is responsible for performing them. To prevent any misunderstanding it is as well to write this down in a contract which can then be reviewed and validated by the customer and if necessary signed by both parties. Certainly, there should be a written contract in place if there will be a professional services fee involved.

At this stage the CSM should propose a preferred method and cadence of reporting and communication—for example, weekly email update reports, fortnightly phone calls and a formal written monthly report, with face-to-face or virtual meetings by arrangement as and when necessary. Make sure that the customer is comfortable with the proposal or has the opportunity to propose their preferences. Again, review any important deadlines and agree on any major milestones en route to onboarding completion. For each milestone, try to have a way of measuring its achievement. This needn't be intricate or onerous—in fact the simpler the better, and could be as straightforward as simply ticking off completed tasks on a task checklist.

6.6.4 Capturing and Analyzing Onboarding Requirements

Once you move from discussions about onboarding to performing the onboarding work itself, the CSM will need to capture more detailed information about the customer requirements. To capture the information the CSM can use the Onboarding Requirements Capture template which you will find in the Downloads section at www.practicalcsm.com. The "templates" is a Microsoft Excel workbook. The first worksheet provides a list of information pertaining to generic onboarding requirements and the second worksheet provides a list of information pertaining to customized onboarding requirements.

6.6.5 The Onboarding Project Plan

For more complex customized onboarding engagements and especially where the CSM's company will play a role in delivering the onboarding materials to end users it may be necessary for the CSM to treat the onboarding process as its own project. In those circumstances, the project should create a project plan that includes well-defined work phases where the following information is provided for each phase:

■ Activities: What activities will occur during the phase
■ Assets and resources: What assets will be required and what resources will be consumed by the phase, and who will be providing these

- Timing: In which order the phases are to be delivered and where relevant the agreed start and end dates for each phase
- Dependencies: Which other phases must be completed before this phase can commence
- Roles and responsibilities: Who will be responsible for performing which activities during this phase
- Targets and Measurements: How the phase will be measured and what targets are set for determining satisfactory phase completion

In addition, the CSM should also think about the following:

- Risks and Contingencies: What risks have been identified for the onboarding project and what plans are in place to manage those risks?
- Reporting: Who is governing or otherwise overseeing the onboarding process, what information do they require at each stage and in what format should that information be?

6.6.6 *Measuring, Reporting and Handoff to Customer*

The basic rule of thumb for any work that the CSM performs on behalf of the customer, or indeed for any results that accrue from that work is this: *if it wasn't documented and measured it didn't happen.* Wherever possible, the CSM should ensure there is a way to document activity and measure results arising from that activity. This helps the CSM to track and monitor their own productivity and the results they help to achieve, which they can use for their own purposes in learning how to improve upon their performance in the future and to justify their company's investment in their salary (see the later chapter on performance evaluation for more information on this). The information relating to the activity that the CSM records need not be onerous, but should include the following (Table 6.3):

Table 6.3   Information to Be Documented

Item	Description
Task	A brief description of the specific activity
Time	How many hours the CSM spent in performing the activity
Outputs	The results of performing the activity (may be a physical entity, but may also be, for example, an increase in knowledge)
Customer outcomes	The benefits attained by the customer from the performance of the activity
Company outcomes	The benefits attained by the CSM's company from the performance of the activity
Success rating	A level from 0 to 5 that the CSM attribute to the activity to rate its overall success
Comments	Comments on any lessons learned that can be used in the performance of similar activities in the future

Table 6.4   Example of Documentation

Item	Description
Task	Customized onboarding PDF for System X users for Customer A
Time	4 h for CSM, 4 h for Marketing
Outputs	A customized version of the standard onboarding PDF for System X based upon requirements specified by Customer A
Customer outcomes	PDF was sent to all of Customer A's System X users and feedback was gathered by the customer that the message was positively received
Company outcomes	End-user onboarding for Customer A's System X users was completed
Success rating	4
Comments	In the future, we can use this customized version as a template. This will reduce the time spent both for the CSM to determine customer requirements and for the Marketing team to create the customized documentation

A template for documenting CSM activity is provided in the Downloads section at www. practicalcsm.com.

So, for example, let's say that as a part of the customer onboarding process, a communication is crafted that will go out to all end users of a new software application that the customer purchased from the CSM's company. The communication will tell the users all about why the new software was purchased and what it will help the customer's organization to achieve, but most importantly it will explain in general terms how these users will be impacted by the new system in their day to day work. Let's assume that the communication is in the form of a PDF and that is was created by the CSM's company's Marketing department, based upon a brief that the CSM drafted in collaboration with the customer as well as borrowing text and images from an existing generic onboarding PDF for the software system which the CSM's company already possessed. In this example the documentation might look something like this (Table 6.4).

In addition to internal documentation, it is also good practice for the CSM to provide progress reports to the customer. This report may be formal (i.e., written up as a formal report) or informal (for example, the information might be included within an email) depending upon circumstances. Commonly the customer will need regular informal updates and more formal reports can then be created when each major milestone within the overall engagement is reached. The report can then include documentation for all activity, outputs and outcomes attained since the previous milestone. The report will be simple for the CSM to create since they can refer back to their own internal activity documentation to remind themselves as to what has happened and to copy and paste information as necessary.

6.7   Tools for PCSMF Phase 3: Onboarding

- Customer onboarding scoring tool
- Onboarding requirements capture template

- Onboarding project plan template
- CSM activity documentation template

6.7.1 Tools for Capturing Onboarding Requirements

There are two tools for use when identifying onboarding requirements:

Firstly, there is the *Customer_Onboarding_Scoring_Tool*. This tool is provided as a Microsoft Excel workbook, and provides a fast and simple way to determine the overall level of work required for onboarding a particular customer, based upon the four criteria of *product/service complexity*, *customization work*, *adoption requirements* and *customer maturity levels*, as discussed in the section above relating to scoring the customer.

Secondly, there is the *Onboarding_Requirements_Capture_Template*. This template is also in Microsoft Excel format and the workbook contains two worksheets. The first worksheet provides a list of information to capture for generic or standard onboarding requirements. The second worksheet provides a list of information to capture for complex or customized onboarding requirements. While the information captured within the second sheet is likely to vary considerably per customer, some at least of the information captured within the first sheet will tend to remain the same for each specific product or service. As such it may be possible for the CSM to save some time and effort by copying this information across from previous projects.

6.7.2 Tools for Managing Onboarding Activity

For project management of onboarding activities there is the *Onboarding_Work_Plan_Template*. This template is in Microsoft Excel format and the workbook contains five worksheets, each sheet representing a phase of work within the overall project with a space for each outcome for the phase to be clearly defined and explained. The plan itself then contains rows for activities, and each activity can be named and described in terms of what each activity is, who is responsible for performing it, how it will be accomplished, when it will start and end and what the outputs from the activity will be. Additional worksheets can be copied by the CSM and added in as necessary for the management of more complex onboarding projects.

Once the onboarding plan is created the CSM and other colleagues can use it both as a guide for performing activities and also as a mechanism for tracking and measuring and reporting on progress.

6.7.3 Tools for Measuring and Tracking CSM Activity

The final tool that relates to onboarding is the *CSM_Activity_Tracking_Template*. This is another Microsoft Excel workbook which provides a way to quickly and easily document the amount of time CSMs spend on a project against the results achieved. It includes space to record activities and time spent, together with descriptions of outputs and outcomes attained by these activities. It also provides a way to document lessons learned from the performance of these activities that can be applied when performing similar tasks in the future.

While the *CSM_Activity_Tracking_Template* is intended for internal use by the CSM (perhaps in collaboration with their team and/or line manager), the information captured within it can be used within an externally facing report that the CSM may need to create for presentation to the customer.

6.8 Summary of Activities and Outputs for PCSMF Phase 3: Onboarding

6.8.1 Activities for PCSMF Phase 3: Onboarding

The Activities for Phase 3: Onboarding include:

1. Review the completed *Customer_Research_Checklist* for this customer (or other tool you use in handovers) which you created in Phase 1: Preparation.
2. If there are any information gaps that need to be filled or assumptions that need to be validated make a note of them and prepare questions for the customer
3. Review the completed *Customer_Engagement_Strategy* together with any other documents that have also already been created in the Central Repository for this customer to ensure you are up-to-date on requirements from the engagement
4. Use the *Customer_Onboarding_Scoring_Tool* to gain an initial understanding of the likely needs and level of complexity of the customer for onboarding.
5. Hold an initial conversation with the customer to discuss their onboarding needs and explain the options available to them
6. Follow-up as necessary to learn more information and to negotiate an agreement as to the scope and level of help you will be providing for customer onboarding together with other relevant information such as start times and important deadlines, communication and reporting and any professional services fees
7. Use the *Onboarding_Requirements_Capture_Template* to complete a detailed onboarding requirements capture for the customer and analyze this information to determine a phased onboarding project plan
8. Document the onboarding project plan using the *Onboarding_Work_Plan_Template* and share the plan with colleagues and customer as necessary. The plan should include phases, milestones, activities and responsibilities as well as outputs and outcomes for each phase.
9. Work the plan! Make adjustments as necessary along the way due to changes in customer needs or additional information uncovered in these later stages that provide you with additional insight into customer onboarding requirements. Liaise with colleagues and customer regularly during this time to ensure activities are being completed and outputs and outcomes are being attained.
10. Use the *CSM_Activity_Tracking_Template* to record and manage your own time and to learn lessons for future similar engagements
11. Use the information contained both within the *Onboarding_Work_Plan_Template* and the *CSM_Activity_Tracking_Template* to create customer-facing reports at each major milestone and at the end of the onboarding process.

6.8.2 Outputs for PCSMF Phase 3: Onboarding

The Output for Phase 3: Commitment is the successful completion of all onboarding activities, which should be signed off by the customer and detailed in the *Onboarding_Work_Plan_Template* together with lessons learned which should be documented within the *CSM_Activity_Tracking_Template*. By the end of the onboarding phase you will be ready to move forward to PCSMF Phase 4: Adoption Planning.

Chapter 7

Practical CSM Framework Phase 4: Adoption Planning Part 1—Concepts

7.1 What Is Adoption All About?

7.1.1 Defining "Adoption"

Due to the breadth and depth of activities involved and the crossover both between initial onboarding and full adoption at the front end, and between completion of onboarding and commencement

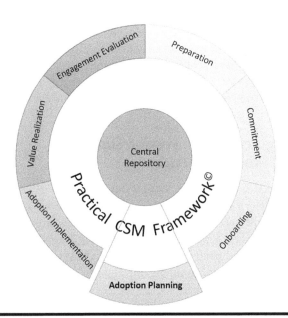

Figure 7.1   PCSMF Phase 4: Adoption Planning.

of value realization at the back end, it is harder to define the term "Adoption" than it might at first seem. The best definition I can think of for it would be:

> The accomplishment of everything that is necessary in order for maximum value realization to occur.

For some situations, this might mean nothing more than plugging something in and switching it on; however, in that sort of very simple adoption situation, it is unlikely that a CSM would be deployed. For more complex situations, there is likely to be a wide variety of tasks that will need to be completed in order for adoption to be accomplished in full. This is particularly the case where there are many people involved. Effectively the more people that are directly or indirectly impacted by the initiative, the more need there will likely be for adoption services.

7.1.2 Proof of Concept and Proof of Value Pilots

In some situations, the customer may have "bought in" to the idea but requires further evidence of the benefits that they can derive from the proposed products, services and/or solutions before they are ready to make a full commitment. In these circumstances, there may be an initial, limited-size implementation that will serve as a test case, after which the customer will be better placed to make a decision over a full implementation.

A *proof of concept pilot* is usually either very limited in size, or even not fully featured and tends to be fairly short in duration. It provides just sufficient functionality to answer specific "does it work?" and "does it do what you say it will do?" type questions. These might, for example, relate to the use of new innovative technology for the first time, or to integration with the customer's existing systems, or to customization based upon the customer's specific requirements.

A *proof of value pilot* is generally fully fledged in terms of features and functionality and longer in duration. It might, for example, take the form of a complete implementation of the solution for a specific department or team. The idea of the proof of value pilot is to go further than merely finding out if the solution works, to learn how much *value* the solution will return. Value only gets realized as the solution gets utilized over time; hence, a short, simple pilot is often insufficient for this purpose, and the proof of value pilot may need to provide full functionality and run for multiple weeks or months in order for value to be measured.

The point here is that CSMs need to make sure they are aware of any proof of concept and/or proof of value pilot requirements, and allow for these within the adoption planning process.

7.1.3 The Changing Role of the Vendor/Supplier in Providing Adoption Services

Traditionally, the performance of adoption services was often left entirely in the hands of the customer. Once the product/service had been purchased, installed, configured, etc., and some basic onboarding had occurred the vendor's (or other seller's) job was largely over except for ongoing product/service maintenance and support services. However, now that the relationship between customer and supplier has moved away from that of simple buyer/supplier and is much more that of a partnership, the role of the vendor in supporting and enabling good quality adoption to occur has very much changed.

Additionally, many technology sales these days are highly complex in nature, combining as they do multiple products and services into a single solution that might also include customization, configuration, integration, security and other considerations. It is therefore simultaneously harder for the customer to perform high-quality adoption without any assistance from the vendor/supplier and in the interests of that vendor/supplier now to provide that assistance. This is one of the major factors behind the exponential rise in popularity of customer success management over the last few years. Helping customers with their adoption needs is often therefore the most important aspect of many CSM's role, and also the most complex part, which can of course make it the hardest part to perform well.

7.1.4 Adoption Is the Successful Management of Change

The process of adoption is effectively the process of managing the change from how the customer's organization used to be before the solution it has purchased was implemented, to how the customer's organization needs to become after the implementation has occurred. As such it could be described as the management of all changes required within the customer's organization to enable the customer to realize value from their initiative. This will include changes to capabilities and processes and the subsequent preparation of users of these processes to enable them to perform their new duties effectively.

Of course, there is a whole profession aimed at effective change management. This includes academic research and study into change management best practices, third-party change management specialist organizations, and change management professionals employed within customer organizations' HR teams to assist that specific company through the changes it experiences.

Different organizations in different industries and with different strategies will experience different rates of change. Additionally, some organizations will have more maturity than other similar companies in terms of their experience of handling change. Some companies may have a different cash flow situation and/or a different attitude toward using external services versus paying for outside help. All of the above considerations and more will means that every customer organization that the CSM gets involved in should be treated as unique in terms of its change management requirements.

7.1.5 Helping Users to Undergo Change

The major part of adoption is helping users through change. Discussion on how to find out who these users are and how they will be impacted by the change occurs later in this chapter, but the point to make here is that when it comes to adoption it is the people aspect of change that requires the most time and energy to be spent in order to get the adoption right. The fundamental aspects of any adoption initiative will likely include (Table 7.1):

Table 7.1 Aspects of an Adoption Initiative

Aspect	Description
Communicating change	This occurs well prior to any change actually occurring. The proposed changes are announced and explained. Implications for each user are explained and discussions may take place where reactions are gauged and concerns are discussed. The idea here is to ensure that when the change does finally occur, users are already on board and problems regarding fears and concerns are already dealt with, so that users come to the change with the attitude of readiness and acceptance of it.

(Continued)

Table 7.1 (*Continued*)   Aspects of an Adoption Initiative

Aspect	Description
Preparing users for change	Where necessary, users need to be provided with additional knowledge and skills to enable them to perform new tasks and/or perform existing tasks in new ways. This will necessitate reviewing each user's knowledge and skill gaps (what they need to know compared with what they already know) and then devising and implementing training, communication and support programs to cover those knowledge and skill gaps.
Assisting users through the change	When the change occurs, some users may be very comfortable with it, but others might be less so. This might be for a variety of reasons, some practical and some more emotional. On the emotional side, users may experience fear or anxiety around whether they are able to perform new tasks well and what will happen to them if they cannot. On the practical side, problems with the change or unexpected side effects from it may be experienced that cause legitimate issues that need to be dealt with. Whatever the problems, users need to have the support and assistance in place to monitor and help them as necessary.
Supporting users after the change	Once the change has occurred, users may require ongoing support so that they can resolve unexpected issues that come up, or can be reminded as to how certain tasks are now performed. It may take a while for users to become as familiar and comfortable with the new way of doing things as they were previously with the old and more familiar way. Support should continue until all unexpected issues have been resolved and users do now feel comfortable and familiar with the new ways of working.
Monitoring and measuring change	Outputs from users' work needs to be measured to ensure that productivity, efficiency, quality or other targets are being met and where they are not met that this is recognized so that corrective action can be taken. This might, for example, include further training, reconfiguration of the technology being used, or additional process changes. Information relating to measurement of outputs may need to be reported to senior decision makers—particularly to sponsors who have funded the initiative—in order to assure them of the value being returned.
Encouraging new behavior	People by their nature tend to be conservative by nature, in the sense that it is generally more comfortable for people to do things the old (though perhaps less efficient or effective) way than to learn a new way of doing it. Where this applies it might take some encouragement to reinforce the desired new behaviors in users. This encouragement might contain both positive aspects such as rewards for completion of new task within a certain timeframes, and negative aspects such as needing to explain to line managers if users do not complete their new tasks within a certain timeframe.

7.1.6 Adoption as a Paid for Professional Service

Just as with onboarding, there is no reason why a company could not offer adoption as a chargeable professional service. Indeed there is every reason for organizations to carefully consider the financial implications of offering adoption as a value-added professional service for customers to elect to purchase or not as they choose. There are many different strategies that companies can take here, based upon their business model and, in particular, upon the value proposition they are offering to their customers. If, for example, the value proposition (i.e., the reason why customers should purchase their product or service from *this* organization instead from a competitor) is about the very best possible quality then it could be argued that customers might expect to have to pay extra for additional value added services such as adoption services.

If, on the other hand, the value proposition is about the lowest possible prices and/or fastest availability then again an argument could be made for adoption services to be a separately billable professional service that customers can choose either to have or not to have based upon their needs. However, if the value proposition is about *business outcomes*—i.e., the customers' purchase decisions are made not based upon the features or other qualities of the products or services themselves but instead upon how those products and services will help the customers to achieve strategic end results within their organizations—then there is a very strong argument to suggest that adoption services should be a recognized and nonoptional component of the solution that is being offered. This is because in the circumstances where the attainment of end results (or outcomes) are what are being sold to the customer, change management (i.e., adoption) cannot be an option—it *has* to happen and it has to happen to the right quality and at the right time in order for the value promised in the value proposition to occur.

Needless to say, as a CSM it is important to ensure you are clear as to exactly *what* adoption services your own organization offers and how much of those services are offered at no additional charge via customer success management, versus being paid for as an additional professional service fee.

7.1.7 The Role of the CSM in Adoption Planning and Implementation

Because there is so much complexity within the topic of adoption services, I have divided the subject into two separate Practical CSM Framework phases. Phase 4 of the Framework is called Adoption Planning and deals with the preparation stages for product/service adoption, and this is the focus of this chapter. Phase 5 of the Framework is called Adoption Implementation and this will be dealt with in the next chapter. Due to the focus of the CSM role on providing advice, assistance and guidance to the customer rather than on actually *doing* the work themselves, CSMs will find that they are likely to be as busy if not more busy during the Adoption Planning stage compared to the Adoption Implementation stage which follows.

When you think about it, customers who have just purchased a particular product, service or solution are highly likely to know much less at the early "just purchased" stage about that product, service or solution than the vendor or other supplier does. Of course over time as they use the solution the customer's knowledge will grow with the experience of using it, but initially it makes sense that they will be relying to greater or lesser extent upon the expertise of the supplier or of a third-party systems integrator to help them get things right. This knowledge of how to "get things right" based upon knowledge of the solution itself and upon multiple real-world experiences of assisting with the adoption of the solution in other customer organizations is what the CSM brings to the table as being uniquely qualified to help the customer with their own adoption requirements.

This is what sets the supplier's CSM apart as being someone with very special knowledge that is potentially of high value to the customer. Effectively it is the CSM's *raison d'etre* or "reason for existence," or if you prefer to you could think of it as the CSM's USP (unique selling point).

In any case, the point is that because the CSM themselves will (or if newly appointed to the role then will eventually through the role-related training and coaching they receive) have been through the process of helping other previous customers with the adoption of this solution, they are well placed to help *this* customer with its own adoption needs. Additionally, due to the ongoing need to provide high-quality adoption assistance to its customers, the CSM's company will over time have developed best practices for the adoption of its products and services, and will have created assets such as task lists and templates that simplify the adoption process and ensure that best practices are adhered to, and then evolved those best practices and assets over time as they are used in each new customer engagement.

7.1.8 Comparing Onboarding and Adoption

There are similarities and overlaps between onboarding and adoption. Both deal with preparing the customer organization for undergoing change in order to generate value from the solution they have purchased, and the CSM might experience different engagement where the same activity occurs for one engagement at the onboarding stage and for another, different engagement during adoption. Care should also be taken around language, since different organizations may well use the two terms differently—sometimes even interchangeably—and customers may also either have their own specific definitions for each terms or conversely might struggle to understand the differences between the two.

The main differences are:

Onboarding: Onboarding occurs earlier in the engagement (typically either immediately before, during or immediately after solution implementation) and focuses more on immediacy (i.e., getting the customer up and running and generating some immediate initial value from the solution). Typically it focuses on the communication of basic solution information to those that require it.

Adoption: Adoption occurs when the customer is ready for its users to start utilizing the solution within their day-to-day activities and therefore focuses on managing change. It tends to be more comprehensive in its scope than onboarding. It is likely to include aspects of communication, education and ongoing support for impacted users. It needs careful planning prior to implementation and may be implemented in phases.

7.1.9 Adoption Complexity

As a simple yet effective way of gaining an immediate understanding of the likely level of complexity of your customer's adoption needs, use the customer adoption scoring tool that is provided for you in the Downloads section of www.practicalcsm.com. This follows the same format as the customer onboarding scoring tool discussed and reviewed in Chapter 6. To use the tool you simply rate the customer's adoption needs according to the same four influencers of complexity that were discussed for onboarding in the previous chapter, namely; *product/service complexity, customization work, adoption requirements* and *customer maturity levels.*

For each influencer, you will be asked to provide a score from 0 to 5, where 0 means no complexity due to this influencer and 5 means a very high level of complexity due to this influencer.

In this way, you will come up with an overall score between 0 and 20, which you can then use to help understand the overall adoption complexity for that customer. The larger the total number the more complex the customer's adoption needs. As for onboarding, it's only a broad indicator, but it's a good starting point to prepare the CSM for more detailed discussions about adoption needs with the customer's stakeholders.

7.2 Understanding Impacted Users

7.2.1 Adoption Complexity and Impacted Users

You will recall our definition for "adoption" as being "the accomplishment of everything that is necessary in order for maximum value realization to occur." We will now briefly discuss what this "everything that is necessary" might include. In particular, we will focus on the link between adoption complexity (how easy or difficult it is to complete the adoption process) and the numbers and types of impacted users (people who will be either directly or indirectly impacted by change due to the initiative taking place). Essentially the relationship between these two factors is nonlinear. It may not be precisely logarithmic in nature, but there's definitely a curve to the line, whereby complexity increases more and more rapidly as additional users get involved (Figure 7.2).

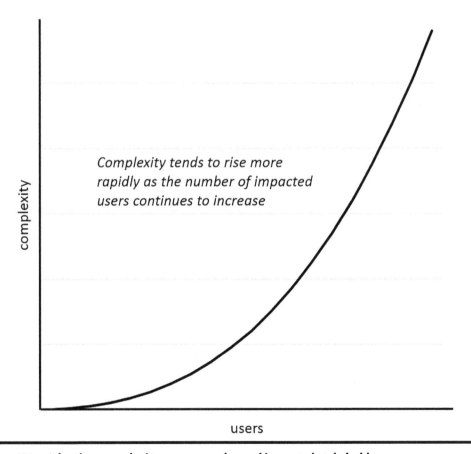

Figure 7.2   Adoption complexity versus numbers of impacted stakeholders.

Of course, this doesn't mean that CSMs should try in any way to curtail either the overall number of impacted users or the different needs that those users have. In fact, the reverse is true—it is in fact essential for the CSM to help their customer to ensure they have uncovered *all* the impacts on *all* potentially impacted users (which may sometimes include users from outside of the customer's own organization) in order for adoption to be completed successfully. What it does mean though, is that for situations that involve larger numbers and/or types of impacted users, CSMs should anticipate there being a much greater level of complexity in adoption requirements and should therefore plan their time allocation accordingly.

7.2.2 Identifying Users' Knowledge, Skill and Attitude (KSA) Needs

KSA stands for knowledge, skill and attitude, and these can be thought of as the three aspects of change management needs that each user may have and which must therefore be handled by the adoption plan. Let's examine each aspect (Table 7.2):

Table 7.2 Understanding KSA

Aspect	Description
Knowledge	Knowledge is often described as "book learning," and refers to a cognitive understanding of what the stakeholder is required to do and how they are required to do it. The reason that it is sometimes referred to as "book learning" is because increasing knowledge is the traditional role of academic organizations such as schools and colleges, and because knowledge is (or at least was) generally transferred through books and lectures. Having an understanding of what needs to be done generates the ability for the person to think and act independently rather than having to be told what to do by a supervisor at every stage of the performance of a task. Knowledge is therefore of particular importance in jobs that require autonomous decision-making by the person involved, such as in sales, customer service or consultancy roles.
Skill	Skill is the ability to perform a task adequately, and this performance ability tends to increase in quality over time as more experience of performing the activity is gained. Different types of tasks have more or less of a skill-related component. For example, tasks requiring precise brain-to-body motor skills such as dentistry or fork lift truck driving will tend to require a high level of skill, which in turn requires at least a degree of on-the-job style training to be completed before a person gains the desired skill. Because skill cannot be taught through books but through experience, it tends to be taught in situ by coaching and/or mentoring rather than just by instructing (for example, think about how you might teach someone how to swim or ride a bicycle).

(Continued)

Table 7.2 (*Continued*) Understanding KSA

Aspect	Description
Attitude	Attitude is the emotional and personality-related aspect of capability. Regardless of how knowledgeable and/or skillful a person might be, if their attitude toward performing the task is wrong, they will either perform the task less well than otherwise, or even not perform the task at all. Emotions that might negatively affect a person's attitude toward performing a task might include ignorance (not understanding why it is important, for example), anger (caused, for example, by feelings of being unjustly imposed upon by being ordered to perform the task) and fear (perhaps due to feelings of insecurity around the ability to perform the task sufficiently well, and concerns about being sanctioned in some way of they cannot do so). An individual's personality will at least to some extent dictate the level of impact that attitude may have to the performance of the tasks they are asked to perform. People with high emotional IQs and mature personalities will be more likely to need less support with attitudinal problems than their counterparts with lower levels of emotional IQ and less maturity.

7.2.3 Directly and Indirectly Impacted Users

You may recall our discussion in previous chapters about the differences between directly and indirectly impacted stakeholders. We defined directly impacted stakeholders as those who will actually use the solution itself (either to perform the same or similar task/s as they previously performed but now using the new solution components), whereas indirectly impacted stakeholders will still do or at least experience something different due to the initiative, but will not themselves use the new solution (for example, the output produced by a directly impacted stakeholder group's activity may form the input for an indirectly impacted stakeholder group's activity). In this chapter, we will describe directly and indirectly impacted stakeholders as "users."

Although the focus of adoption activity may be on directly impacted users, it may still be essential to have considered the needs of indirectly impacted users and allowed for those needs within the overall adoption plan. For example, a directly impacted user might need an initial communication to explain what will be happening, followed by training on the new or changed activity and then may need to be provided with ongoing support and management. Whereas an indirectly impacted user might just need the initial communication only, or perhaps the initial communication and some basic support in case they have questions or run into difficulties. Whatever the case, it is up to the CSM to make sure they and/or the customer has fully investigated all possible users and identified in what ways each one will be impacted by the initiative.

7.2.4 User Adoption Requirements Information Gathering

First, let's deal with a very simple piece of terminology. Groups of users who share the same (or sufficiently similar for the differences to be of no great consequence) adoption requirements can be grouped together and treated as one unit for the purposes of adoption. Doing this has the obvious advantage of reducing the amount of admin and makes planning for adoption a lot easier. Some groups may be quite large and contain hundreds or occasionally even thousands of users. Others may be a lot smaller and contain merely a handful of similar users. You may also come across individual users who have unique adoption requirements, in which case they are effectively their own group—a group containing just one individual. These groups are referred to within the Practical CSM Framework as Impacted Groups (IGs).

For each IG, the CSM needs to ensure that the following information has been identified and recorded (Table 7.3):

Table 7.3   Information Gathering for Impacted Groups

Info	Description
Name	An identifying name for the IG
Location/s and numbers	The location or locations in which the IG members reside, and the numbers of users at each location
Impact scope	A description of how this IG will be impacted by the initiative. This should be made as comprehensive as necessary to ensure all aspects of the scope of the impact on them is fully documented
Directly or indirectly impacted	Although this information should be easily inferred from reading the Impact Scope, it is useful to note separately whether the IG is directly or indirectly impacted by the solution
Knowledge requirement (K)	A full description of what knowledge is currently not known by the IG that its members will require in order to perform their role adequately
Skill requirement (S)	A full description of what skills are currently not possessed by the IG that its members will require in order to perform their role adequately
Attitude requirement (A)	A full description of what attitudinal issues may be present in the IG that will need to be managed in order for its members to perform their role adequately
Initiative phase	If the initiative will be delivered across a series of phases, the phase in which each IG will become impacted should be recorded here. (Note that this is not the same things as "Adoption Phases" which are phases within the adoption plan itself, rather than within the overall initiative).
Deadlines	Any time-related information should be noted. For example, this might include deadlines by which particular IGs must be ready and able to use the new solution
Priority level	What priority level this IG has in terms of importance for dealing with first. This could be termed simply as "High," "Medium" or "Low," or numbered from say 1 to 5 where 1 is a very low priority and 5 is a very high priority

7.2.5 The Specific Role of the CSM in Uncovering and Recording User Information

Note that what we said was that the CSM needs to ensure that the above information has been identified and recorded. What we did not say was that the CSM needs to uncover this information directly themselves. In point of fact, CSMs are rarely the people who are best placed to access this information if it already exists, or to research and uncover this information if it does not already exist. Instead, the CSM should act as adviser and consultant to the customer, and help the SPL as much or as little as is necessary to uncover these facts for themselves.

How this is done depends upon the existing relationship with and the needs of the SPL and of the customer more widely. Assuming a good trust relationship exists between SPL and CSM, and where the SPL and the customer more widely is relatively inexperienced in adoption best practices for this sort of initiative, the CSM is likely to play a more active role than would otherwise be required or appropriate. In these circumstances, the CSM may take the lead in organizing and project managing the process of uncovering the required information. This might include explaining and specifying *what* information needs to be obtained and also in determining or at least recommending *how* that information might best be gathered.

The CSM might also in this sort of situation take control of managing the information itself as it is uncovered. Even if this is not the case, it is extremely helpful either for the CSM to have access to the user-related information that the customer records or to keep such recordings themselves for their own reference purposes.

7.2.6 Obtaining User Information from Key Stakeholders

As mentioned above, when it comes to the actual research, the CSM will be liaising with the SPL and other key stakeholders within the customer organization to get the job completed. They may play a direct role in uncovering this information, but they may be more likely to perform an indirect, advisory role. In either case the CSM must make sure they are aware of the primary ways in which research might be conducted and the types of key stakeholders within the customer's organization (apart from the SPL of course) who might already hold this information or have access to it or worst case scenario have the ability to create it. These key stakeholders might include the following:

7.2.6.1 Human Resources (HR)

The Human Resources (or HR) department (which might be referred to by other names such as Personnel Management or Human Capital Management) is always a good port of call for information relating to job roles. Parts of the HR management team's responsibilities are to manage and maintain detailed job role descriptions for each job role. Assuming it is up to date and accurate (both of which assumptions should most definitely be carefully validated before the information is trusted) this job role information is a gold mine for uncovering user information for adoption. This is because it should clearly identify which job roles will be impacted by the initiative and in what ways they will be impacted.

As a side note, HR managers may also be important people for CSMs to form good working relationships with since at the Value Realization stage (occurring in Phase 6 of the Practical CSM

Framework) the CSM may well need their assistance in ensuring that new job roles and changes to existing job roles are officially sanctioned and properly documented.

7.2.6.2 Department Heads

Department Heads are responsible for ensuring both the success of the department itself in terms of achievement of its own targets and the contributions of that department toward the wider achievement of overall corporate goals. They are generally appointed by and report to the company's senior management team. They are involved in determining and implementing departmental strategy and in communicating that strategy to their workforce as well as in providing leadership and management to "steer the ship." They will generally be ultimately responsible for managing and allocating departmental budgets and be involved in decision-making for hiring and firing new workers.

Departmental Heads can be of use to the CSM both directly in terms of their knowledge of how the initiative the CSM is working on impacts their department and indirectly in leveraging the time of team leaders, people managers, process owners and capability owners who have ownership of specific activities and who oftentimes have more detailed and explicit knowledge that the CSM needs than the Department Heads themselves.

7.2.6.3 Team Leaders and People Managers

These are the people who control, manage, guide and lead teams of workers on a day-to-day basis. They are intimately involved with and have an in-depth understanding of what the people within their management team do and how they do it, and they are generally responsible for making sure that activity and/or productivity targets are met. These leaders and managers are therefore very well placed to know exactly and in detail which members of their teams will be directly or indirectly impacted by the initiative and how they will be impacted.

Team Leaders and People Managers are very useful contacts later in the adoption planning process as well as in the adoption implementation phase, when availability for adoption-related activities (particularly training) may need to be discussed, negotiated and agreed.

7.2.6.4 Process Owners and Capability Owners

These are managers not of people but of operations that include one or more processes or capabilities. Their responsibility is to ensure that the operations they are responsible for happen to the right levels of quality, efficiency and productivity, while also ensuring other types of considerations are managed—for example, safety and security—and that best practices are followed. These types of managers will again have detailed knowledge about eh areas of the business they are responsible for, and are therefore ideal candidates for learning about in what ways each process will be impacted by the initiative and how this affects the workers who are involved in auctioning those processes.

As with Team Leaders and People Managers, Process Owners and Capability Owners are also very useful contacts later in the adoption planning process as well as in the adoption implementation phase, when availability for adoption-related activities (particularly training) may need to be discussed, negotiated and agreed.

Note: There may be some (or even much) overlap between these different types of managers and leaders. In smaller organizations particularly, it will be quite common to come across senior leaders who are also responsible for day-to-day people and/or process management, and people managers may also be process or capability owners.

7.2.7 Who Will Perform the Research Activities?

It is generally the case that the CSM will not have met the majority or even any of these key stakeholders before. It is also possible that due to business etiquette and/or corporate culture within the customer organization, it would be better for the SPL or one or two other key stakeholders from the customer organization who are already involved in the initiative to approach and hold discussions with these managers and leaders than for the CSM to attempt to do it themselves. Even if it is feasible for the CSM to perform the work, for practical reasons of time and availability the CSM may need the customer to take responsibility for conducting all or at least a part of this type of research. Whatever the case, the CSM needs to agree on what work needs to be done and how it will be done as well as who will be tasked with performing it and a deadline for the work's completion.

On the other side of the coin, CSMs may wish to meet and start to form relationships with at least some of these business managers and leaders, since they may be influential in terms of their authority and decision-making powers which make them very useful contacts for the CSM to cultivate.

7.3 Research Techniques

7.3.1 Understanding Research Options

If the CSM will be conducting all or at least some of the research directly through their own efforts then they will need to be familiar with the ways in which the required information can be gathered. Even if they are not directly involved in the research gathering themselves, they may sometimes need to make recommendations to the SPL or other key stakeholders as to what methodologies can be employed to get the best results.

7.3.2 Technique 1: Interview

The most obvious research technique is the interview. This will often be a one-on-one interview with an individual stakeholder (for example, a specific Team Leader or Process Owner) to discuss aspects of the initiative that relate to that specific stakeholder's area of authority and responsibility. It could also be an interview that involves multiple stakeholders in one go, which can be useful where there needs to be discussion and consensus forming around which users will be impacted and in what ways they will be impacted.

A typical interview might last between 30 and 90 min and it could be conducted face to face or by phone or virtual meeting over the Internet. CSMs should prepare their questions in advance so that vital information is not omitted. They should also make sure they have a way of recording outputs from the interview that will not get in the way of the flow of the discussion. A simple checklist of topics for discussion with space to record findings from each topic might be suitable for this.

It might also be worth noting in passing that information obtained via interview (and to some extent by survey also) tends to only be as good as the honesty and accuracy of the information provided by the person or people being interviewed. It is entirely possible for researchers to be misled by interviewees either deliberately through dishonestly answering questions by providing false information, or accidentally through either misunderstanding what is being asked or simply through errors in memory or judgment (just ask a police detective about the reliability and accuracy of witness statements to see how often this occurs). While I am not suggesting that CSMs should suspect every interviewee of being dishonest or inaccurate, I am suggesting that they should bear the reliability of information obtained through interviews in mind and where possible look for ways to validate the most important types of information—perhaps through correlation of this information from multiple sources, for example.

7.3.3 Technique 2: Workshop

The concept of the workshop is to take the process of discussion and consensus forming described above a stage further and to provide a forum for in-depth brainstorming, debate, negotiation and ultimately decision-making around whatever topic the workshop relates to. In this case, the workshops would of course relate to determining which users will be impacted and in what ways they will be impacted.

If the customer organization has already thought through this information and made the necessary decisions then simple interviews with Team leaders and Process Owners will be all that is required. On the other hand if the customer organization has not yet thought through this information and/or made the necessary decisions then a workshop where all relevant key stakeholders are invited to attend and where the CSM leads these stakeholders through this thinking and decision-making process would be a very powerful way to attain the required results.

It is worth noting however that workshops are generally quite complex and sophisticated types of meetings that require a great deal of planning, management and leadership in order to be productive. Getting it right and leading a high-quality workshop that helps the customer's key stakeholders to determine which members of their workforce will be impacted by an initiative and in what ways that impact will be experienced is a fantastic way to move the engagement forwards and will likely have a very positive effect on the trust relationships that the CSM is forming with these key stakeholders.

On the other hand, getting it wrong and not really reaching consensus on who will be impacted and how they will be impacted and perhaps running the risk of being perceived either as wasting important senior leaders' time or being incompetent in the CSM role may actually be harmful to these relationships. Care should therefore be taken to prepare well for a workshop, and if the CSM does not feel confident to lead the workshop then they should consider ways in which to gain that confidence (such as training on workshop leadership or gaining practical experience through attending other colleagues' workshops and participating as an assistant) beforehand. If a workshop is required and the CSM does not feel comfortable to lead it, it may well make sense to ask a colleague who does already have the right skills and experience to perform the task instead, in which case the CSM can attend to assist this person and to gain further workshop experience.

Another point to consider is that besides the CSM, other key people from within the CSM's company may potentially add value to and/or gain value from participating in this type of customer workshop. Given this is the case, the CSM might want to consider who else they might wish to invite, and how the work of facilitating the workshop might be shared between them.

Other factors that the CSM needs to consider when organizing a workshop include (Table 7.4):

Table 7.4 Factors for Workshops

Factor	*Description*
Duration	Workshops of this kind might last from around half a day (say 3–4 h) to several days in duration, depending upon size and complexity of the initiative and the numbers of key stakeholders attending
Attendees	The more stakeholders that attend the workshop the harder it will be for everyone to fully voice their opinions and for consensus to be reached. On the other hand, too few stakeholders make it hard to discuss everything fully since there will be less perspectives in the room from which to brainstorm and debate any given topic
Availability	One factor to consider in organizing a workshop or even in determining whether a workshop is feasible in the first place is key stakeholder availability. From a practical perspective there is little point in running a workshop if not everyone whose opinion is essential is available to attend. The CSM might need to be creative around this—for example, by inviting senior execs to attend a short part rather than the entirety of a workshop, or by inviting geographically distant stakeholders to attend remotely
Agenda	Careful thought should be given to the agenda to ensure that all topics that need to be raised, discussed and agreed upon are covered. This is particularly the case when senior leaders are invited to the workshop, since this may be the one and only opportunity to get their input
Facilitation	The role of the CSM (which might potentially be delegated to someone else if the CSM does not feel sufficiently confident to perform it) is to facilitate the workshop. This means that they need to co-ordinate activities and discussions, encourage participation, ensure all stakeholders' opinions are listened to and considered equally, decisions are reached (where necessary) and outputs are recorded
Time management	An important aspect of workshop facilitation is time management. Whoever is managing time needs to ensure that the workshop stays on track as it works through the agenda. This means making sure that sufficient time is devoted to each topic or section, but that the workshop moves forwards with enough speed to get through all agenda items. Where the workshop gets stuck (perhaps in debate or disagreement on a specific topic) the workshop facilitator needs to recognize this and step in to deal with it in an appropriate way
Energy levels	Workshops can sometimes be quite intense in their nature, and discussions can get quite heated or technical or complex—sometimes all three at once! With this in mind, the CSM should be aware of energy levels in the room and where necessary give attendees short breaks to refresh themselves. It may also be a good idea in longer sessions to sometimes get attendees standing up and moving around the room in order to cause disruptive change and to get more oxygen flowing to the brain

(Continued)

Table 7.4 (*Continued*) Factors for Workshops

Factor	Description
Preparation and administration	The key to success in most activities is good preparation. CSMs should spend time planning and preparing for the workshop. Important aspects of planning and administration includes practical considerations such as inviting and reminding attendees, briefing them on what to expect, selecting and where necessary preparing appropriate facilities and providing refreshments
Recording outputs	It is essential that outputs from the workshop (especially any decisions made) are recorded and may also need to be distributed to attendees afterwards. If the CSM is going to be busy facilitating and time keeping, they may not have time available to also record outputs. The CSM must therefore think in advance as to who will perform this important task
Follow up	It is not uncommon for workshops to turn up issues or uncover aspects of the initiative that had not previously been realized, or to simply not be able to reach an essential decision due to disagreement in the room or perhaps because of lack of needed information. Whatever the case, there is likely to be a number of follow up activities generated from the workshop that need to be recorded and then (of course) need to be assigned to someone to perform

7.3.4 Technique 3: Survey

If the opinions of a large number of people with a similar perspective (for example, a group of several hundred or more similarly impacted users) is sought (for example, it might be necessary to ask an IG how they currently perform a particular task, or what the impact of a proposed change to the process for performing that task will be on them) then it may well be difficult or impossible to meet with them all personally to interview them. In this instance, a survey might be a better way forwards.

Surveys are useful because they can address information from a lot of people very efficiently. Where they are not so good is in getting much detail from those who are surveyed. This is both because survey respondents don't tend to want to respond with very detailed answers to questions since it is very time-consuming for them to do so, and also because it is very difficult and time-consuming for survey owners to even read a lot of detail from many hundreds or respondents, let alone correlate this data into any meaningful information.

Surveys are therefore best used where quantitative information is required rather than qualitative information. For example, a survey that asks questions with Yes/No answers, or that gets respondents to select from a number of pre-written options, or that asks them to rate things from 1 to 5 or 1 to 10 are all very feasible. On the other hand, surveys that ask respondents to describe things in their own words and provide lengthy written answers to open questions are much harder both to get people to respond to and to administrate afterwards.

7.3.5 Technique 4: Focus Groups

One way to overcome the limitations of survey techniques where qualitative information such as opinions, experiences and preferences is required from a large cohort of similar users is to use a focus group. A focus group is a small but representative sample of a larger group. For example, the customer may have 2,000 call center workers who operate call centers in several locations across the country. It would be very time-consuming and expensive to interview them all individually or even in groups, but the limitations on qualitative information from surveys means that this is not going to work either. Instead, a carefully selected representative sample of say 20 call center workers drawn from across the different locations could be invited to form a focus group. A meeting can then be conducted with this focus group and the necessary questions asked so that the thoughts and opinions of this small group on the necessary topics can be recorded. Because care was taken to ensure that the focus group is a true representative sample of the larger group, their outputs should reflect the outputs that would have been gained had all members of the larger group been interviewed.

As with workshops, focus group management and facilitation is a skill in its own right. Care needs to be taken in selecting the right focus group members, in preparing the right questions for the focus group to discuss and debate, and in recording the outputs from the group's discussions. However, it is a very effective way of solving the specific problem of eliciting qualitative information from a large user group, where this is necessary. There may also be confidentiality issues that need to be managed carefully. This can arise because the people who are invited to form a focus group tend to be from more junior ranks within the customer organization, and either may not be allowed to know certain information ahead of time, or may be concerned about their concerns and opinions being expressed to more senior management. An experienced focus group facilitator should be able to deal with both of these issues effectively. Also as with running workshops, it may be a good idea for a CSM with limited experience of running focus groups to first gain some training or first-hand experience of focus group facilitation before attempting to lead a focus group themselves.

7.3.6 Technique 5: Existing Documentation

Rather than needing to talk to key stakeholders, it may be possible to bypass them altogether and go directly to existing documentation. This does assume that the researcher has the authority and ability to access such documentation of course. But this technique does have the distinct advantage of usually being much more efficient in terms of time, and requires less organization and liaison with others around diary management and availability to attend meetings. The most obvious types of documentation include:

- Process maps and workflows
- Capability definitions and use cases
- Customer journey maps
- Job descriptions
- Detailed task descriptions and step-by-step instructions for fulfilling each task
- Task or activity-relate training guides
- ISO 9001 documentation (or equivalent)

If the CSM and/or SPL does not have knowledge of or access to the necessary documentation, the first step might be to conduct interviews with key stakeholders to gain an understanding of what documentation is available that is relevant and to gain permission to access it.

7.3.7 Technique 6: Observation

This is where the researcher physically or remotely observes users during the performance of their duties in order to learn what activities they perform and how they execute these activities. Direct observation has the obvious benefit of being accurate since the researcher experiences what happens for themselves at first-hand rather than relying upon what others tell them (as occurs, for example, in interviews and surveys). However, this only holds true if the actor (the person being observed) is not aware of the observation occurring, since otherwise they might alter what they normally do in order to appear better in front of the researcher in some way (for example, they might decide to follow the correct procedure to the letter while under observation, even though they would normally take many shortcuts when not observed). The problem that this raises though is a problem of ethics, since the CSM and/or the customer may not consider it ethical to observe workers without their prior knowledge and awareness of it and their consent for it to occur.

7.3.8 Technique 7: Shared Previous Customer Experience

The final technique for research that we will cover is shared previous customer experience. This is where a friendly, previous customer that has already gone through the adoption and value realization stages of the same (or substantially similar) products, services and solutions in similar circumstances is invited in to share the experiences they had with this customer. This can be a very powerful way for the customer to gain useful insight into how best to adopt the solution and generate maximum value from doing so. If this technique is used it can sometimes be a good idea for the CSM merely to act as introducer and liaison, but then to leave the two customers alone to share their knowledge and experiences without oversight or interference.

7.4 CSM Involvement in Adoption Research

7.4.1 Performing the Research Itself

As we discussed earlier, it is often not useful or necessary for the CSM to perform detailed user-related research themselves. In most cases, this should be left as the responsibility of the customer organization. However, even if the CSM will not be directly involved in performing the research, it is still important for CSMs to understand the benefits and limitations of each of the four techniques described above and to have at least a passing understanding of when and how each technique should be deployed. This is because one important aspect of the CSM's role is that of coach, consultant and adviser to the SPL and other key stakeholders within the customer organization.

Oftentimes the CSM may find the customer key stakeholders are already well versed in research techniques and may even have already pre-researched and recorded all necessary information relating to the needs of impacted users. However, this cannot be relied upon to occur in every customer engagement. Depending upon the customer organization's size and maturity in managing change of this kind, the CSM may well need to explain what research needs to be undertaken and propose ways in which that research could be conducted.

Whatever the situation, as stated previously the CSM is responsible for ensuring as best they can that adequate research is undertaken in order for sufficient information about user requirements to be uncovered.

7.4.2 How Will Research Findings Be Recorded?

However, much or little the CSM is involved in the actual research; they will certainly want to review and discuss the research findings. They will therefore want to make sure that research findings are documented in a format that makes sense and either that this documentation is placed in a location that is accessible to them or they are able to make a copy of it for their own purposes. As well as this they will want to have agreed to meet with the SPL (and other key stakeholders as necessary) to discuss the research findings and agree the implications of these findings in terms of adoption requirements.

7.4.3 Professional Services Opportunities

Because the CSM is unlikely to have the time available to perform all of the necessary research on users—especially in situations where the information is not currently available and will need to be created from scratch, adoption tends to become a partnership between customer and solution provider. As previously discussed earlier in this chapter, the non-chargeable services that the CSM can offer the customer to assist them with adoption should be made explicitly clear at the outset. However, during the engagement both the customer and the CSM may well learn more about the true adoption needs of the customer and the level of help that they could use to complete this adoption. As such, the CSM should always be looking for professional services opportunities and be ready to discuss and propose further assistance on a paid for professional services basis to the customer as appropriate.

7.5 Working with Multiple Stakeholders

7.5.1 The Management of Stakeholders Is Harder with Adoption

Because it addresses the change management needs of all impacted users, adoption is generally the most complex part of a CSM's engagement. One reason for this is the number of different stakeholders that may be involved both in the research and planning activities, but also in the implementation phase (covered in the next chapter). It may be the case that team leaders, process owners and the like are all very open with the information that the CSM needs to obtain from them, in agreement between themselves as to what changes are required, and compliant with the CSM and SPLs' plans as to how those change requirements will be met. It is also entirely possible that the reverse is true, and that getting information from the relevant stakeholders proves very difficult, that there is not one consensus opinion within the management team on which users will be impacted, or in what ways those users will be impacted, and there is disagreement on what should be done about it. Typically of course the CSM is likely to find elements of helpfulness and/or consensus, and elements of unhelpfulness and/or disagreement.

7.5.2 Using the Stakeholder Management Matrix and Stakeholder Management Plan

In Section 5.5 of Chapter 5, we looked at how to develop a stakeholder management strategy. In this section, we review the use of the RACI Matric, the Stakeholder Management Matrix and the Stakeholder Management Plan. If the CSM has not yet needed to use these tools, it may well be the case that they need to do so now that the Adoption Planning phase has been reached. It may also be the case that while the CSM did use these tools in earlier stages of the engagement, the need for their more detailed utilization is now evident. In any case, the development of an RACI Matrix, a Stakeholder Management Matrix and a Stakeholder Management Plan is strongly recommended when tackling complex Adoption engagements that have multiple stakeholder involvements. Templates for these tools can be found in the Downloads section of www.practicalcsm.com.

7.5.3 Dealing with Uncooperative Stakeholders

Naturally, the CSM must always bear in mind that they are the representative of a supplier to the customer's company, and as such they do not themselves carry any authority or level of seniority within the customer's organization. They are in effect a guest who has been invited in to assist with a particular problem. That said, the CSM does have a job to do, and regardless of whether the engagement is directly paid for via a professional services fee or whether the work of the CSM is simply offered as a part of the overall deal and is not separately billable, one way or another the customer *is still paying for the CSM's time.*

The CSM should therefore expect to be treated in a professional manner and be met with helpfulness rather than hostility. It is very rare that key stakeholders (i.e., senior managers) cause any real issues due to negative attitudes toward the CSM. If it does happen and if the CSM cannot deal with it through their own efforts then if (and only if) the CSM perceives it as a problem that needs to be dealt with for the good of the initiative—in other words of there is a legitimate reason of value to the customer organization itself rather than just being an inconvenience to the CSM— then the CSM may need to raise the matter with the SPL. This should be done diplomatically and discretely, and the CSM should stick to factual information about what the problem is and why it needs to be fixed, rather than expressing any feelings or emotions about the issue. If at all possible, the CSM should propose a way forwards for dealing with the issue for the SPL to consider.

Almost certainly the "problem" stakeholder will be known to cause such issues and the revelation of difficulties will not come as a surprise to the SPL. If the CSM has developed a good working relationship with the SPL then they should find the SPL to be supportive and cooperative around fixing the issue. Remember to keep the conversation professional at all times and not to bring up feelings and emotions. The discussion should focus entirely on what the problem is, why it matters to the customer organization and what should be done about it, not on how the CSM feels about it.

The resolutions to such problems will typically take one or more of the following forms (Table 7.5):

Table 7.5 Resolving Stakeholder Issues

Form	Description
Upward pressure	This is achieved by (diplomatically) showing the difficult stakeholder the value of cooperation to themselves or to their team/department/process, and/or the negative consequences to themselves or to their team/department/process of noncooperation
Peer pressure	This is where support is requested from the overall group of similar-level stakeholders is sought to help change the difficult stakeholder's mind. This might be done non-threateningly by, for example, raising appropriate discussions in meetings and gaining commitment from all attendees to abide by the overall consensus of the group

(Continued)

Table 7.5 (*Continued*)   Resolving Stakeholder Issues

Form	Description
Downward pressure	This is where managers of a higher seniority level get involved to request cooperation from the difficult stakeholder on the CSM and SPL's behalf. Care must be taken if this route is used, since it may have deeper or wider impacts than other routes. Use only when necessary and use carefully
Circumnavigation	If cooperation from the difficult stakeholder just cannot be attained by any reasonable means, it may be possible to go around them. This might be achieved either by gaining the necessary information and/or authority elsewhere, or by planning the Adoption in a different way that removes or reduces the importance of the difficult stakeholder's involvement

Whatever steps the CSM takes to deal with difficult stakeholders, the CSM should always ensure they maintain the highest levels of their own professionality and accord this stakeholder (and indeed all stakeholders) respect and friendliness. Aside from any ethical issues, treating *all* people this way will help the CSM to develop the best possible professional relationships with customers and colleagues alike, and it is entirely possible to win difficult stakeholders around over time, such that they may eventually even become some of the CSM's strongest allies.

Chapter 8

Practical CSM Framework Stage 4: Adoption Planning Part 2—Implementation

8.1 Step 1: Determine Adoption Requirements

8.1.1 Understanding the Customer's Adoption Requirements

The adoption start point from a practical perspective is to ensure there is consensus within the customer's key stakeholder group on adoption outcomes and other adoption-related needs—in other words on what it is the customer needs to achieve through the implementation of the adoption plan, and how they intend to go about planning, implementing and measuring that adoption plan. This may often be as straightforward for the CSM to learn as asking the SPL and documenting what they say. However, in more complex situations this might need much more careful handling—particularly when multiple key stakeholders with perhaps very differing and sometimes even opposing viewpoints are involved in the decision-making and/or where there is less experience within the customer organization of managing the sorts of changes required by the current initiative. What needs to be decided and documented includes (Figure 8.1):

1. Key objectives (outcome requirements)
2. Who will be involved in the research and planning processes
3. Which users are impacted by the initiative and whose adoption needs therefore need to be included
4. Who will be involved in funding and implementing the plan
5. How progress will be measured
6. Who will take those measurements and provide progress reports
7. Who will provide the ultimate sign off on a "job well done" and confirm the investment was worth it?

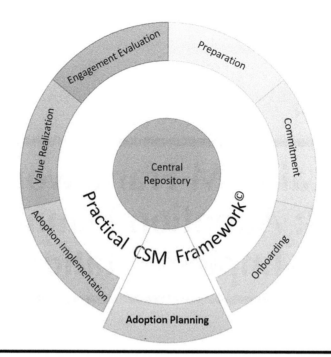

Figure 8.1   PCSMF Phase 4: Adoption Planning (continued).

Readers may recall that Chapter 4 contained information relating to performing basic research during Practical CSM Framework Phase 1: Preparation. CSMs who performed this activity can refer back to the *Customer_Research_Checklist* document which they created and stored in the Central Repository to refresh their memory as to how much of this information is already known and documented and how much of it is as yet unknown and still needs to be determined. An *Adoption_Requirements_Questionnaire* is provided as a Microsoft Excel workbook in the Downloads section of www.practicalcsm.com which the CSM can use to document all this information in one place within the first worksheet of this workbook.

8.1.2 The Workshop as a Forum for Determining Adoption Requirements

Readers may recall the information relating to research techniques in the previous chapter. In the section of Chapter 7 that dealt with this topic there was a discussion about workshops. The workshop is an ideal forum to use when multiple stakeholders with differing opinions need to come together to discuss, argue, negotiate, and where necessary make compromises in order ultimately to facilitate agreement on a chosen way forward for something. This fits well for situations where several customer stakeholders from a variety of departments need to work out and agree on these details.

The role of the CSM is to provide advice and assistance to the SPL to help them decide whether a workshop is required or not. If so, the CSM and SPL must also discuss agree who would be the right person to lead it and also the CSM should advise the SPL whether workshop facilitation is included within the services offered by the customer success team at no charge or whether it should be offered as a separately billable professional service. There is no right or wrong answer to the above, as it really does depend upon the specific circumstances of the customer, the CSM's company and the relationship that exists between them. If CSMs decide to take on the role of facilitating an adoption requirements workshop themselves they should consider liaising closely with and perhaps jointly leading this workshop with the SPL. Other options might include business architects and management consultants from the customer organization, the CSM's company or third-party specialist organizations.

8.1.3 Other Ways of Determining Adoption Requirements

What if the workshop does not seem to be the right way forwards for determining the customer's adoption requirements, but information regarding these requirements is missing and needs to be researched and/or determined? In this circumstance, the CSM might use a combination of other research techniques including one-to-one or group meetings with key stakeholders and follow-up research to uncover specific user groups' needs and/or opinions using techniques such as focus groups, surveys and observation. Whereas there may be a case to be made for the CSM performing the role of workshop facilitator, it may be harder for the CSM to take on these tasks since they are likely to be quite onerous in terms of time and also will require access to various groups of users within the customer's organization that it may be easier for the customer to access themselves.

Whichever way the job is done, the CSM must ensure that the information is collected and validated by the SPL as being accurate and complete. The CSM should then make sure that the information is documented, either by completing the first workbook within the *Adoption_ Requirements_Questionnaire* or using some other way as desired.

8.2 Step 2: Identify Process Changes

8.2.1 Processes and Capabilities

The start point for performing research to understand which users will be impacted by change and in what ways they will be impacted is to identify the process changes within each capability that will be impacted by the initiative. The output from this first step will be a list of impacted capabilities and for each impacted capability an explanation for what process changes will occur and who is involved in each process.

As we have seen in previous chapters, a *process* is a series of steps that are followed in the performance of an activity. These steps are predefined and are repeated each time that activity takes place. Processes are therefore contained within each business capability, which you may recall we defined as the ability of the customer's business to perform a specific task in order to attain an output.

Note that the customer organization may refer to "processes" as "workflows." Technically there is a small difference between a process and a workflow (though it depends which authority you decide to reference as to exactly what that difference is), but to all practical intents and purposes these two terms are interchangeable and therefore either term is fine to use, so my recommendation is to use whichever term the customer is most familiar and comfortable with.

8.2.2 Utilizing Previous Customer Research

The likelihood is that this task will already have been completed by the customer organization (with or without the help of the CSM's own company or other third parties) during the pre-sales process. However, it is also perfectly possible that either this task was performed but in a summary rather than detailed fashion since this was all that was necessary at the time, or that it was not performed at all. If any existing research *was* performed the CSM should review it to determine its level of completion and accuracy.

8.2.3 Practical Steps for Researching Impacted Capabilities and Processes

One way or another, the CSM needs to ensure that the necessary research takes place to understand and document which business capabilities will be impacted by the initiative. The process changes for each impacted business capability can either be researched at the same time or as a follow-up activity, depending upon circumstances. It can often be easier to combine these two tasks, since it may well be the same stakeholder/s that have both sets of information and it may make sense to interview them once rather than twice.

In terms of practical steps to take, the CSM should discuss the task with the SPL and start by reviewing any existing documentation from previous activities. The SPL and CSM can then discuss what details are missing and can come to an agreement as to what research needs to be done and who will perform it. As discussed in Chapter 7, it may not be the role of the CSM to actually perform this research, because the information is internal to the customer organization and will be held by process owners, team leaders and so on. However, it *is* the role of the CSM to help to make sure it is performed correctly and thoroughly and that the information obtained is documented in an appropriate format. If necessary the CSM can make recommendations to the SPL regarding the appropriate research techniques to deploy and the types of stakeholders within the customer's organization to approach (see Chapter 7 for information about these).

8.2.4 Documenting Impacted Capabilities and Processes

The resulting information from these activities is likely to be in the form of access to or copies of documentation that already existed in a variety of locations within the customer organization and that was created for other purposes. As such, it may need to be reformatted into one comprehensive document that contains just the information required by the CSM and SPL for the purposes of adoption planning. A template for this purpose is provided in the second worksheet of the *Adoption_Requirements_Questionnaire*. This provides a way to list the different processes that will be impacted together with who is involved with the performance with them, and to document the anticipated changes for each process.

8.3 Step 3: Create Impacted Groups

8.3.1 Determining Which Workers Are Impacted

Once all of the changes to processes within all impacted capabilities has been documented, the CSM and SPL can now review this information to determine who within the customer organization will be impacted and in what ways that impact will be felt. In less complex initiatives, this task may be very obvious—even self-evident—from a casual glance at the process change-related information contained in the second worksheet within the *Adoption_Requirements_Questionnaire* that was created in Step 1. However, for more complex situations where many processes from within many business capabilities were identified as being impacted, and where many different types of users were identified as being involved in these processes the situation may be more difficult.

8.3.2 Understanding Impacted Groups

An impacted group (IG) is simply a group of users that share the same impacts or changes on their activities. What the CSM needs to ensure gets completed is to group the impacted users into relevant IGs and to document the impacts for each IG. Grouping up users into IGs is just a matter of pattern spotting and it is done to simplify the process of planning change management needs for these users. As stated, an IG should contain all of the users who share the exact same impact on the activities they perform. So, for example, a customer organization might have a workforce of 500 call center workers, all of whom will impacted in the same way by the implementation of new call center software. Rather than worry about the change management needs of each call center worker individually it might make sense to treat all 500 of them as one single IG which can be given a meaningful name such as "Call Center Workers."

8.3.3 Determining IG Membership in More Complex Situations

Where the determination of IGs can get trickier is in more complex situations. Let's use the same example of a customer organization which is implementing new call center software and which has a workforce containing 500 call center workers. Perhaps this workforce is divided between two physical call centers—one in New York and another in San Diego. Perhaps the 250 workers at each call center further divides up into 220 customer support workers who respond to phone call queries from customers, 22 customer support team leaders who also respond to phone call queries from customers but who also manage their team of 10 customer support workers, and 8 call center managers who oversee the entire workforce at that call center. So the question is: "Are each of these different roles impacted in the same way by the proposed changes?" If the answer is "Yes," then just one IG can be created that contains all 500 workers.

8.3.4 Creating IGs to Cover Different Roles

However, it is very likely that the answer is "No" in which case it might be necessary to create further IGs to define the different needs of all of the users, based upon their different *roles*. One way to do this may be to create an IG called something like "Call Center Customer Support Workers," another IG called "Call Center Team Leaders" and a final IG called "Call Center Managers." The correspondent workers can now be placed in their relevant groups. Note that the "Call Center Team Leaders" act as team leaders to their teams of 10 customer support workers but they also act as customer support workers themselves. Since these workers will be impacted by changes to processes in both roles, the team leaders should therefore be placed into *both* the "Call Center Customer Support Workers" and the "Call Center Team Leaders" IGs.

8.3.5 Creating IGs to Cover Different KSA Gaps

Readers will recall the information about KSA—knowledge, skills and attitude—that was discussed in Chapter 7. For each IG the CSM needs to ensure that the KSA "gaps" are recorded accurately. These gaps are what will be addressed within the adoption planning that will come next, and therefore represent what will actually get implemented as practical assistance to the impacted users to help them perform their roles adequately.

KSA gaps can be defined as the knowledge, skills and or attitude that each impacted user within the group is missing (i.e., do not already have) but which will be required by them in order to fulfill their role once the planned changes have occurred. To calculate KSA gaps the CSM (and those they work alongside to perform this task) will therefore need to understand both what KSA are needed *and* what KSA already exist. This gap may be different for different workers, even when the role is the same. If this is the case then those workers may need to be further divided into separate IGs rather than all placed into the same IG which is defined purely by role.

Going back to our example situation, perhaps the situation at each physical call center is different. Perhaps the New York call center was recently acquired by the customer organization and currently uses completely different call center software than the new software which is going to be implemented during this initiative. Conversely, perhaps the San Diego call center already uses a previous version of the same software. So for the New York workers the change they will undergo will be greater than for the San Diego workers, since the New York workers will need ground-up training and familiarization with the new software package whereas for the San Diego workers it may just be a matter of upgrade training that identifies the changes between the previous software version and the latest version. Note that the *role* the same workers in each call center performs remains the same, but the difference is in existing knowledge. The San Diego workers are already familiar with the software package in general terms, but for the New York workers the software is completely new. There may therefore be a need to create two entire sets of IGs—a set with "New York…" at the start of each title and a similar set with "San Diego…" at the start of each title.

Is that everything? Perhaps, or perhaps not. What about new employees? From time to time this customer organization will no doubt be recruiting new employees to work in its call centers. These new employees might be existing call center workers switching employers or might even be graduates or others with no previous call center work experience. In either case, there may be a need for further IGs to be created that define the further and differing KSA needs of these groups.

8.3.6 Additional IG Considerations

Going back to our example, another issue that might raise its head is availability. It would be unreasonable to expect all of the customer support workers and customer support team leaders in say the New York call center to be available to undergo training at the same time, since that would mean that no one would be left in the call center to manage customer calls. Since there are 22 teams at the New York site (each comprising 10 workers and 1 team leader), perhaps the training could be arranged so that it will be delivered two one or perhaps two teams at a time, therefore always leaving the remaining 20 or 21 teams available to cover the telephones. The CSM *could* create separate IGs for each group, but in practice this will create a lot of additional project management complexity and is unnecessary since it is a consideration about how the training needs to be delivered rather than about any difference in actual needs. The recommendation here would therefore not be to create separate IGs for each team, but instead to note any such requirements as information *about* the IG so that when the time comes to determine *how* the training will be delivered this sort of practical consideration will be allowed for.

8.3.7 The Importance of Getting the IGs Right

The above fictitious situation is purely an example of the types of complexity that the CSM may face when determining IGs and placing impacted users into those IGs. What it hopefully has illustrated is the need for CSMs to think very carefully about which IGs need to be created and which impacted users need to be placed into each IG. Performing this task well is very important, since the formulation of all change management services (communications, training, certification, coaching, support and so on) will be based on these groups' change management requirements.

8.3.8 How to Define Accurate and Useful IGs

In summary, to define accurate and useful IGs the CSM should follow these steps (or make sure that the customer has done so):

1. Thoroughly research all impacted processes and document how each impacted process will change
2. For each impacted process document which users are involved—these are your impacted users
3. Create IGs where each IG represents a defined change that needs to be addressed within the change management process
4. Place impacted users into the IGs based upon role within each process
5. If necessary subdivide these IGs into additional IGs to represent different KSA gaps (e.g., the difference between workers with existing familiarity and those with no familiarity of a software package) and place the relevant users into each IG
6. Do not subdivide into further IGs that do not denote any difference in knowledge, skills and/or attitude gaps. Instead, note any additional considerations (such as availability issues) as information about the IG

8.3.9 Documenting IGs

It is possible that some or even all of the above work on identifying impact users and grouping them by change management needs has already been accomplished by the customer prior to the CSM's involvement. If this is the case then the existing documentation of this information may already be satisfactory to use as the basis for creating the adoption roadmap. However, the likelihood is that while the SPL and/or other key stakeholders within the customer organization have (or have access to) the information, it is not all in one place, it is not all in one format, it is incomplete and it is not centrally stored and managed. If this is the case it makes sense to create new documentation that is specifically designed for the purposes of adoption planning and that is accessible by the CSM, the SPL and whoever else needs to view or edit it. A template for this purpose is provided in the third worksheet within the *Adoption_Requirements_Questionnaire* workbook. This provides a way to list the different IGs that will be impacted together with impacted user membership for each group, KSA gaps for each group and notation of any additional information that needs to be considered at the adoption planning step.

8.4 Step 4: Document Practical Considerations

8.4.1 Types of Practical Considerations

There are a number of different considerations relating to an adoption program that need to be dealt with up front during the adoption planning stage. These include (though are not limited to) (Table 8.1):

Table 8.1 Practical Considerations for Adoption

Consideration	Description
Implementation phases	Will the solution be rolled out all together or will it be rolled out in a series of phases? If the former, when will the implementation be completed? If the latter, when will each phase occur, what happens in each phase, and how will this impact the adoption plan?
User availability	When are the users available, especially if they need to undergo any lengthy training? Are all users within an IG available together or will they need to be separated into multiple groups that undergo separate training in order to maintain productivity levels?
External dependencies	Are there any activities that are outside of this initiative but which this initiative relies upon being completed prior to commencing the adoption? (For example do a group of new recruits need general induction training first before being exposed to the specific task-oriented training contained within the adoption plan?)
Internal dependencies	Are there any activities that are outside of within this initiative and which must be completed prior to commencing the adoption? (For example is there some customization or integration work that must be completed before the adoption commences?)
Financing	Are there sufficient funds available for the completion of the adoption program and where will this funding come from? If cash is tight would it be better for cash flow reasons to divide the adoption roadmap into a series of phases where essential training is completed straight away and other training is left to be completed at a later stage when it becomes affordable?
Deadlines and timeframes	Are there any hard deadlines by which or timeframes in which all or certain aspects of the adoption must be completed? For example a new piece of legislation, or the launch of a new product may each engender specific deadlines that must be met
Milestones and KPIs	What does the customer require in terms of milestones en route to overall completion of the adoption program, and how will those milestones be measured?
Internal and external standards	Must all or parts of the adoption program ensure conformity to internal and external standards, such as best practice guidelines and government or industry regulations?

The CSM may be able to deal with these types of considerations in one-to-one conversations with the SPL, or may wish to agree with the SPL to include discussions on one or more of these points in the conversations that will take place with other key stakeholders around outcome requirements and impacted users. However, the information is gathered, the CSM should ensure it is fully documented ready for the adoption planning step. A separate tab within the *Adoption_Requirements_Questionnaire* document has been created for this purpose.

8.5 Step 5: Determine Communication, Training and Support Requirements

8.5.1 Types of Adoption Activities

There are many types of activities that might be specified for inclusion within an adoption program. The simplest way to consider what types of activities are required for each IG is to divide these activities into three types: communication activities, training activities and support activities. These can be defined as follows:

8.5.1.1 Communication Activities

8.5.1.1.1 Communication for Disseminating Information

This is usually the first type of activity to occur, and it is used early on to inform everyone about the upcoming change in order to help prepare them for that change ahead of time. Communication is also used throughout the adoption process to keep people informed about *what* is currently happening (and what will happen next), *who* will be affected, *why* it is happening, *when* it is happening, *where* it will happen and *how* it is happening. Its primary role could therefore be described as *information dissemination*. This might include schedules of upcoming training events, explanations about how processes will change, contact information for people to use to ask questions or get help, and so on. It could also include communicating requirements for additional information—for example, the CSM and SPL might need to send out survey questionnaires to learn more about certain impacted users' training and/or support requirements (readers may wish to refer back to Section 3 of Chapter 7 for more discussion on research techniques, including surveys).

All sorts of communication formats can be used—emails, texts, intranet posts, letters, posters, leaflets, phone calls and face-to-face and virtual meetings can all be used as appropriate to share the necessary information with those that need to receive it and (where relevant) to give the opportunity for employees to ask questions and give their feedback.

8.5.1.1.2 Communication for Addressing Attitudinal Issues

As well as its practical role to disseminate necessary information, communication is also used to impact the "A" in KSA—in other words where potential attitudinal problems with one or more IGs have been identified, communication is likely to be the main way of addressing these issues. "Problem" attitudes might include fear about coping, anger about being required to perform additional tasks, concerns about job security, and worries about not getting adequate support through the change.

While not all fears can necessarily be completely allayed, and while not all stakeholders can be turned into raving fans who cannot wait for the change to occur, what the CSM and SPL need to ensure is that impacted users are at least *acceptant*. What this means in a practical sense is that impacted users accept that the change is going to happen and that they will need to play their part both in undergoing the change (for example, by attending any required training) and in performing the new tasks post-change (i.e., by following the new processes and not reverting to doing what they used to do prior to the change). Without this minimum requirement of acceptance from impacted users it will be very difficult to make the change occur successfully. Effective communication is therefore an essential component of any adoption plan, not just for information dissemination but also for addressing attitudinal issues.

Communication activities for addressing attitudinal issues will need to be carefully crafted to address the issues that have been identified in the IGs. A good way of getting employees on board is to ask a "C" level or other senior leader to help out. A personal message from the CEO, COO or some other high-level authority figure really helps to gain acceptance from employees. This needn't become an onerous burden on the senior leader—it could, for example, be delivered as an address during an "all hands meeting," or it could be a recorded message that is sent to all employees, or it could even be a short letter or email signed by the senior leader, or some combination of the above.

8.5.1.1.3 The Role of the CSM in Communications

CSMs should not generally get involved directly in communicating information to IGs. Instead, their role is consultative and advisory, helping the SPL and other key stakeholders to develop a strong communications strategy that enables appropriate dissemination of information and which addresses any attitudinal issues as needed.

8.5.1.2 Training Activities

8.5.1.2.1 Training for Knowledge and Skills

Training is aimed at filling the "K" (knowledge) and "S" (skills) component gaps of KSA (more information on KSA and the differences between knowledge and skills can be found in Section 2 of Chapter 7). Some customers may use specific terminology to define differences between knowledge and skill training activities. For example a customer might refer only to learning new skills with the term *training* and might use another term such as *education* to refer to learning new knowledge. Whatever terminology the customer uses, it might be worth the CSM referring to knowledge and skills training in the same way to avoid misunderstandings and to ensure the customer's stakeholders are comfortable with any learning-related conversations.

8.5.1.2.2 Meeting Different Knowledge and Skill Requirements

Different IGs will have different levels of these two needs, so each training activity should be carefully planned to meet a combination of one, other or both of these specific requirements.

Knowledge is often best provided by providing both *concepts* and *examples* and following these up with *exercises*. Concepts explain the knowledge to the trainee, whereas examples illustrate it. Concepts can sometimes be hard to understand in isolation, especially where the trainees do not have any real-world experience that they can relate these concepts to. On the other hand, exercises usually cannot get the knowledge itself across on their own, but can often make the concepts much easier to understand because they contextualize those concepts by providing examples of real-world situations that trainees can relate to. Exercises are used to try out the newly learned knowledge in a safe environment, such as working through a fictitious case study, or answering a series of questions.

Skills generally cannot be learned without repeatedly performing the activity itself, and generally speaking skills are both learned and improved through this repetitive performance of the activity, during which users are given feedback and advice on how to improve their performance. Skills training often takes the route of breaking down complex activities into a number of tasks and teaching the tasks one at a time. Then when the trainees are ready tasks can be gradually recombined, until finally the trainees can perform all tasks simultaneously. For example when teaching someone to swim it is common to hand the trainee a float to hold in their hands so that they can concentrate just on learning how to move their legs. Then they are asked to hold the float between their feet to keep their legs still while they learn the correct movement with their arms. Finally, the float can be taken away and the trainee can use both arms and legs to swim without any flotation aid.

8.5.1.2.3 Task-Based Learning Versus Functionality-Based Learning

Rather than learning about all the different features and functions of the various tools that the trainees will need to use in the performance of their role, it may be better for the training to follow the specific tasks that need to be performed in each step of the new process that the trainees will be asked to perform.

This can sometimes reduce the amount of training needed to cover just the specific features and functions required by the tasks within the process. It can also make the training much easier for trainees to understand and to learn and then to repeat afterwards when back at work, since it contextualizes the training and links it directly to the actual steps of the process. This methodology works really well in situations where processes are highly defined and are repeated with little or no change each time they are performed.

On the other hand, where users will have a lot more autonomy over how they go about performing tasks and will potentially need to know how to select which tasks to perform and then perform those tasks in different orders and in different ways each time, it may be necessary to provide bother broader and deeper training on all relevant features and functions. These features and functions can then be used as a *toolkit* from which users can select each time a task must be performed. This latter type of training is more comprehensive in scope and therefore tends to be more expensive and time-consuming to deliver since it is likely to cover more profound and in-depth knowledge on every relevant feature and function rather than just those ones that a particular process uses.

Neither task-based nor functionality-based training is "better," it is purely a question of the CSM pointing out the pros and cons of each and then helping the SPL to select whichever is appropriate to the needs of the IG in ensuring they are able to perform their new role.

8.5.1.2.4 Determining Training Needs and Training Effectiveness

How do you know exactly what training an individual or an IG needs? Also, once you have delivered the training, how do you know if the training was effective? These are two very reasonable questions to ask, and CSMs should ensure that the answers to both of these questions are addressed within the customer's adoption plan.

8.5.1.2.5 Determining Training Needs During the Planning Phase and/or During Training Delivery

Training needs can be assessed up front to predetermine the specific training requirements for each IG or even for each individual worker within each IG and prior to performing the adoption planning process. This can be done by interviewing or surveying each worker, or by interviewing and/or surveying relevant managers (including team leaders and process owners as necessary) and recording this information as additional information to consider during adoption planning. This is potentially the best way of doing things if it is possible, because it will tend to produce an adoption plan that is more specifically pointed toward fulfilling the known training needs of each impacted user. This can make the adoption plan both more productive in its results and more efficient in its utilization of key resources—including time and money of course.

The potential issue with performing up front training needs assessment is that it is yet another task that needs to be performed prior to implementing the training. This means that adoption implementation can be delayed—perhaps unnecessarily—and costs can be increased. It may be very difficult and/or expensive to perform this up front research. It may be a lot easier to build the training assessment into the adoption plan itself as an activity that takes place *during* the adoption implementation rather than beforehand. This might be done the same way (e.g., through interviews and surveys of workers and/or managers) or it might even be done as a just-in-time activity where users and/or their managers determine their training needs at or just before the time that training will be delivered. This works particularly well for self-service style training where users are given a range of training options as a menu from which they can select their own personalized training plan. The disadvantage to this route is that it relies upon users and their managers knowing (and being honest about) their training needs, which might not always be the case, especially where new tools and processes that the users and/or their managers are not yet aware of are being introduced to them.

8.5.1.2.6 Informal Training Versus Formal Training

Formal training is training that is determined and organized by the organization and the users are then told what training activities to attend and when to attend them. Informal training is training that users can select themselves based upon their own understanding of their personal needs and or preferred learning styles.

Formal training is useful for ensuring that *all* users within a particular IG fulfill specific training obligations—perhaps in order to put these users through an externally awarded certification of competency, for example, or simply to ensure uniformity of learning between all members of the group. The disadvantage of the formal route is that it can be inefficient or frustrating when viewed from the perspective of an individual user, since they will be forced through a prescribed training program that may not suit their personal needs or preferred training style.

Users' needs may differ from individual to individual even within the same IG, since one user may already know more or less than another user (perhaps, for example, due to their previous experiences in other roles). Users' preferences may also differ, since some people may, for example, respond better to face-to-face training from an instructor, whereas others may prefer to self-study from books or multimedia content, and so on. The informal route can therefore be a great choice where the customer organization wants to provide multiple training options for users to select from. This is great where individual workers are trusted and encouraged to create personalized training paths to suit their own needs and/or preferences.

8.5.1.2.7 Accessing Existing Training Assets and Resources

An important aspect of the value to the customer of the CSM is the CSM's knowledge of what is already available in terms of training assets and resources related to the CSM's company's products and services. This will of course include any training courses or content which the CSM's own company offers, as well as other training courses or content that are produced, managed and delivered by third-party training organizations and other companies.

CSMs should be well prepared with relevant information regarding what is currently already available, which should include where the training content comes from, what the costs are, what its availability is (including locations and languages) and its relative strengths and weaknesses compared with the other offerings. The CSM should make sure that they do not come across as a salesperson or promotor of their own company's training offerings over other organization's offerings, but should instead make sure they have done their research well on this topic and then provide open, honest and realistic advice as to what is available and what might best suit the specific requirements of this customer.

8.5.1.2.8 Developing Customized Training Content

If the "right" training content to meet one or more specific user training requirement does not already exist then it may be necessary to create it. This can add further costs in both time and money to complete, but of course if the training is required but is not already available then there is nothing for it but for it to be developed, and the appropriate time and money will need to be assigned for this to happen.

Generally speaking there will be some existing training content that can be adapted. This will reduce costs considerably since it will only be a percentage of the overall content that will need to be written rather than all of it. Assuming there is an existing generic course that is available, oftentimes it is only a small percentage of this generic course that needs any change. These changes might deal with any customization of the standard products and services that have taken place, or might explain the utilization of one or more tools within the customer's own processes, for example.

As a general rule, any customization of training content that the CSM's own company performs on behalf of the customer will not be included at no charge, even if the generic training content is usually provided at no charge, since it incurs development time to create the customized version.

8.5.1.2.9 Phased and/or Staggered Training Delivery

Training for any one IG does not necessarily need to all be delivered at the same time, or during the same phase of the adoption program. It may be more efficient and/or effective to "sheep dip" a group of users through the entire training they require all in one go, before moving on to performing the same operation with another group of users. This is especially the case with geographically widespread users where either trainers or users will need to travel in order for the training to be delivered.

On the other hand, it may be more efficient and/or effective to perform the training across multiple rounds or phases over time where certain aspects are covered initially and other aspects are covered later. This might be phased based upon difficulty (for example, a foundation course at the beginning followed by an advanced course at some later stage), or it might be phased based upon functionality (for example, the essential functions covered in the first course followed by additional non-essential but still useful functionality covered in a later course).

The decision for delivering the training in one go or in phases is generally a practical one, based upon availability of training materials and instructors, availability of users to attend training and the level of urgency of the users' training needs.

8.5.1.2.10 Post-Training Assessment and Certification

Once the training has been delivered its effectiveness will need to be measured, and the level of readiness of the users who have undergone the training for performing the new or changed processes will need to be assessed. It may also be necessary for users to undergo either internal (to the customer) or external testing or examination to gain certification of accomplishing a minimum standard of knowledge and/or skills. Obvious examples of this would be for performing roles such as operating dangerous machinery (for example, fork lift truck drivers) or managing critical corporate resources (for example, IT security managers) or providing professional services advice to customers (for example, the accountants in an Accountancy firm who provide the accounting services to the firm's customers). In these cases both the training and the passing of required exams to gain certification needs to be very carefully managed and records need to be securely kept.

Even without formal internal or external certification it may still be important to informally assess training effectiveness, either to ensure that users are ready to perform their new roles and/or to measure the effectiveness of the training program in order to show the ROI (return on investment) to the project sponsors. This assessment can be done in a number of different ways including (though not necessarily limited to):

User appraisal: Let the users themselves determine whether the training has met their needs through a post-training assessment survey. This is generally the simplest and least cost method for assessing training.

Trainer appraisal: If the training has been delivered by an instructor then the instructor can be asked to assess the level of preparedness of users to perform their role. This does however require the trainer to understand the users' roles and to spend the time to perform the task for every user who undergoes their training

Testing: This could be done by practical (e.g., skills-based) or theoretical (e.g., knowledge-based) testing which might be to a less formal and/or rigorous standard than formal or external certification

Manager appraisal: Managers (including team leaders or process owners) could be asked to appraise the post-training capabilities of the users and determine whether the users are now able to perform their required tasks effectively

Further discussion on measuring training effectiveness in order to determine adoption program ROI will be covered in Chapter 9: Adoption Implementation.

8.5.1.2.11 The Role of the CSM in Training

There are circumstances where the CSM may deliver some informal training on aspects of the solution. This will tend to be one-to-one or small group training that might only cover certain features and functions, and is typically delivered to the SPL and/or other key stakeholders rather than impacted users. In almost all situations, even if the CSM has the knowledge and skills to perform training it is recommended that they do not do so. This is to ensure that they maintain their persona as a business outcomes focused customer success consultant in the eyes of customer stakeholders, so that they can develop and maintain strong trust relationships with key business stakeholders.

What the CSM's role *is* regarding training is to act as expert adviser to the SPL and other key customer stakeholders, helping them to understand what the different training options are for each training need that the customer and CSM uncovers during the analysis and planning processes, and acting as liaison between the customer and external resources owners such as the CSM's own company's training department and third-party training companies with whom the CSM's company has relationships. Performing this task well can add enormous value for the SPL and can be a great way to reinforce and develop the CSM/SPL relationship. Indeed it is one of the key ways in which CSMs can prove their specific value to the initiative.

8.5.1.3 Support Requirements

8.5.1.3.1 Post-Change Support

The third and final type of requirement that should be incorporated within an adoption plan is the requirement for post-change user support. Once the change has occurred (in other words once the changes have been implemented and any necessary training has been delivered, and the users have now stopped performing the old processes and started performing the new processes) users can still run into all sorts of difficulties that will need to be dealt with. These might include (though not be limited to) (Table 8.2):

Table 8.2　Common User Support Difficulties

Difficulty	Description
Process-related problems	A particular process or specific process step may be found to be inefficient or to not perform as required and need to be changed
Tool-related problems	A particular tool or a specific feature or function of the tool may be found to be inefficient, or to not function as required and may need to be reconfigured or adapted/changed
Missing knowledge	Users may find that the training did not provide them with all of the knowledge they need to fulfill their new role
Missing skills	Users may find that the training did not provide them with all of the skills they need to fulfill their new role
User errors	Users might forget what they have been taught, or might make mistakes while performing their role. This is to be anticipated, especially in the early stages immediately post-training as it typically takes a while for users to gain familiarity with the changes
Additional user needs	Users might find additional uses for any new tools they have been provided with, and might have further questions about the tools' features and functions
Emotional support	Some users may need some level of emotional support to help them through what might for them be a stressful process of dealing with change
Technical problems	Any tool or system can malfunction, break or otherwise go wrong in some way or another and require a relevant expert such as a mechanic or an IT engineer to identify and fix the problem

8.5.1.3.2 Types of Support Services

Perhaps the most obvious support service is the formal telephone support line or Internet-based support tool where users can log a support request and get access to support professionals who will respond to their questions and help resolve their problems.

Other support services might include self-service tools such as automated "help" systems or pre-created FAQ (frequently asked questions) answers. Support tools might also include access to just-in-time training VODs (Video on Demand) that show users how to perform particular tasks or user particular features or functions of a system.

Also included within support services would be human-resourced support such as coaching and mentoring services. Mentoring means providing less experienced users with access to the time of a more experienced user who can share their expertise with the more junior user and in doing so transfer knowledge and skills. Coaching is where a user is provided with in-the-job training from a trainer or coach. Both coaching and mentoring can be very effective for the right users. Mentoring works well when there are sufficient numbers of more experienced users who are available to provide the mentoring services to more junior or less seasoned users. Coaching works well when the subject matter requires expert trainers or coaches who have specific coaching and training skills, or simply when mentoring would not be practical.

8.5.1.3.3 Support Service Packages

Support for users can be provided in a variety of ways to suit the specific needs of different user groups. Best practice generally dictates that a package of suitable support needs to be identified, developed and put into place to fulfill the support requirements of each IG. Some of these support services might be fairly short term but more intensive in terms of cost and time involvement, whereas other components might be longer term. An example might be coaching or mentoring for just the first month after training, followed by ongoing access to a telephone support line, a self-service online help system and a FAQ tool.

8.5.1.3.4 The Role of the CSM in Support Activities

As with both the previously discussed communication and training activities, the role of the CSM in support activities is to help the SPL and other customer key stakeholders to determine what each IG's support requirements are and then to design a package of support services to meet those requirements. CSMs should be familiar with the pros and cons of the different types of support activities so that they can provide good quality advice to the customer. CSMs should of course also be aware of what the CSM's own company offers as included and additional (for a professional fee) support services and what other third-party organizations offer, and the main differences between each offering.

8.5.1.3.5 The Adoption Activities Checklist

Since there is a lot to consider when determining appropriate adoption activities to meet the needs of each IG, I have provided a tool called *Adoption_Activities_Checklist* which can be accessed from the Downloads section at www.practicalcsm.com. This checklist provides a simple way to work through and document the communication, training and support needs of each IG in an orderly manner in order to reduce mistakes or omissions and to increase efficiency.

8.6 Step 6: Capture Adoption Barriers and Risks

8.6.1 Defining Adoption Barriers

An adoption barrier is a challenge or obstacle that needs to be dealt with first in order for adoption to take place satisfactorily. Adoption barriers may include (but are by no means limited to):

- Political issues such as lack of support from one or more areas of the business (and especially important if lack of support from senior management)
- Lack of support from the workforce to engage with and support the adoption plan
- Financial issues such as inadequate funding or disagreements relating to which parts of the businesses should contribute toward the budget, or cash flow concerns
- Lack of certainty regarding adoption outcome requirements
- Lack of clarity regarding the changes to one or more processes
- Lack of clarity regarding the impact to one or more IGs
- Lack of authority to proceed with implementing the adoption plan, including authority to take employees' time away from their work for training or other activities relating to the adoption plan
- Lack of assets and resources required to perform the adoption, including training materials, support services, etc.
- Lack of expertise to perform adoption activities, including subject matter experts, trainers, support workers, etc.
- Cultural issues relating to the regional and/or corporate culture that might place limitations on the way in which adoption should be planned (for example, managers may need to be briefed first before their teams are trained, in order to ensure no loss of face occurs due to managers not knowing what their team knows)

8.6.2 Capturing Adoption Barriers

The topic of adoption barriers should be brought up with the SPL and/or other key stakeholders within the customer's organization and the SPL should be encouraged to compile a list of potential barriers either with the CSM and/or with help from their colleagues. This list should be as definitive as possible; however, it should be recognized that not all adoption barriers can be known up front, and further barriers may be uncovered after the adoption plan has been created, or even during adoption implementation. An adoption barriers questionnaire has been included as a separate worksheet within the *Adoption_Requirements_Questionnaire*.

8.6.3 Defining Adoption Risks

Adoption barriers are known obstacles that can therefore be dealt with up front prior to planning or certainly prior to implementing the adoption plan. Adoption risks, on the other hand, are *potential* obstacles that *may* occur if certain circumstances prevail. In other words, adoption barriers deal with what is known, whereas adoption risks deal with what is unknown but possible. Adoption risks may include (but are by no means limited to):

- Changes to corporate strategy leading to changed adoption outcome requirements
- Changes to customer (as in the customer's customer) requirements, leading to changed adoption outcome requirements

- The unsuccessful completion of other projects or initiatives (for example, a dependency on the launch of a new support service)
- Problems with the performance of products or services within the solution (for example, a product feature may not work as promised, or a service feature may not function to the promised quality level)
- Changes to external conditions (for example, a macro economic downturn, new legislation, or new competitive offerings)
- Changes to senior personnel, leading to business reorganization and reduction in support or necessity for the implementation
- Mergers or acquisitions that might take precedence in terms of time and availability of assets and resources away from the implementation and/or might significantly impact the adoption requirements

8.6.4 Capturing Adoption Risks

The topic of adoption risks should also be brought up with the SPL and/or other key stakeholders within the customer's organization and as with barriers the SPL should be encouraged to compile a list of potential risks either with the CSM and/or with help from their colleagues. Again as before, this list should be as definitive as possible; however, it should be recognized that not all adoption risks can be known up front, and further risks may be uncovered after the adoption plan has been created, or even during adoption implementation. An adoption risks questionnaire has also been included as a separate worksheet within the *Adoption_Requirements_Questionnaire*.

8.7 Step 7: Create Outline Adoption Plan

8.7.1 Ownership of the Adoption Plan

This is the step where all of the information that the CSM and others have researched and collated is analyzed and used to determine the customer's adoption requirements. Generally speaking, the best way to approach this analysis is to work in close partnership with the SPL and/or other relevant customer stakeholders to develop a high-level adoption plan. The plan that is developed should be owned by the SPL and the customer, with the CSM providing input in terms of advice and assistance, rather than being owned by the CSM.

Working in partnership with the customer to help develop an adoption plan which is created and owned by them has several advantages. Firstly, the plan that is developed is likely to be higher quality since it incorporates both the ideas of those who actually work for the customer and know the organization best as well as the ideas of the CSM (and others as necessary from the CSM's organization and third-party organizations who have supplied other parts of the solution) who are experts in the solution itself and who have had useful experience of previous adoption cycles of the same or similar solution in other companies. Secondly, from a political perspective, the initiative's sponsors and other senior decision makers within the customer organization are more likely to be persuaded by and supportive of an adoption proposal that has been created by the company's own experts (with help from the CSM and others). Finally, the responsibility for the plan's completeness and appropriateness to need should ultimately rest with the SPL and the customer rather than with the CSM and the CSM's company. This matches the overall role and responsibilities of the

CSM to provide advice, assistance and access to resources to the customer rather than to make business decisions on behalf of the customer.

8.7.2 Preparing to Analyze the Information

There are various ways in which the planning process can be conducted. The important thing is to find a methodology that suits the needs of the customer and that fits the specific circumstances such as availability of people, format of information, etc. The simplest way or working is often the most effective. My recommendation is to arrange a face-to-face meeting of an appropriate length (depending upon complexity) with the SPL and any others who will participate in the planning process. Make sure that there will be access to all of the information that you have researched and try as much as possible to find a location that is reasonably comfortable and where you will not be interrupted or disturbed.

Try to spend some time reviewing the information on your own and make some personal notes ahead of the meeting, so you are well informed and ready to participate in the meeting itself. This also gives you the opportunity to review some of the documentation you have created in previous Phases within the Practical CSM Framework but which you may not wish to share with customer employees. These might include the *Customer_Engagement_Strategy* created in Phase 1: Preparation and the *RACI_Matrix,* the *Stakeholder_Management_Matrix* and the *Stakeholder_ Management_Plan* created in Phase 2: Commitment.

Information that you might wish to ensure you and others have access to during the meeting include (though is not limited to):

- A company org chart and/or other reference information regarding the customer's organizational model, preferably including information on what each department is responsible for and the roles and numbers of the employees within it.
- The *Customer_Research_Checklist* document that you created in Practical CSM Framework Phase 1: Preparation and have subsequently referenced and updated in Phases 2–4.
- The *Customer_Engagement_Proposal* that you created in Practical CSM Framework Phase 2: Commitment.
- The *Onboarding_Work_Plan* that you created in Practical CSM Framework Phase 3: Onboarding.
- The *Adoption_Requirements_Questionnaire* that you created in this phase; Practical CSM Framework Phase 4: Adoption Planning.

8.7.3 Performing the Analysis and Producing an Outline Adoption Plan

Performing the analysis should be reasonably straightforward. You should now have all (or the vast majority of) the information you need to complete the task, so the job is not unlike putting together a jigsaw puzzle now that you have all the pieces out on the table.

The recommended start point is to review the customer's adoption outcome requirements to make sure that these outcome needs are foremost in everyone's mind during the analysis. Then it is a question of working through the different IGs and agreeing on what the adoption needs of each IG are and how they can best be met given the restraints on assets and resources and any other restrictions or factors to take into account you may have previously noted. These factors might include time, money, availability, deadlines, dependencies, etc. What you are looking to achieve is an outline or high-level plan that simply summarizes what needs to be done and in what order it needs doing without necessarily going into any detail at this early stage.

If the initiative has sufficient complexity to warrant doing so it can be a good idea to first prioritize the adoption needs of each IG into groups of higher and lower priority, and then to deal with each priority group separately, using the *Adoption_Requirements_Questionnaire*, as the core documentation, and using each worksheet contained within it as necessary to ensure that all requirements are met and that barriers and risks are dealt with appropriately within the plan that you formulate. Review and discuss the highest priority group's adoption requirements and formulate an outline or high-level plan for meeting those needs. Once you have dealt with the highest priority group, move to the next highest priority group and so on until all IGs' adoption requirements have been reviewed and discussed and you have an outline plan for all adoption requirements.

It's a good idea to capture discussions and ideas as they come up even if they relate to something you are not discussing at that moment, so that you can refer back to them later when it is the right time to cover that particular topic. The outline adoption plan can be created in any format. If desired the *Outline_Adoption_Plan* template that can be found in the Downloads section at www.practicalcsm.com can be used for this purpose.

8.7.4 Adoption Activities for Successful Change Management

The following are the most common adoption activities or components that should be discussed and where necessary defined for each IG (Table 8.3):

Table 8.3   Adoption Activities for Successful Change Management

Component	Description
Initial communication	Impacted users need to be informed well in advance of the upcoming changes in order to help them prepare both emotionally and practically for these changes. An early communication should explain what will happen, why it is occurring and how those users will be affected. This initial communication should attempt where possible to allay any unnecessary fears or concerns about coping with new activities, and reassure users that they will be fully supported through the change
Follow-up	Opportunities may need to be provided for users who have recently been made aware of upcoming changes to ask further questions about the changes and about the consequences of those changes to their own role and activities. These might be handled partially by direct managers in team or departmental meetings and/or access to HR or change management specialists who can answer questions in confidence
Preparation for change	Any activities that need to occur and/or assets and resources that need to be available prior to the changes occurring should be detailed here. This might include further communications around upcoming important dates when change management activities will occur, testing of new software systems, creation of process documentation, customization of training content, etc.

(Continued)

Table 8.3 (*Continued*)   Adoption Activities for Successful Change Management

Component	Description
Undergoing change	Any activities that need to occur and/or assets and resources that need to be available during the change should be detailed here. This might include communications about accessing new systems and services, training on using new systems and following new processes, access to new systems and services and supporting documentation, access to online and other help and support systems, etc.
Post-change support	Any ongoing activities to continue supporting the users after the change has occurred. This might include coaching and/or mentoring, and ongoing access to help and support services
KPIs and measurement	This section should identify how the change management activities and resulting change in KSA (knowledge, skills and attitude) will be measured and evaluated to ensure effectiveness

8.7.5 Uncovering Further Information Requirements

As you work through the analysis of IG requirements you may find that one or more questions arise that cannot be answered without further research. These questions might relate anything at all, for example, to IG needs, or to availability of an asset or resource, or to suitability of a certain training method, etc. You may therefore need to decide whether to proceed on the basis of an assumption about the missing information which can be validated at a later stage if necessary, or whether the missing information is sufficiently important to need to be researched now, prior to completion of the planning process.

8.7.6 Reviewing the Outline Adoption Plan

Once you have completed a first pass of the adoption planning process, it generally makes good sense to go back through the plan again. This might take place separately once further information requirements have been researched and the information has been added to the documentation. In any case, it is a good idea to do this separately after a few days have elapsed if possible, since it brings fresh energy and perspective to the conversation.

At this point, you are not necessarily trying to fill in all of the detail, but what you do need to do is ensure that the basic outline is correct.

8.7.7 Managing Adoption Barriers

Once the outline adoption plan is created and has been reviewed and amended as necessary, you should review your adoption barrier documentation to make sure that adoption barriers have been addressed sufficiently within the plan and if necessary making further amendments to the plan to ensure they are now addressed.

8.7.8 Managing Adoption Risks

General risk management best practice is to rate risks according to both the level of impact that will be experienced if the risk occurs and the likelihood of the risk occurring. The second tab

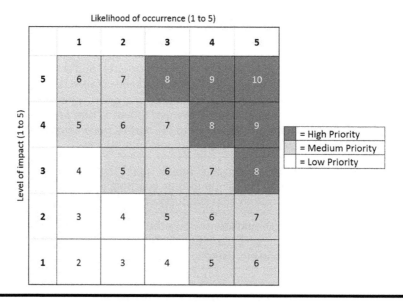

Figure 8.2   A simple risk scoring matrix.

within the *Adoption_Risks_Questionnaire* document contains a simple matrix to help with scoring risks. Each risk is given a rating from 1 to 5 for both the likelihood of its occurrence and the impact to the business if it does occur, and then these two ratings are combined to give an overall score. Risks with a score above a certain number (for example, above 7) can then be classified as High Priority. Risks with a score below a certain number (for example, below 5) can be classified as Low Priority, and risks with an intermediate score can be classified as Medium Priority. The risk scoring matrix is shown in Figure 8.2.

Any risk that is calculated to be a medium or high priority risk will need a strategy either for avoiding the risk entirely through changes made to the adoption plan or through specifying the actions to be taken for dealing with the risk should it occur. Low priority risks can either be treated in the same way as medium or high priority risks or simply ignored if the risk priority is sufficiently low.

A list of risks and actions for dealing with them should be included in the outline adoption plan, and there is a place in the *Outline_Adoption_Plan* template for them.

8.8 Step 8: Create Adoption Proposal and Gain Acceptance

8.8.1 What Is an Adoption Proposal?

An adoption proposal is a simple document that performs a similar function to a business case. Its purpose is to enable project sponsors and other senior authorities to sign off on the adoption plan by providing the basic information they will need in order to do this, set out in simple, clear and business-relevant terms that they will understand. Adoption proposals are not always required, it depends entirely upon the way in which decisions are managed within the customer organization. If acceptance and sign off from sponsor/s has either already been given or is not necessary then the CSM and SPL may decide not to write an adoption proposal and to proceed directly to

Table 8.4 Sections of a Typical Adoption Proposal

Section	Description
Executive summary	A brief (half to one page in length) summary of the content within the proposal, including a summary of the objectives, proposed activities, costs, timescales, measurements and reporting
Adoption objectives	An explanation as to the initiative that the solution supports and the outcomes to be attained from successful solution adoption
Proposed activities	A high-level description of the activities that will be taken to complete each phase within the proposed adoption plan
Finances and timescales	Details of expenditures and timeframes for each adoption phase and overall
Measurements and reporting	Details of measurements and reporting for each adoption phase and overall
Key risks	Details of any substantial risks that have been identified but that were not avoided within the plan, together with the proposed steps for managing them should they occur
Appendices	Other information to support the proposal. This might include details around personnel to be deployed, third parties who will be involved, research and planning methodologies and research findings

Step 8: Complete Full Adoption Plan and Publish Adoption Roadmap. However, for more complex situations there may be value in creating an adoption proposal just purely as a checksum for ensuring the adoption plan is complete.

The recommendation is to keep the adoption proposal as brief and succinct as possible, although of course it is very important to ensure it is accurate and contains all of the information necessary for project sponsors to make any funding or other decisions. The Adoption Proposal should be created to suit the needs of the specific situation, but might include the following sections (Table 8.4).

An *Adoption_Proposal_Template* that follows the above format has been included in the Downloads section at www.practicalcsm.com.

8.8.2 Getting Approval

Once the adoption proposal has been completed and validated, the SPL (with support from the CSM as required) can submit it to the initiative's sponsor/s and other senior decision makers for discussion and approval. The sponsor/s may request amendments, in which case the necessary changes should be completed as swiftly as possible and the proposal resubmitted for final approval.

Note that in some circumstances it may be necessary for other key stakeholders including team leaders and process owners to sign off on those parts of the proposal that impact their teams and/or processes. It is the responsibility of the SPL to know who needs to view and approve the adoption proposal, but as with everything, it is best practice for the CSM in their advisory capacity to do their best to ensure that all necessary approvals have been granted.

8.9 Step 9: Complete Full Adoption Plan and Publish Adoption Roadmap

8.9.1 The Full Adoption Plan

The adoption plan is a fully detailed document (or collection of documents) that will be used by the CSM, SPL and others to manage the implementation of the adoption program. It makes sense to gain approval and acceptance of the high-level plan prior to completing all of the details of the full adoption plan, especially in more complex situations. Once approval has been gained, the CSM and SPL can be confident that it is worthwhile to invest the necessary further time that will need to be spent on fleshing out the details of the plan.

By this stage all the creative decisions will have been made and therefore the vast majority or perhaps even all of what remains to be done is the administration work around availability of personnel and resources and scheduling activities. The CSM need only take an advisory role here and should not take on the role of completing all the details. There may be others (for example, Training and HR professionals from within the customer organization or from third parties) who will need to be liaised with to complete this work. The CSM may need to perform some of this liaison and "project management" to ensure that collaboration between the necessary partners takes place in a timely and efficient manner.

In terms of documentation, for more simple adoption programs the full adoption plan can be documented within a spreadsheet program such as Microsoft Excel. A more complex, multi-phased adoption program with multiple IGs and multiple outcome requirements may need to be documented in a project management tool such as Microsoft Project, or whatever project management system the customer and/or the CSM's company uses. As with any complex document, it always pays to get someone who was not involved in its creation to review the document once created to check for errors and omissions.

8.9.2 The Adoption Roadmap and Other Marketing Collateral

As stated above, the adoption plan is a fully detailed document (or collection of documents) that will be used by the CSM, SPL and others to manage the implementation of the adoption program. This document is of course invaluable for those who will actually manage the implementation of the adoption program, but it may also be a good idea to provide a summary roadmap of adoption activities that can be published more widely for everyone—or at least for key stakeholders—to see, so that they can prepare themselves and their teams for any impact of the adoption implementation in terms of their time and workload ahead of time.

An adoption roadmap can also be considered to be a great marketing tool. As such it might be a good idea to include creative personnel such as graphic designers and marketing specialists in the team to help design and create the roadmap itself. The roadmap might typically be created in the form of a PDF that can also be printed as a large-sized poster that can be displayed on office walls.

Your adoption plan may also call for other marketing collateral such as posters, videos, email campaigns etc., to be created. Again, you will need to ensure that this work is completed as appropriate.

The look and feel of the adoption roadmap and other collateral should be tailored to suit the culture and requirements of the customer organization. What the marketing campaign needs to convey is an explanation for:

- What will be happening (a description of the initiative and the changes it will engender)
- Why it is happening (the benefits to the customer's organization that the initiative will bring)
- Who will be impacted by the change
- When the changes will take place (for the roadmap particularly, this will be the majority of what it contains, showing the major phases of the adoption program and summarizing what will happen during each phase)
- Expectations of the workforce (typically to make sure they understand the implications to their own role and to prepare themselves for the change ahead of time)
- Reassurance of support (to allay doubts, fears and concerns)

8.10 Tools for PCSMF Phase 4: Adoption Planning

- Adoption Requirements Questionnaire
- Adoption Activities Checklist
- Outline Adoption Plan
- Adoption Proposal Template

8.10.1 Tools for Capturing Adoption Requirements

The tool that has been provided for identifying adoption requirements is called the *Adoption_ Requirements_Questionnaire* and this contains six worksheets as follows:

- Firstly, there is the *Adoption Requirements* worksheet. This is where basic outcome requirements plus other requirements which the adoption program must fulfill can be documented.
- Secondly, there is the *Process Change* worksheet, which can be used to document changes to processes within each business capability that will be impacted by the initiative.
- Thirdly, there is the *IG Questionnaire* worksheet. The purpose of this worksheet is to provide a way of recording the names and relevant details for each group of users that will be impacted by the initiative.
- The fourth worksheet is called *Practical Considerations* and this can be used by the CSM to record any additional information that needs to be considered when developing the adoption plan.
- The fifth worksheet is the *Adoption Barriers* worksheet where potential barriers that may be obstacles to the successful completion of the adoption program can be noted and described.
- The sixth and final worksheet is the *Adoption Risks* worksheet where potential risks that may arise during the adoption program can also be noted and described.

The second tool for determining adoption requirements is the *Adoption_Activities_Checklist*. This is also a Microsoft Excel workbook and it contains three worksheets as follows:

- The first worksheet is called *Communication Activities* and this can be used by the CSM to record the communication activity needs of each IG.
- The second worksheet is called *Training Activities* and this can be used by the CSM to record the training activity needs of each IG.
- The third worksheet is called *Support Activities* and this can be used by the CSM to record the support activity needs of each IG.

8.10.2 Tools for Creating the Outline Adoption Plan

The tool provided for creating the outline adoption plan is called *Outline_Adoption_Plan* and this is just a template that contains headings which the CSM and SPL may want to consider using within the outline plan they create.

8.10.3 Tools for Creating the Adoption Proposal

The tool provided for creating an adoption proposal (if required) is called *Adoption_Proposal_Template* and not unlike the format for the outline adoption plan, this is a template that contains headings which the CSM and SPL may want to consider using within the adoption proposal they create.

8.11 Activities and Outputs for PCSMF Phase 4: Adoption Planning

8.11.1 Activities for PCSMF Phase 4: Adoption Planning

The Activities for Phase 4: Adoption Planning include:

1. Review the completed *Customer_Research_Checklist* for this customer (or other tool you use in handovers) which you created in Phase 1: Preparation.
2. If there are any information gaps that need to be filled or assumptions that need to be validated make a note of them and prepare questions for the customer
3. Review the completed *Customer_Engagement_Strategy* together with any other documents that have also already been created in the Central Repository for this customer to ensure you are up-to-date on requirements from the engagement
4. Use the *Customer_Onboarding_Scoring_Tool* to gain an initial understanding of the needs and level of complexity of the customer for adoption, or if you wish you can just refer back to the *Customer_Onboarding_Scoring_Tool* to gain an understanding of the likely needs and level of complexity of the customer for adoption, as this is likely to be similar in complexity to their onboarding needs.
5. Hold a series of meetings with the customer to discuss their adoption needs and determine their adoption requirements, using the *Customer_Research_Checklist* from Phase 1: Preparation to remind you of any previous information, and recording discussion findings in the first worksheet within the *Adoption_Requirements_Questionnaire* workbook.
6. Follow-up as necessary to learn and document additional information where any information gaps were uncovered
7. Use the Process Change worksheet within the *Adoption_Requirements_Questionnaire* workbook to document each process that will be impacted by the initiative and described the changes
8. Use the information gained in Step 7 to determine which users will be impacted and then group them into IGs. Document each group and their KSA change requirements in the IG Questionnaire worksheet within the *Adoption_Requirements_Questionnaire* workbook
9. Capture all practical considerations that need to be regarded during the adoption planning process in the Practical Considerations worksheet within the *Adoption_Requirements_Questionnaire* workbook

10. Work through the communication, training and support needs for each IG and document these needs within the *Adoption_Activities_Checklist* workbook
11. Capture potential adoption barriers that need to be regarded during the adoption planning process in the Adoption Barriers worksheet within the *Adoption_Requirements_Questionnaire* workbook
12. Capture potential risks that need to be regarded during the adoption planning process in the Adoption Risks worksheet within the *Adoption_Requirements_Questionnaire* workbook
13. Now work with SPL and other customer stakeholder as necessary to create an outline adoption plan. Use the information now contained within the *Adoption_Requirements_Questionnaire* and *Adoption_Activities_Checklist* workbooks as well as information pertaining to the customer's overall needs contained within the *Customer_Research_Checklist* that you created in Phase 1 and information pertaining to stakeholders that you documented within the *RACI_Matrix,* the *Stakeholder_Management_Matrix* and the *Stakeholder_Management_Plan* in Phase 2 to help you as necessary. Document the outline adoption plan using the *Outline_Adoption_Plan* template.
14. Create an adoption proposal using the *Adoption_Proposal_Template* and gain acceptance and approval for your adoption plan. This may necessitate amendments which you should document in the *Outline_Adoption_Plan* template as necessary.
15. Once the outline adoption plan has been approved, proceed to help the customer to flesh out the adoption plan into a fully detailed version, using project management tools to do so if necessary. This may involve multiple stakeholders from HR and Training departments, change management professionals, and team leaders and process owners as necessary.
16. Create a summarized version of the full adoption plan that can be published more widely as an adoption roadmap for all workers (or at least for managers) to see, and start work on any other marketing collateral needed for marketing the upcoming adoption program.
17. Capture a summary of the work you have accomplished plus any lessons you have learned in the *CSM_Activity_Tracking_Template.*

8.11.2 Outputs for PCSMF Phase 4: Adoption Planning

The main Output for Phase 4: Adoption Planning is a fully detailed adoption plan. If possible, the CSM should store a copy of this document together with other documents created during this phase in the Central Repository, together with lessons learned which should be documented within the *CSM_Activity_Tracking_Template.* By the end of this adoption planning phase you and the customer will be ready to move forward to PCSMF Phase 5: Adoption Implementation.

Chapter 9

Practical CSM Framework
Phase 5: Adoption
Implementation

9.1 What Is Adoption Implementation?

9.1.1 The Adoption Implementation Process as a Project

The adoption implementation process can be defined as being all those activities which combine together to prepare impacted users for change. The adoption implementation process will usually have defined start and end dates and may also contain multiple phases, each with their own start and end dates and with defined responsibilities for performing and overseeing activities and carefully defined milestones for achievement by the end of each phase. The adoption implementation process can therefore be viewed and treated as its own project, which needs to be funded, managed and measured just like any other project. That said, adoption can also be thought of as an ongoing lifecycle that doesn't happen overnight but instead occur cyclically over time (Figure 9.1).

9.1.2 The Role of the CSM in Adoption Implementation

Unless the entire adoption implementation process has been handed over as a paid for professional services piece of work for the CSM's company (or other third-party company) to manage on behalf of the customer, the responsibility for managing the adoption process remains with the customer, and specifically with the SPL or other nominated key stakeholder. Assuming this to be the case, the CSM's role is supportive. They should be available as necessary to provide advice and access to any relevant assets or resources that the CSM's company owns or has access to. They should not, however, take on the role of project manager or take responsibility for the positive delivery of the adoption program—these should rest squarely with the customer itself.

With that said, it may be the case with some customers—especially those with less experience or maturity around implementing adoption programs—that the SPL or other nominated stakeholder does not have much or even any project management training or experience. If this is the

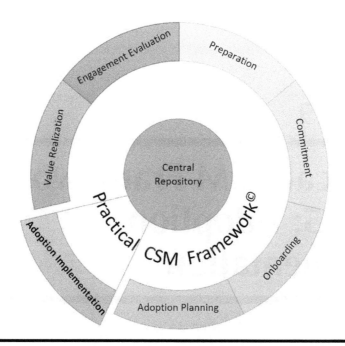

Figure 9.1 PCSMF Phase 5: Adoption Implementation.

situation and given that the successful adoption of the solution is equally important to the CSM's company as to the customer, it may well be in the CSM's interests to play some sort of proactive role in project managing the adoption process on an informal rather than formal basis. In this situation, it needs to be clear that the formal project management responsibility still lies with the customer and their nominated stakeholder and that the CSM's role is purely advisory.

This is important because the CSM is not likely to have the time available to take on a full project management role, neither are they likely to have the necessary level of authority nor access to resources, assets and people within the customer organization to fulfill the role. Additionally, there are many aspects of the adoption process that will remain outside of the control of any third party and for which it is important that the customer organization rather than the CSM's organization remains responsible for. An example of this would be negotiating how much time sales people should take away from their sales duties to undergo training on new systems and processes, or how employees who will be taking on new responsibilities should be rewarded or remunerated for doing so.

9.2 Project Management and the Role of the CSM

9.2.1 The Need for Project Management

Although in theory customers should either take the lead in project managing their adoption program or appoint a third party to do so on their behalf, this cannot always be relied upon to occur either at all or to a sufficient quality. Since it is in the CSM's company's interests that the adoption program is successful, it is part of the CSM's duties to do what they can to ensure that this happens. Therefore, while CSMs do not need to be professionally qualified project managers (though having the customer's own experienced project managers involved can greatly help in the project's success), they most definitely do need to be competent at managing (or helping to manage) small projects such as a customer's adoption program.

CSMs tend to come into the customer success management role not as a first job but with experience of performing other roles beforehand. I have certainly met CSMs whose background included a formal project management role. If this happens to be the case for you and you are trained, experienced and perhaps even qualified in project management best practices then these skills you have previously acquired will undoubtedly prove very useful to you in your CSM role. If on the other hand you do not have any knowledge or experience of project management best practices then my recommendation would be to consider purchasing and reading a book on the topic or maybe even attending a foundation level course on it, since the skills learned from such a book or course will likely stand you in good stead throughout your customer success management career.

9.2.2 Defining Projects and Project Management

A project could be defined as *an undertaking comprising a defined start date, end date, and a series of activities in between that combine to create a predefined outcome.* The outcome is the result of the project, and this result is generated by completion of the project's activities. In the case of an adoption program, the outcome will be the successful adoption of the new solution, and the activities within the project will include tasks relating to assessing users' training needs, communicating to users, training users and supporting users.

Project management can be defined as *managing the project's activities to ensure the best possible outcome is attained.* At a minimum, this outcome should include that the project was completed on time, within budget, and to the satisfaction of the customer's key stakeholders including the senior sponsor.

9.2.3 Classic Versus Agile Project Management

Classic project management assumes that outcomes will be defined up front and that the project will follow a "waterfall" approach where everything is first planned and then when the plan is completed and approved the activities within the plan will commence and will continue until completion.

Agile project management takes the view that outcomes can be more loosely defined at first and then activities can be planned and enacted and results measured in short activity cycles. At the end of each cycle lessons are learned and if necessary the direction of the project can then be changed for subsequent cycles.

The cyclical approach allows for learning to take place along the way, and can therefore lead to a better result, especially where the project entails a high level of innovation. Where requirements are known and defined in advance the classic approach tends to be easier and simpler to manage. In the case of an adoption program, it is likely that CSMs will generally find that the classic approach to project management will work best.

9.2.4 Typical Project Management Tasks

Project management is quite broad in scope and generally includes the following tasks (Table 9.1).

Table 9.1 Typical Project Management Tasks

Task	Description
Defining outcome requirements	Working out what the project needs to achieve and setting the scope and deadlines for the project
Research and analysis	Finding, documenting and understanding relevant information that will be needed for planning purposes
Planning	Determining what activities will occur, how they will occur, who will perform them, when and in what order they will occur, how they will be measured, what resources they will require, how much they will cost, who will pay for them and how they will be measured
Orchestration	Ensuring that activities occur according to the plan by controlling, influencing and leading those responsible for performing those activities
Measuring and reporting	Taking measurements to determine progress, comparing these measurements against predetermined KPIs and creating progress reports for presentation to project sponsors
Handling obstacles and risks	Dealing with any unforeseen obstacles or challenges as they occur and reacting to risks if they occur by following the predetermined risk mitigation plan or if necessary by determining a risk management plan and then enacting that plan
Handling changes to project outcomes	If after the project commences the project sponsors require modified or even completely new outcomes from the project the project manager will need to alter the project plan to manage these changed requirements

Of these tasks, the first three (namely defining outcome requirements, research and analysis, and planning) have already been covered in Chapters 7 and 8 that dealt with Practical CSM Framework Phase 4: Adoption Planning. The focus of this chapter is on the last four items in the list (namely orchestration, measuring and reporting, handling obstacles and risks, and handling changes to project outcomes).

9.2.5 Typical Project Management Skills

As with customer success management, project management can call upon a wide and diverse range of personal and technical skills in order to get the job done. Most notable among these might be:

- Administration
- Communication
- Negotiation
- Relationship building
- Stakeholder management and team management
- Leadership and influencing
- Documentation and reporting
- Problem-solving

- Financial management
- Time management
- Integration skills
- Scoping and defining project boundaries
- Identifying possible risks

Note that personal skills (for example, leadership, communication and relationship building) feature as much if not more on this list as practical or technical skills (for example, administration or problem-solving). This list is by no means exhaustive but will give a good idea to CSMs as to what they will need to be good at in order to succeed as a project manager or in an advisory role to the actual project manager.

9.2.6 Defining the CSM's Role in Project Managing an Adoption Plan

As stated above, unless the entire adoption program has been contracted out as a professional service to either the CSM's company or a third party, it is up to the customer organization to appoint a project manager to oversee the implementation of their adoption program, and CSMs should not attempt to formally take on the role. However, it is perfectly acceptable and even encouraged to "lend a hand" on an informal basis, certainly in terms of advice, support and liaison with other parties as had been described before, and even with a degree of hands-on administration and leadership if the circumstances call for it. It is down to the CSM to decide how active a role they play in their customers' adoption implementations, based upon their own skills, experience and availability and upon the needs of each individual customer.

9.3 Benefits of a Multi-Phased Adoption Program

9.3.1 The Value of a Phase Approach to Adoption

There are lots of advantages to taking a phased approach to the adoption process. The table below lists some of the care benefits (Table 9.2).

If the adoption process has been planned as a single and undivided program, it might therefore be worthwhile for the CSM to consider discussing the pros and cons of dividing it into multiple shorter phases with the SPL and other key stakeholders.

Table 9.2 Benefits of a Phased Approach to Implementation

Benefit	Explanation
Manageability	Breaking down a complex project into several smaller sections and then treating each section as its own separate mini-project with its own funding, activities, responsibilities and outcome requirements tends to make the management easier, which in turn reduces the likelihood of mistakes or omissions being made and increases the efficiency and efficacy of the adoption process itself
Flexibility	Increased flexibility comes from allowing for lessons to be learned in earlier phases of the adoption process. The results of those lessons can then be applied in refinements and improvements to later phases

(Continued)

Table 9.2 (*Continued*)   Benefits of a Phased Approach to Implementation

Benefit	Explanation
Agility	By leaving later phases open to be determined at a later stage, the adoption process becomes more agile. This means that as the company's needs change, the later phases of the adoption process can be designed to allow for those changes since the design process is delayed until the phase is required
Finance	By separating the adoption activities into a number of phases, it may be possible to treat the funding for each phase separately, thus reducing the need to find funding for the entirety of the adoption process in one go or from one source
Productivity	Instead of one major push, the adoption process could spread out the phases over time, reducing the time burden on both impacted users to attend activities outside of their normal working role (such as training) and therefore maintaining necessary levels of corporate productivity
Adoption requirements	It may be the case that not all adoptions requirements occur at the same time. For example, if the implementation of one or more new tools or systems occurs as a phased activity over time (perhaps being rolled out to different departments or different locations at different times) then the adoption program may need to follow this same pattern of phased implementation
Adaptability	Each customer can be very different in terms of the customer's values, culture, comfort around rate of change, organizational hierarchy and overall environment. The CSM must be comfortable with working in the style and manner that best suits the customer and not try to insist on the customer adapting what they do to suit the CSM's working style and preferences

9.4 Preparing for Project Kick-Off

9.4.1 Readiness through Good Preparation

I have always liked the expression "getting all your ducks in a row." While I've never had the necessity to arrange ducks or indeed any other aquatic birds into neat, orderly lines, I have certainly experienced the difficulties involved in attempting to perform a complex task without everything being completely ready. The moral here is that a little extra time spent up front making sure everything is good to go can save a lot of frustration down the line when, for example, everything gets delayed while a forgotten asset is created, or while a missing resource is secured, or while an additional group of user's needs are identified and activities for them are added to the program.

9.4.2 The Readiness Checklist

One good way to handle the concept of readiness is to prepare a "readiness checklist" and then to run through the items on this list with the customer prior to project launch, signing off on each item on the list or where necessary stopping and taking any further preparation actions so that an item can then be signed off. Some items for consideration on such a list are show below:

- Have all project outcomes been clearly defined and agreed?
- Have all processes that will undergo change been identified?
- Has the nature of each process change been accurately documented?
- Have all impacted users been identified?
- Have impacted users been correctly assigned into IGs (impacted user groups)?
- Have the KSA needs of each IG been assessed and documented?
- Have appropriate requirements for communication, training and support been identified for each IG?
- Have all activities to deliver these requirements been selected, costed and approved?
- Have appropriate ways for measuring the results of these activities been identified?
- Have all activities been assigned into project phases?
- Have all assets and/or resources needed for the performance of these activities been created and/or assigned (and if team members are global, consider time zone constraints)?
- Have all mechanisms for delivery of activities (including third parties) been identified and made ready?
- Have all activities (or at least those in upcoming phases) been scheduled as necessary?
- Have all necessary communications occurred?
- Have all necessary validations and approvals occurred?
- Have all adoption barriers or challenges been addressed?
- Have all potential risks been identified and plans for mitigation should they occurred been created?
- Is there anything else that has not been done that needs to be done prior to project launch?
- Are we ready to go?

This final question can be thought of as a sign off by the formal project manager (for example, the SPL) that all preparations have been adequately made and that everything is ready for the adoption program to commence.

An *Adoption_Program_Readiness_Checklist* document has been created as a template for CSMs to use as a start point for defining their own adoption readiness checklists, and this can be accessed from the Downloads section at www.practicalcsm.com.

9.4.3 Maintaining a Flexible, "Can Do" Attitude

As discussed above, it is far better to have been well prepared in the first place than to have to deal with unnecessary problems en route. However, it is still entirely possible in even the most carefully of prepared for situation for new needs or missing information to be uncovered that necessitate changes to the plan even after the program has gone live. General Dwight D. Eisenhower is famously quoted as saying, "In preparing for battle I have always found that plans are useless, but planning is indispensable." While it's very important to *have* a plan, it is also important not to become so attached to that plan that the project team becomes rigid and inflexible in their attitude to change. Last minute changes are not perhaps a complete inevitability but are certainly to be expected and when they occur should be dealt with cheerfully and professionally.

The advice therefore is not to get so attached to the plan you have created that you become rigid or inflexible in your attitude, or get frustrated when unanticipated problems come up during the implementation of the adoption program that needs dealing with *in situ*. In fact, it could be argued that it is precisely when these sorts of issues arise that CSMs are best able to help and support the SPL and other customer stakeholders by the use of their expertise, experience and creative problem-solving skills to help resolve these problems and get the project back on track.

9.5 Managing People

9.5.1 Many More People Are Likely to Be Involved

People management is a critical skill of any project manager and indeed of any CSM. Prior to launching the adoption program and during the research and planning phases, it may well be the case that only a small number of key stakeholders have been involved. Now however it is entirely likely that not only a much greater number of people will be involved but also that they will come from a wider and more diverse range of backgrounds and have a wider and diverse range of opinions about the initiative itself and the adoption program that you have developed to support that initiative.

9.5.2 Some People May Not Be Supportive of the Adoption Program

The CSM may well find therefore that there are different levels of support for the project and that not all people are comfortable or happy with the role that has been allocated to them within this project and/or the use of their assets and/or resources by the project. Some might not be happy but are still acceptant and compliant. Others however may be reluctant to agree to whatever needs of them the project may have. For example, a sales person may not wish to take time away from their selling activities to attend training on what they perceive as unimportant administrative tasks that they are not interested in, or a manager may be reluctant to allow access to their team because they are concerned about meeting productivity targets.

9.5.3 Some People Are Difficult by Nature

Not all people who end up presenting difficulties are doing it deliberately. Some peoples' personalities or the circumstances they find themselves in that are causing them emotional problems might make them awkward to deal with regardless of whether or not they agree or disagree with what is happening or have any rationale for their behavior. This might include people with behavior traits such as unreliability or those with poor people skills.

This category of people also includes those who may even be in favor of the adoption program, but still end up providing difficulties due to external circumstances beyond their control. They might, for example, fall ill, or be transferred at the last minute to a different role, or be stuck at an airport, or have to deal with an emergency of some kind.

9.5.4 Forewarned Is Forearmed

Some people do not present as being difficult but later they turn out to be so. Others however may already be known for being difficult to get on with or awkward to deal with. This sort of information about known personality traits that may need careful handling can be very useful for the CSM to learn, especially regarding key stakeholders whom they will need to communicate and/or negotiate with on a regular basis. Aside from the CSM's own colleagues who might already know the some of the key stakeholders within a customer organization, it may be possible to approach the SPL or other customer stakeholder with whom the CSM has struck up a sufficiently close and trusting relationship, and ask them as an internal resource who may have worked with these stakeholders for several years to provide a rundown of any useful advice they might be able to give the CSM regarding the personalities and characteristics of their colleagues.

If the CSM elects to raise this topic with the SPL or other customer stakeholder they should, first of all, make sure they have established a sufficiently close and trusting relationship to enable that stakeholder to feel comfortable about opening up and revealing this sort of personal information about their colleagues to an "outsider." Additionally, they should try to make it as comfortable as possible for the stakeholder. For example, do not raise the issue in a formal meeting or in front of others. Instead wait for an opportunity in a more informal setting (for example, over lunch or a coffee) and when the two of you are alone and not in danger of your discussion being overheard by others. Raise this issue carefully and ensure you give the stakeholder room to answer in as much or little detail as they wish without it being awkward for them. For example, rather than asking "Which of your colleagues are the most awkward to deal with, and in what ways are they difficult?" you could instead ask "Is there anything else about any of the people we will be working with that you think it might be useful for me to know about in advance, and which might help me to deal with them more effectively?". This softer approach gives the stakeholder much more scope for answering in a way that they feel comfortable with.

A final point is not to record what they are saying, so that they do not feel that their words are "on the record." If it is a voice or video call do not press the Record button on the conferencing tool, or if the meeting is already being recorded, now is the time to pause or stop recording and make the stakeholder aware that you have done so. If the meeting is face to face do not make notes in front of them to document what they are telling you and instead just listen and remember.

9.5.5 Dealing with Difficult People

The important thing about dealing with difficult, awkward or unresponsive people or with people who let you down is not to take it personally and not to let it affect one's own personality or behavior. Assisting with project managing an adoption program can be stressful, so if unexpected additional difficulties are suddenly thrust upon the CSM it can sometimes be tempting to respond emotionally. It is therefore a good idea to prevent this from occurring in the first place by anticipating in advance that problems of this sort are very likely to occur, and preparing oneself for responding appropriately when they do. This reduces the emotional impact when they do occur since it does not come entirely out of the blue, and it also enables the "autopilot" to take over and perform the prepared response while any initial emotional impact is being absorbed and dealt with.

In short however, the best way to deal with difficult people is to be an emotionally resilient person who has the strength of personality to deal with difficult people in a friendly and professional manner without allowing it to impact their own emotional wellbeing. CSMs are advised to continually work at increasing their emotional resilience and strength of personality as these are in any case characteristics that tend to improve all round happiness and wellbeing and I would suggest that no one can have too much of them.

9.5.6 Be a Good Negotiator and Be a Great Listener

Note every desired requirement that you may have of someone's time, money or other resources can be gotten from them. Sometimes you might get everything you want, sometimes you might get nothing at all, but oftentimes you may need to reach a compromise with the other person.

Learning when and how to gain commitments and make compromises is a very important skill for project management of people, and this is referred to as the skill of negotiation. Sometimes the CSM may need to negotiate on their own behalf, and sometimes the CSM may need to step in to assist negotiations between two or more key stakeholders who, for example, might disagree on a detail such as responsibilities for performing activities or for funding those activities.

Whatever the case, the CSM should be aware of the basics of negotiation. My recommended eight steps for high-quality negotiation are as follows:

Step 1: Do not allow emotions to enter into the discussion. Instead, leave all such personal considerations at the door—they have no part to play in work-related negotiations, which should be conducted professionally and with regard only to objective not emotional criteria.

Step 2: Determine your minimum position. This is the absolute worst case result from the negotiation that you would be prepared to accept. Once you have defined it and validated it, do not budge from it and if necessary walk away from the negotiation if this minimum position cannot be met.

Step 3: Determine your ideal position. This is the best case result that you might be able to attain from the negotiation. Make sure it is clearly defined and includes all the possible things you wish to achieve. This might include both positive and negative aspects (e.g., you might state what activities you want to have included within a task whose details are being negotiated and also what activities you want to make sure are left out of the task).

Step 4: Define the agreement. Before commencing the negotiations with the other party or parties, first define and agree with those parties what an agreement will mean. For example, this might include start and end dates for taking any agreed actions, commitments to report back on activity, and so on. If this is done ahead of any negotiation then everyone is already clear on what an agreement will look like and what will happen after it has been reached.

Step 5: Start by sharing your ideal position. This will now become your *starting position* which you can share with and explain to the other parties. At the same time learn from the other parties what their starting positions are, and again make sure you understand them fully.

Step 6: Look for the commonalities and differences between each party's starting position. If there are sufficient commonalities between starting positions such that all parties can get what they have stated they want within these starting positions then an agreement can probably be concluded straight away.

Step 7: Negotiate fair trade-offs between each party's position. If an agreement cannot be concluded from the starting positions, the parties can trade-off desired aspects of their starting position against aspects of the other parties' starting positions to find a single position where all parties at least maintain their minimum position while equally winning and losing in terms of any additional desired aspects.

Step 8: Conclude the negotiation. Make sure that each party is 100% clear as to what has been agreed, document the details of the agreement and distribute to each party. If necessary get contracts drawn up and signed. Don't feel you have to do this on your own—include the account team when necessary.

The above eight steps can be used equally as an interested party (i.e., as one of the parties with a position that needs to be negotiated) or as a disinterested third party acting purely as an unbiased negotiator. The CSM may find themselves in either or both of these positions from time to time.

9.5.7 Maintain Your Own Personal Integrity at All Times

Above all else, when managing people within the project management of an adoption program or indeed at any other time, always remember your own center in terms of your personal code of ethics and morality and philosophy on what is right and wrong. Trust your instincts to give ground where it feels right to do so and to maintain your position when that feels like the right thing to do. Treat others with politeness, kindness and consideration at all times, but never allow anyone else to dictate your emotions.

9.6 Managing Tasks

9.6.1 Apply the Rule of "Divide and Conquer"

Managing all of the activities in a complex project can sometimes feel overwhelming or even impossible. Stress levels can very quickly rise when faced with hundreds or even thousands of tasks to manage, many of them simultaneously. The basic rule of *divide and conquer* can be applied here, and this division of a project into smaller, more manageable chunks is often referred to within the project management professional as a WBS (work breakdown structure).

The concept of WBS is to break down a complex project into a series of smaller component parts called *work packages*, where each work package (i.e., each part of the total project) has its own specific *deliverable* (i.e., a definable and measurable result to be achieved from completing that particular part). In the context of an adoption program a WBS work package might project ect might have used the concepts within WBS to define a work package called "Initial Global Communication" which comprises a series of activities relating to creating and delivering an initial communication about the upcoming changes that will go out to everyone in the company. The deliverable might have been defined as "All employees have been made aware of the upcoming change, and now have a high level understanding of its impact to the company and to themselves." and this can be measured to see if it has successfully occurred, for example, by surveying a small sample subset of all employees from across the organization.

9.6.2 Using Work Packages within a WBS

To apply the concept of WBS within their own project, a project manager will need to first break down the project into multiple phases and then secondly to within each phase break down the activities into work packages. Each work package should be given the following attributes (Table 9.3).

The work packages can now be handed out or assigned to those stakeholders who are responsible for them and work can commence.

9.7 Measuring and Reporting

9.7.1 Why Take Measurements?

The only way to know whether something is working or not is to measure it. If you're not measuring it then you're only guessing as to what results you are getting. If you *do* take measurements then you might not know every detail about the results you are getting, but you will at least have some idea.

Table 9.3   Work Package Attributes

Attribute	Description
Name	A meaningful name that should help to identify the purpose of the activities contained within the work package
Deliverables	A clear definition of the outcomes that should be attained from the successful completion of the work contained within the work package
Activities	A list of the actions or tasks that will be performed within the work package
Responsibilities	A list of who will be involved in performing the activities and their roles
Schedule	A list of start and end dates and times for activities and for the work package overall
Measurements	An explanation as to how the work package will be measured
Governance	Who will take the measurements, will be reported to once the work package is completed and who will sign off to accept the work has been satisfactorily completed
Status	Each work package can be provided with a status of green, yellow or red and a summary of known issues can be provided

9.7.2 More Measurements Create a Fuller Picture but Cost More

The more measurements you take, the more information you have on which to judge the results you are getting. This works both in terms of the different *types* of measurements you take and the *frequency* with you take them. Taking multiple different types of measurement about a particular activity provides you with multiple sets of different data to analyze. It's a bit like viewing something in three dimensions rather than just in two dimensions—the more measurement types you add, the better you understand the results you are getting. Likewise if you take measurements more frequently you will also build up a more detailed and accurate picture as to what is happening, and of course you will not have to wait so long between measurements to check on progress.

One downside of taking more measurements is that you create more work, particularly where the measurement taking process involves some element of manual intervention. If the measuring is fully automated then this may not be a large factor to consider. Another downside is that you end up with more data, and of course if you combine both multiple measurement types with increased frequency of measurements then you will potentially get many times more data. The data needs storing which carries both a cost and a risk of loss or theft, and it also needs analyzing and interpreting, so again more work is required.

There is therefore a trade-off between taking enough measurements to be able to sufficiently understand what is happening but not taking too many measurements so that unnecessary expenditure is incurred. What the precise trade-off should be in any given situation will vary based on all sorts of factors. It is up to the SPL and fellow customer stakeholders to make this decision, but it is also up the CSM both to provide their own advice on this topic and to provide access to subject matter experts who can give more qualified and detailed advice when necessary.

9.7.3 The Difference between Indicators and Outcomes

As we know from our previous definition of the word, the term "outcome" refers to the end result and it defines the reason why an initiative has been undertaken (i.e., in order to attain the results or outcomes). As we have also stated, an outcome should be specified with three criteria—*what it is (quality), how much is required (quantity)*, and *when it must be achieved by (deadline)*. For example, a well-defined outcome might be "Minimum revenues of $100m must be generated by the AsiaPac region during this financial year." The only way to know for sure and certain whether an outcome such as this one will be achieved is to wait until the end of the financial year and then count the revenues in the AsiaPac region for the year that has just ended to see whether it is greater or less than $100m. In other words you can only definitely know that an outcome has been attained *afterwards*.

This is great for the purposes of reporting on outcome attainment, but pretty much useless if you want to be able to know in advance whether or not you are on target to achieve your outcome. This is because if you are not on target then learning this as early on as possible enables corrective action to be taken throughout the remainder of the financial year to ensure you get back on target before the end of the year. A leading indicator is a measurement that is taken in advance of the deadline for outcome attainment and which gives you useful information about whether or not you are on track for attaining your desired outcome in the future. In our example, a simple was of doing this might be to measure revenues on a weekly or monthly basis. So, for example, we might take monthly revenue measurements and we might find that by end of month 3 (i.e., at one-quarter of the way through the financial year) the AsiaPac region has taken $20m in revenues. Assuming that we believe the year to be smooth and consistent in terms of revenues coming in, this might tell us that we are $5m down on where we need to be if we are going to hit out target of $100m by financial year end. Knowing this in advance has helped us to know that we need to take some corrective actions (for example, through additional marketing or sales activities) in order to get our revenues back on track.

9.7.4 Selecting Leading Indicators in the Real World

This simple example works well as a straightforward illustration of the concept of leading indicators. However, the reality is sometimes much harder. Take the example of the launch of a brand new and highly innovative product into the market. In this example can we simply take the first Quarter's revenue figure and multiply by four to project the likely revenues that will be received by financial year end, or is it a little more complicated than that? The chances are that it might take several months or even several years for a brand new product or service to become established in the market and for revenues to begin to pick up. So if, for example, you wanted to know how much revenues you might receive overall from the entire lifetime of a particular product (which for the sake of argument we will say will remain in production for 5 years), you cannot just take the first three month's revenue figures and multiply by 20 and expect to get the result you are hoping for. So in the case of launching new products, revenues may prove to be a very poor measurement to select as a leading indicator, since it does not accurately portray at an early stage what is likely to occur at later stages.

Leading indicator selections therefore needs to be thought about very carefully. To illustrate this point, here is a quote from Microsoft Corporation's CEO Satya Nadella about measuring early activity after launching a new software product: "*Revenue is a lagging indicator, usage is a leading indicator.*" So for software, Nadella sees the measurement of early adopters' activity (things like how often they log in to the software, how long they stay engaged with it and how many different features and function of it they use) are better leading indicators of the likely success of the software than just measuring revenues coming in during the early stages. CSMs should advise their customers to think very carefully about what measurements to take, and advice from industry and product/service experts should be sought to ensure that the measurements that get taken really do help to determine progress toward outcome attainment.

9.8 Handling Problems

9.8.1 Defining Adoption Barriers and Risks (Again)

Problems can come in all sorts of shapes and sizes, but for the sale of simplicity we will divide them into two types—adoption barriers and risks. An adoption barrier is any obstacle or challenge that we know is there and which we need to surmount, remove or deal with in some way in order to attain our desired outcomes. A risk is an obstacle or challenge that *might* occur. If it does happen then again we will need to surmount, remove or deal with it in some way in order to attain our desired outcomes.

9.8.2 Project Managing the Activities Relating to Handling Adoption Barriers and Risks

The processes for the identification, the analyses and the planning for the management of both adoption barriers and risks were all explained in Chapter 8. What we will briefly touch on here in Chapter 9 is the actual implementation and project management of those plans to ensure that adoption barriers and risks are adequately handled throughout the lifetime of the adoption program.

As with so much in life, the secret to simplifying the handling of adoption barriers and risks is to carry out good quality planning. If during the planning process you and your customer have spent sufficient time in identifying the relevant adoption barriers and risks and designing and documenting activities to manage them, it should just be a case of following your plan (in the case of adoption barriers) and following your plan *should the risk occur* (in the case of risks) to ensure that all issues are handled and all obstacles to outcome attainment are removed.

9.8.3 Handling New Challenges When They Arise

The above is all well and good in its way; however, it does rely upon knowing in advance what the actual adoption barriers and risks will be so that they can be carefully prepared for ahead of time. Sometimes however a new challenge that threatens the attainment of the project's outcomes arises without prior knowledge. This might happen either due to a lack of sufficiently careful or detailed research (let's face it the world is very complex and nobody is or should be expected to be perfect), or it might be the case that brand new threats arise that simply had not previously existed.

If this occurs, the CSM, SPL and any other relevant stakeholders need to go back to the processes for researching and determining responses to each newly identified threat, and then carrying out those responses appropriately. What the CSM should also do is ensure that these new challenges together with the responses and the results of taking those responses are documented so that for future adoption programs with other customers those particular challenges can be identified and planned for in advance.

9.9 Dealing with Change

9.9.1 Change Is Inevitable

As we have already discussed elsewhere in this book, the one constant in life is change, and change can and will occur at any time. CSMs should therefore expect to find that despite even the most careful and detailed of plans, when it comes to implementation the adoption requirements and needs will change and therefore the plan will need to be amended on the fly. Of course this might *not* happen, but the chances are that it will and it is better to be prepared for change and for it not to happen than for changes to occur and to be caught off guard by them.

9.9.2 The Rule of Thumb—Allow 5%–10% for Contingency

Of course it is difficult to prepare specifically in advance for unanticipated changes that will occur in the future, since if you knew what the changes would be then they would no longer be unanticipated. Assuming that like me you are not clairvoyant or have access to anyone who *is* clairvoyant, the only answer is to simply allow for a certain amount of slack within the project in terms of time and cost and then this additional slack can be used to deal with the changes that *do* occur. How much contingency time and budget to allow will be up to the SPL and their colleagues to determine, but a rule of thumb might be somewhere around 5%–10%, depending upon the size and complexity of the adoption program and the maturity and sophistication of the adoption team.

9.10 Completing the Project

9.10.1 Completion of Major Milestones

While it may not be the entire project, the completion of a major milestone is nevertheless a major achievement which should be at least acknowledged if not celebrated. If they have not already been taken, measurements should definitely be made at this stage to analyze actual performance against predetermined goals to ensure that the project remains on track. At this stage of course if the measurements show that the project is not on track then the SPL and CSM need to investigate to discover why this is and take corrective actions as necessary to ensure that the adoption program gets back on target.

9.10.2 Governance

You may recall (or indeed already be familiar with the fact) that governance is the process of overseeing a project. A governance committee or team will be appointed by the project sponsors to perform this role. Their responsibilities are to receive regular reports on progress and in turn to report this progress back to project sponsors as required, and to provide help and advice if any problems arise that the project management team cannot themselves resolve. They may also have powers of authority to make high-level decisions, for example, to release the finances for Phase 2 upon successful completion of Phase 1, or to make the decision to push out an important deadline by a month to allow for a previously unexpected delay.

As can be seen the governance committee is an important body, and it is therefore a good idea for the CSM to make themselves aware of how it is formed, who it comprises, how often they sit, what decisions they are responsible for and what information they require and in what format they require it. The CSM can then assist the SPL to take appropriate measurements and compile such reports ready for presentation to the governance committee as required. The CSM may or may not be asked to attend governance meetings, but doing so can be a great opportunity to meet and start to form relationships with senior managers who may be on the panel.

Attending regular governance meetings can also be a great opportunity for CSMs to request feedback and advocacy from customers, to ensure contract renewals occur and to position additional products, services and solutions with the customers as upselling and cross-selling activities. This is just mentioned here in passing, but all of these topics are covered in more detailed in Chapter 10 which discusses the Value Realization phase of the Practical CSM Framework.

9.10.3 Completion of the Adoption Program

Once the final phase has been completed and any additional work that may have arisen in an ad hoc fashion is done, the adoption program is completed. This can therefore be treated in the same way as the completion of any other milestone.

9.10.4 ...Or Is It Really Completed After All?

So in one sense the adoption program is done, but perhaps in another sense only the major part of it is done. Adoption can be seen as a formal project with a beginning point, multiple milestones for achievement and an end point with predetermined outcomes. But in addition, adoption can also be thought of as an ongoing process with no actual end at all.

Customers can be thought of as having *adopted* the solution when they have been through the process of communicating to, training and otherwise supporting their users through the change and those users are now busy using the new solution to generate the desired outputs that will ultimately combine over time to attain the overall outcomes for the customer's entire initiative. However, it may well be the case that as customers use the solution they will learn more about what it can do for them and will start to use more of its features and functions to perform a wider range of tasks and to generate additional value for them. More users may start to use the solution, and more processes connected to more business capabilities may be changed to take advantage of improvements that the solution can offer. In this way, the customer does not simply adopt the solution at the beginning for a specific time, but continues to adopt the solution in different ways as that customer's requirements grow and as their knowledge of and confidence in the capabilities of the solution grows.

This is especially the case where customers are purchasing service contracts such as SaaS but indeed where anything is provided as a service. Sometimes that service is only required for a specific need at a specific time, but the hope is that many customers will find uncover additional uses for the service that will necessitate ongoing renewals and preferable renewals at higher levels than previously. Again, there will be more discussion about renewals in Chapter 10.

9.11 Tools and Tasks for Practical CSM Framework Phase 5: Adoption Implementation

9.11.1 Tools for Implementing the Adoption Plan

The main documents that the CSM, SPL and others will use for implementing the adoption plan is the adoption plan itself together with any other deliverables such as an adoption roadmap which have been created during Practical CSM Framework Phase 4: Adoption Implementation. No tools or templates have been provided for the creation of these documents, since they need to be created in a style and format that is relevant to the needs of the specific customer, and will usually actually be created *by* the customer with appropriate input and assistance from the CSM, rather than being created by the CSM.

One tool has been created to assist with adoption implementation, and this is the *Adoption_ Program_Readiness_Checklist* and this contains a generic list of items that can be amended as required to provide a customized checklist for the CSM and SPL to use to ensure that nothing has been forgotten during the launch of the adoption program.

9.11.2 Activities for PCSMF Phase 5: Adoption Implementation

The Activities for Phase 5: Adoption Implementation include:

1. Review the completed *Customer_Research_Checklist* for this customer (or other tool you use in handovers) which you created in Phase 1: Preparation.
2. If there are any information gaps that need to be filled or assumptions that need to be validated make a note of them and prepare questions for the customer
3. Review the completed *Customer_Engagement_Strategy* together with any other documents that have also already been created in the Central Repository for this customer to ensure you are up-to-date on requirements from the engagement
4. Take some time with the SPL and other key stakeholders to review the adoption plan, adoption roadmap and any other documentation that was created by the customer to project manage the adoption program with
5. If necessary break the project phases down into smaller, *work packages* that can be assigned to individuals to complete and which each have their own deliverables.
6. Customize the *Adoption_Program_Readiness_Checklist* and then work through the list in a project readiness workshop. Attend to any issues that are uncovered by this process.
7. Commence the adoption program. Allocate time in your schedule to support, advise, counsel and otherwise assist the SPL or whoever is formally project managing the adoption program. Pay special attention to managing people and to ensure that tasks are completed and measurements are taken.
8. Collate and documents measurements and compile reports (or make sure that those who are responsible for performing those tasks are doing so)
9. Respond to unexpected challenges that turn up, and make sure to document these challenges for reference in the planning for future similar adoption programs with other customers.
10. Attend governance committee meetings or other management meetings as necessary to report on progress and to help determine any changes to the adoption program if any are necessary.

9.11.3 Outputs for PCSMF Phase 5: Adoption Implementation

The main Output for Phase 5: Adoption Implementation is the completion of the adoption program—or at least the initial or formal part of it (see discussions above about whether an adoption program can be said to ever fully reach a completion). The CSM should store a copy of any documentation created during this phase in the Central Repository, together with lessons learned which should be documented within the *CSM_Activity_Tracking_Template*. By the end of this adoption planning phase you and the customer will be ready to move forward to PCSMF Phase 6: Value Creation.

Chapter 10

Practical CSM Framework Phase 6: Value Realization

10.1 What Do We Mean by Value Realization?

10.1.1 What Is Value Realization?

As we have already discussed in previous chapters, the reason why the customer has purchased products, services and/or solutions from us is to support their business and to facilitate the outcomes that their business needs to attain. The products, services or solutions usually form a part of a specific initiative with its own outcomes that in term combine with the outcomes from other initiatives to deliver the overall strategic outcomes of the business. One aspect of the CSM's role is to understand these strategic and initiative-based outcome requirements so that the CSM can assist the customer on its journey to attaining them and report on progress toward them (Figure 10.1).

These outcomes form the "specific value" that the customer is aiming to achieve. However, there may well be "additional value" in the form of other advantages and benefits from using these products, services and solutions that the customer can also attain en route to the achievement of their pre-defined outcomes.

The CSM can help the customer both with attaining their stated outcome requirements as quickly and efficiently as possible and also in gaining as many additional benefits from their company's products, services and solutions as possible. In doing so, the CSM is assisting the customer to realize maximum value from the relationship with and the products, services and solutions purchased from the CSM's company. This of course enhances the likelihood of contract renewals and further sales.

In addition to corporate value, value can also be personal to an individual customer stakeholder such as the SPL or other key stakeholders who have a strong investment in the outcomes of the initiative. This value may, for example, be around the enhancement to their own or their team's or department's image and status internally within their company if the project succeeds, or related to financial rewards and bonuses for hitting targets.

Figure 10.1   PCSMF Phase 6: Value Realization.

10.2 Comparative Duration of the Value Realization Phase

10.2.1 The Long Haul to Outcomes Attainment

Everything that has happened thus far that the CSM has been involved in has been relatively short term in duration and tends to have a fixed start and end date. This includes requirements gathering, onboarding, adoption planning and adoption implementation, each of which could be thought of as its own mini project within the overall project of supporting the customer's initiative. Of these, adoption implementation can perhaps be said to potentially have a longer duration, since it may sometimes be delivered in phases over months or even years, and some aspects of adoption implementation can be thought of as ongoing rather than falling within a specific term. However, by and large, all these activities can be thought of as being the stuff that happens at the beginning, and that happens *purely as an enabler for this phase—the value creation phase.* In a very real sense, from the customer's perspective everything that has occurred up until now (both pre- and post-sales) is preparation working that leads up to the *real* start of the project which happens now. And this is the start of actually using the products, services and solutions to generate outputs that over time will help to attain the company's desired outcomes.

How long will it take from the completion of adoption to the company attaining all of its anticipated outcomes? It could be *any* amount of time, but it would not untypically be a period of 3–5 years, although this pattern will of course differ between industries. From the customer's perspective therefore it is likely to be perceived as a long haul journey, and journey which for them has only just commenced.

10.2.2 Most Customers Will Be in the Value Realization Phase

Given that everything else happens relatively briefly whereas value realization is generally a long haul operation over multiple months or years, the likelihood is that at any one moment in time the majority of a CSM's customer accounts will be in this value realization phase, and only a relatively small number of customers will currently have an initiative in one of the earlier stages. For example, a CSM who has 30 customer accounts to manage may find that perhaps one or two of those customers have initiatives that are currently at the preparation or onboarding stage, and maybe one or two other customers have initiatives that are currently at the adoption planning or implementation stage, with the remainder in various stages of value realization.

10.2.3 Most Activity Will Be in the Previous Phases

From the CSM's perspective, most activity occurs during the earlier stages of a customer engagement, from initial preparation of self and customer through to completing the initial adoption process. Once the value realization stage has been reached the major hard work of research, analysis, planning and implementation is largely over, and it is now a case of taking ongoing measurements, compiling and communicating routine reports and where necessary taking any corrective actions to keep the initiative on track. So although at any one moment of time the majority of customers' initiatives will be somewhere within the value realization stage, this does not necessarily mean that most of the CSM's *time* will be spent performing tasks relating to this stage.

10.3 Balancing the Needs of Multiple Customers

10.3.1 The Balance of the CSM's Time

What the CSM is likely to find is that despite there being a relatively small number of customer engagements that are in these preparations through to adoption stages, these are the engagements that will take up the majority of their time. So again going to our example of the CSM who manages 30 customer accounts, it may be that only say three or four of these customers' engagements are in these early stages, but that between them those few engagements take up perhaps half to two-thirds of the CSM's time, leaving the remaining one-third to one-half of the CSM's time to be available for activity relating to the other 26–27 customers and to any additional non-customer-related activities (for example, attending training courses, internal meetings and report writing, etc.) (Figure 10.2).

The same principle applies whether you manage just 3 customers or 30,000 customers, although the precise way in which time balances out between early-stage engagements, late-stage engagements and non-customer-facing activities will vary considerably between different CSMs working in different industries and for companies selling different products, services and solutions to different customers. Your own personal schedule may look quite different to the example shown; however, the important thing is to recognize that there *will be* a balance that needs to be understood so that it can be managed.

10.3.2 Finding Time for Late-Stage Engagements

As we have seen, early-stage engagements are generally quite time intensive. Additionally, they tend to be more visible both within the customer organization and within the CSM's own company

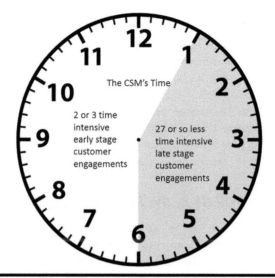

Figure 10.2 The balance of available time.

and they also tend to come with important completion deadlines and therefore often generate a certain amount of stress and pressure on the CSM to maximize the amount of assistance given to them. However, the CSM needs to remain aware of *all* of the calls upon their time and will have to manage their schedule according to the needs of *all* customers plus other duties as best they can. This may take some thinking about, because it is not always easy to determine whether it is better to spend more time with Customer A or to divide up that time and spend it with Customers B to D, or instead to attend a training course to improve skills or knowledge, and so on.

It may also be the case that customers in earlier stages (and the CSM's own colleagues such as sales executives) will be more demanding in their needs and apply more pressure to gain a CSM's time and attention than will customers in the later stage. If a CSM is not careful they may find that too much of their time gets utilized by early-stage customers, leaving insufficient time for other duties. This is one of the reasons why the CSM is encouraged during Section 4 of Chapter 2 of this book to plan and manage their time carefully. If necessary it may be worth reviewing this section again, but in summary my five rules for managing time are:

- Prioritize activity based upon your company's customer success strategy
- Prioritize activity based upon practical considerations
- Keep your customers satisfied
- Determine your unscheduled time needs
- Determine your routine activity requirements

Once you have applied all five rules you can go to your diary or scheduling system and start filling it in, starting with prioritized Rules 1 and 2 activities and then working other activities from Rules 3–5 in as appropriate.

10.3.3 Measuring Is Important

Peter Drucker is famously quoted as saying: *"If you can't measure it, you can't improve it."* This rule applies equally to the world of customer success management as to any other part of a company's operations. CSMs need to make sure that the right measurements are being taken and (equally importantly) that the right actions to analyze, report and where necessary take corrective actions occur, based upon the data that is collected. This includes taking per customer measurements that can be reported within a health score or similar software system and which allows CSMs to monitor the health of the relationship between their own company and a specific customer. It also includes taking measurements of all activity and of all activity relating to a particular product or services and comparing these measurements over time to spot patterns and trends either overall or per product/service and again to analyze, report on and take action relating to these patterns as necessary.

10.3.4 Software Systems for Managing CSM Activity

The work of the CSM is varied and complex. This means that it is not always easy for the CSM to track, manage and report on their activities so that senior management can determine how much value is being created by the CSM's activities. It is also not always easy for CSMs to work out which of the customers they are responsible for managing need their help and assistance, what type of help and assistance is needed, when it is required, and how much of it to give. As a result of this need, early adopters of customer success management concepts (who also happened to be SaaS companies of course) designed and developed software systems to provide these types of assistance to their CSMs. These software systems were originally designed for internal use, but eventually became part of the portfolio of some of these companies' software services for sale to other companies who were experiencing similar difficulties.

These customer success software systems are often referred to as *Health Score* systems. An example of a prominent vendor of this type of system today is Gainsight, which offers a very feature rich product that integrates with CRM systems such as Salesforce or NetSuite that might suit the needs of larger customer success departments from within larger organizations, and there are many other vendors such as Totango and ClientSuccess that make similar, competitive products, as well as a wide range of companies that provide less fully-featured systems that are aimed at smaller businesses' needs.

10.3.5 The Role of CSM Software Vendors in Shaping the Customer Success Industry

Because of the way in which the customer success profession has itself grown from within the SaaS market, the leading vendors of customer success software systems have had a major role in shaping and driving the direction in which customer success management has taken. This can be seen, for example, by the fact that the best-selling book on the theories, concepts and philosophies of customer success management is *Customer Success*, written by Nick Mehta, the CEO of Gainsight, and another best seller in this field is *Farm Don't Hunt*, written by Guy Nirpaz, the CEO of Totango, both of which are great books which this author recommends to his readers. This influence has not necessarily been a bad thing, and indeed without a doubt much of the achievement in driving customer success management forwards as a professional is due to the hard work and creative insight that has come from these individuals and organizations, who have truly been pioneers in customer success practices. As customer success management widens out further and becomes more mainstream adopted by all types of businesses rather than being dominated by SaaS companies (as is already now the case to some extent), this influence may reduce and the theories, concepts and philosophies of customer success management will mature further and become less reliant upon a relatively small number of companies to determine its future growth and direction. This also is no bad thing in the opinion of the author.

10.3.6 Trying to Do It Manually Does not Work

What is clear is that CSMs do need some kind of software to help them to analyze their customer's needs, to report on their activity and results and to manage their time effectively. While it is possible to do these things manually (and indeed I know of several small customer success teams who do just that) I would not recommend it for the following reasons (Table 10.1).

10.3.7 Choosing a Customer Success Management Software System

There are currently many companies that offer either dedicated systems that have been developed from the ground up to provide for the needs of CSMs or existing systems (such as CRM systems) that offer add-on modules that provide CSM-related functionality. In fact, there is perhaps a bewildering array of options for newly set-up customer success management teams to choose from. I am not an expert in customer success software systems, but there are plenty of consultants and

Table 10.1　Reasons for Using a Proper Software System

Reason	Explanation
Time taken to document information	Working everything out manually is very time-consuming. It's often much quicker to use a system that, for example, allows you to select information from a drop-down list instead of having to write it all manually
Accuracy of data entry	Manual data entry leads to mistakes. Words can easily be misspelled and numerical information can be easily entered incorrectly. Even relatively small mistakes of these kinds can have far-reaching consequences
Sharing of information	If each CSM is managing their own information it can be very difficult to share that information either between themselves (to develop best practices and to collaborate on activities) or with senior management (to monitor performance and determine ROI)
Consistency of information	If each CSM is managing their own information in their own way it can be very difficult to compare (or even at times understand) information from each CSM within a team, and it can be very time-consuming to compile team results
Control of information	If a centralized software system that is managed by the IT team is not being used, then this raises questions about where and how information (potentially including customer data) is being stored and who might have access to it
Usefulness of information	Because of all or at least many of the above factors, the information that gets stored becomes less useful and therefore less valuable. As a result, decision-making is less informed and productivity and quality is reduced
Employee recruitment and retention	If the customer success team is looking to grow and mature it will need to attract and retain high-quality employees. The best CSMs will expect to be provided with the right tools to perform their role

sales people who do specialize in providing advice and support to management teams that are trying to decide what customer success software system to purchase to meet their specific needs. My recommendation therefore is where the decision is proving to be a difficult one to make, to engage with a suitable expert who can help with determining needs and selecting appropriate options to select from.

However, I do have one piece of general advice, which is to *keep things simple and flexible*—especially at first. If your customer success team is relatively newly formed and is still in the process of developing and maturing, it is likely that you do not yet fully know what your customer success software system needs are or will be in the near term future. Any decision that you make today should therefore be both *simple* and *flexible*.

Selecting a simpler system, or using only some of the basic functionality of a more complex system can be beneficial at all times, but especially at first. This is because it is all too easy for CSMs and their managers to get tied up by managing data when in fact they should be out there *doing their job*. My strong recommendation is to only use the absolute bare minimum software features at first and then to gradually add more functionality slowly over time as you find you need it and as your sophistication as a customer success team grows and therefore warrants it.

Choosing a flexible consumption model (for example, an annual as-a-service software contract rather than an outright purchase) leaves your options open further down the road when over time you begin to learn what your customer success software system needs truly are. Taking a flexible approach enables you to more easily back out of any early decision that provides to be unsuitable later on in favor of taking a different direction that is now shown to be a better choice to meet your department's needs.

Using simplicity and flexibility as two guides for selecting your customer success software system will also be likely to win you friends and support from the CSMs themselves, since it is likely that a system selected this way is quicker, easier and therefore more effective and less frustrating for them to use.

10.3.8 Criteria for Selecting a Customer Success Management Software System

Aside from simplicity and flexibility, the criteria you use to select a customer success management software system should be based upon the outcomes you are looking to attain from owning it and using it. Outcomes that you might want to consider include (Table 10.2):

Table 10.2 Criteria for Customer Success Management Software Systems

Outcome	Explanation
Secure management and control of data	Any security breach can be damaging to a company, and one that includes loss of customers' data can be disastrous. Ensuring that all data is securely controlled and managed is a no-brainer outcome requirement for all customer success teams
Accurate record keeping for administrative purposes	Leaving aside any "clever" reasons for using a customer success management software system, it may well be necessary simply to know what happened, when it happened, who did it and what the results were for all sorts of general administrative purposes

(Continued)

Table 10.2 (*Continued*)   Criteria for Customer Success Management Software Systems

Outcome	Explanation
Individual CSM effectiveness	Taking each CSM as an individual, any customer success management software system that is chosen should help CSMs to increase both the quality of their work and their productivity levels. It should therefore be simple to understand, straightforward and as non-time-consuming as possible to use and provide the necessary functionality to enable high-quality CSM research, analysis and planning activities
Team effectiveness	The software that is selected should enable the sharing of information between CSMs and provide a mechanism for collaboration on joint engagements. It may also be useful to enable a certain level of access to other colleagues from outside of the CSM team (for example, sales executives and service managers)
Interoperable with existing systems	The general rule of managing and storing data is to try to store it only once, so that it is simpler and more cost effective to manage and to ensure it remains up-to-date. This means that rather than storing all information about, for example, customers and products on the customer success management software system itself, there should be connectivity with other corporate systems that already hold this information (such as CRM tools and product databases) that can then automatically look up and display the information to the CSM within the web page
Enables management reporting	The customer success management software system must provide a way for team leaders, departmental managers and senior business leaders to extract the information they require in the form of reports to determine the effectiveness of individual and team customer success activities and to calculate the return on corporate investment in those activities
Training and support	A software system is only as good as its users, and users need the right training and support to be able to use the software as productively and effectively as possible. The vendor or supplier of the software should be able to provide appropriate training and support options to enable this to happen

10.3.9 Using a Customer Success Management Software System for Health Scoring

The concept of the health score is that it provides a mechanism for rating the health *not* of the customer as a company but instead of the *relationship between the customer and the CSM's company.* So regardless of how well or how poorly the customer is doing as a company, a high health score rating means that the relationship between that particular customer and the CSM's company is currently a good one, and a low health score rating means that the relationship between that particular customer and the CSM's company is currently a poor one.

Naturally, every vendor's customer success management software system differs in the detail, but most of them use a "dashboard" concept that provides the CSM with a bird's eye view of basic

KPI information pertaining to all the customers that they are responsible for managing. Most (if not all) systems provide a rating or *score* for each KPI and for the customer relationship overall—hence, this functionality of software systems is often referred to as a *Health Score System* (if the reader is not familiar with the look and feel of such systems and does not know how they work, it is recommended that they spend a half hour or so on the Internet looking at the offerings from some of the software vendors and getting a feel for what they do).

Different vendors' customer success management software systems will use different KPIs from which a customer's overall health score is determined. Generally though not always, every KPI will be rated from 1 to 5, 1 to 10 or 1 to 100, where 1 is a low rating and 5, 10 or 100 is a high rating, and 0 might be used to indicate no relevance of that particular KPI to that customer. The more sophisticated systems enable their customers (i.e., the customer success team that purchases the software) to select which KPIs they wish to use and also bias the calculation of the overall health score toward one or more of the KPIs over others. For example, if five KPIs are used, the CSM could use a simple average of all five KPI scores to determine the overall health score, meaning that each KPI contributes 20% toward the overall health score. If the customer success team's manager decided that one of those five KPIs was as important on its own as all the other four KPIs combined, then the overall health score could be calculated with this bias, so that this important KPI contributed 50% toward the health score and the other four contributed 12.5% each toward the health score. This would potentially yield a different set of health score values for customers, which of course is the whole point of doing it.

The idea is to select the right KPIs and the right weighting between those KPIs to come up with a health score for each customer that reflects the true nature of the current relationship between the customer and the company as accurately as possible. Figure 10.3 illustrates how this works. The last-but-one column shows customer health scores that reflect a simple average of the scores for each KPI. The final column shows customer health scores that reflect a weighted average of the KPI scores, biased 50% toward KPI 1 and the remaining 50% spread evenly between the other four KPIs. As can be seen by this example, some of the health scores are higher using the KPI 1 bias, and some are lower, and this might have an impact on the CSM's decision-making. For example, the CSM might determine not to waste their time on trying to improve the health of the relationship with customers whose scores are below the value of 2, and instead to focus on helping customers with scores between 2 and 3 to get up to a 4 or a 5. We can see that with the health score that is weighted toward KPI 1, Customers 1 and 7 will be rejected, whereas with the simple average in place Customer 6 will be rejected but Customers 1 and 7 will not (Figure 10.3).

	KPI 1	KPI 2	KPI 3	KPI 4	KPI 5	Health Score (simple average)	Health Score (KPI 1 bias)
Customer 1	1	2	3	1	4	2.20	**1.75**
Customer 2	3	4	3	5	4	3.80	3.50
Customer 3	2	4	3	2	4	3.00	2.63
Customer 4	5	5	4	3	4	4.20	4.50
Customer 5	4	2	4	2	5	3.40	3.63
Customer 6	3	1	2	2	1	**1.80**	2.25
Customer 7	1	4	3	2	2	2.40	**1.88**
Customer 8	3	5	3	1	4	3.20	3.13
Customer 9	3	5	3	4	4	3.80	3.50
Customer 10	3	5	4	4	5	4.20	3.75

Figure 10.3 Using a health score system.

10.3.10 Selecting KPIs to Use in Health Score Systems

As has already been mentioned the exact KPIs that a particular health score system within a vendor's customer success management software provides out of the box will vary, and more sophisticated systems will enable the customer success management team to select whatever KPIs they wish and to set up the maths to reflect as accurate an overall health score for each customer as possible.

Naturally, the selection of which KPIs to include within a health score system is a very important one, as this will have a strong bearing on the overall health score that is calculated. Care should be taken to select sufficient KPIs to reflect each of the different aspects of the customer-to-company relationship. At the same time, too many KPIs can quickly become unwieldy and ponderous, putting additional and sometimes quite onerous administrative strain onto CSMs to keep the data up to date. There is a balance therefore to be had between accuracy and efficiency that needs to be carefully considered.

My recommendation for selecting KPIs is basically the same as for selecting customer success management software systems, which is to use a system that can be adjusted in the future, and then to keep it very simple at first using maybe just two or three KPIs and then to add more KPIs as the CSM team's sophistication and need for more accurate data to analyze grows. Even then however I would still try to stop at around five or maximum six KPIs, since more than this tends merely to increase the admin overhead rather than add much in the way of true value.

The table below lists some of the KPIs that are most commonly used in health score systems and explains where the data might be derived from (Table 10.3):

Table 10.3 Common Health Score System KPIs

KPI	Description	Data
Sponsorship	The level of seniority of the customer's managers that we are dealing with	Entered manually by the CSM or picked up from entries made in a CRM tool by the sales team
Advocacy	How much advocacy the customer has given us in terms of references, case studies, referrals, etc.	Entered manually by the CSM or picked up from entries made in a CRM tool by the sales or marketing teams
Sentiment	Our belief about how the customer views the importance of their relationship with us to be	Entered manually by the CSM or picked up from entries made in a CRM tool by the sales team
Support utilization	How much use the customer makes of our support systems	Entered manually by the CSM or picked up from entries made in a service management tool by the support team
Support feedback	The level of satisfaction around customer support that has been expressed by the customer	Entered manually by the CSM or picked up from entries made in a service management tool by the support team

(Continued)

Table 10.3 (*Continued*)   Common Health Score System KPIs

KPI	Description	Data
Implementation level	How much of the overall product or service has been purchased and implemented by the customer	Entered manually by the CSM or picked up from entries made in a service management tool by the service management team
Utilization level	How much of the overall product or service is actually used by the customer, how often it is used, and in what ways it is used	Entered manually by the CSM or picked up from entries made in a service management tool by the service management team
Company health	How healthy the customer's organization is based upon set criteria such as revenues, profitability, cash flow, market position, investment in R&D, etc.	Usually entered by marketing team or from an outside feed to a specialist third party
Customer satisfaction	The overall level of satisfaction expressed by the customer toward the company and its products, services and solution	Usually managed by the marketing team as a feed from annual customer satisfaction (CSAT) surveys
Net Promoter Score (NPS)	The likelihood expressed by the customer of the customer recommending the company to others	Usually managed by the marketing team as a feed from annual NPS surveys

10.3.11 Retention and Churn

In addition to the per customer measurements taken within the health scores system that are shown above, the customer success team will of course also be taking measurements on the overall and per product/service retention and churn rates experienced by their company, and these too should be stored and displayed within the corporate customer success software system. These are defined as follows (Table 10.4):

Table 10.4   Retention and Churn

KPI	Description	Data
Retention	The proportion of customers who renew their service contract, expressed as a percentage of all customers	Entered manually by the CSM or picked up from entries made in the sales systems by the sales team
Churn	The proportion of customers who do not renew their service contract, expressed as a percentage of all customers	Entered manually by the CSM or picked up from entries made in the sales systems by the sales team

Retention is effectively a mirror image opposite of churn, so, for example, if you have 100 existing customers and 80 of those customers renew then you will have experienced 80% retention and 20% churn during the period you are measuring.

There are various ways in which the retention and churn measurements can be combined and used to generate useful information. One way is to calculate and display retention over the entire lifetime of customers, and then show churn per contract period (for example, per annum if using annual contracts or per month if using monthly contracts). This can help to build up a picture not just of how many customers are retained over the long term, but when within the customer lifecycle they are being lost, and whether this pattern changes over time for more recently acquired customers than for older customers.

Of the two figures, *retention* is the number I recommend CSMs and customer success teams to focus on, since this is the positive number, and is the number that motivates the team more. One final point on retention is that it is no good blaming the renewals team for lower than desirable retention rates. Actions to increase the retention of customers must occur *throughout the lifecycle* of the client's contract term, even though retention itself can only get measured at the end when they either renew or do not renew. Waiting until just before they make that decision to intervene with any positive customer success activity is simply too late!

10.4 Helping Customers to Realize Their Value

10.4.1 Differences in Perspective between the Customer and the CSM

From the customer's perspective their primary or perhaps even their only concern now at this later stage is to make sure that the initiative delivers as much value as possible to their own organization, which is generally attained through the achievement of the initiative's stated outcomes (see Chapter 1 for a discussion about how to define and document outcomes). From their point of view, the whole point of the entire engagement was to get to this value realization stage as quickly and efficiently as possible and then to make sure that as much value as possible does get realized and that this happens as efficiently as possible and as soon as possible.

From the CSM's own company's perspective however, things may look a little different. From this perspective, the later stage engagement requirements are likely to include something like the following:

- To increase the chances of the customer renewing all as-a-service contracts
- To increase the size of all as-a-service contracts as much as possible
- To gain as many upselling and cross-selling opportunities as possible
- To receive useful feedback relating to products, services and solutions that can be used to improve them in the future
- To gain advocacy in the form of references, case studies, referrals, and so on
- To get closer to the customer in terms of both understanding their needs more and developing deeper relationships with key stakeholders
- To continue to provide the best possible customer experience by helping them to attain their desired outcomes
- To learn and develop as an organization based upon the experiences encountered during this engagement

Of the above list it is only the last-but-one item that directly relates to the customer's desires, and the remainder could be thought of as the seller's agenda rather than that of the customer. That is not to say that they are wrong, or even less important for the CSM to consider. This is why as well as working on a customer success plan for each customer it is equally important for the CSM to understand *their own* company's success strategy that takes all the above (or whatever is relevant to that particular CSM) into consideration. For more information on this please review the first two sections of Chapter 2.

10.4.2 Benefits of Working on the Customer's Agenda

As we have seen above, it may not be everything that the CSM needs to concern themselves with but it nevertheless *is* important to help the customer do what they want and need to do, i.e., to maximize value post adoption. After all, if the value that gets realized is insufficient then the, for example, the customer is hardly likely to desire to renew their contract, for example. It is therefore in everyone's interests that value realization occurs and occurs as soon as possible and to the greatest extent possible.

It is also politically expedient for the CSM to show the customer that both they themselves and the company they work for understand the customer's need for value realization and are prepared to work hard on an ongoing basis to help the company achieve their goals. Demonstrating to the customer that the CSM is "there to support them over the long haul" can make for a very positive experience for the customer and can do much to enhance the relationship between customer and supplier organizations.

10.4.3 Leaving Time to Work on the CSM's Own Agenda

As previously stated, the CSM needs to be sure about what else at this later, value realization stage their own company's success strategy requires of them. Only if the CSM is clear about this can they develop a personal timetable that incorporates relevant activities into their schedule to enable these additional objectives to be achieved. It is simply a matter of knowing what is expected of oneself and then planning one's time accordingly.

The good news is that many or even most of these additional goals are very well aligned with the customer's own goals and so the attainment of both sets of goals can often be combined into one set of tasks or activities that contribute toward multiple goals. Some stuff however does still need to be managed specifically, and upcoming sections within this chapter will deal with each of the major areas of these.

10.4.4 Reviewing the Customer's Success Proposal

One of the activities that was discussed in Section 2 of Chapter 5 of this book was the creation of a customer success proposal which documents the overall purpose of the customer success services being offered and explicitly lists the types of help that will be given, together with information on roles and responsibilities (both CSM and customer), timelines, milestones, outcomes, measurements, communication mechanisms and reporting on progress. The success proposal contents are developed in collaboration with the customer.

As was also previously explained, the purpose of the proposal document is to serve as an ongoing reference to both parties. It clarifies what will be done, how it will be done, who will be doing it and how long it will take as well as what the results should look like. Having something that documents these details upfront enables much greater clarity through the engagement on progress being made and value being realized, and of course also serves at the end to show and prove the overall level of success engendered by the engagement.

With this in mind, once the adoption program has been implemented (or perhaps once a significant phase of it has been completed, if the program will be implemented in separate phases over time with gaps in between) it is a good idea for the CSM to propose a meeting with the SPL and other key stakeholders as necessary to review this success proposal and agree how best to move forwards, and what further help and assistance the CSM can continue to provide to the customer on an ongoing basis.

10.4.5 Activities to Help Customers Maximize Their Value

So what *can* a CSM do to help each late-stage customer to realize as much value as possible? The details will of course differ from customer to customer, and the amount of help and assistance will also differ based upon circumstances. The main headings under which later stage CSM assistance can be grouped are:

- KPIs, measurements and milestones
- Reporting and reviewing progress
- Dealing with challenges
- Managing change

We will now deal with each of these in turn, starting with KPIs, measurements and milestones:

10.4.5.1 KPIs, Measurements and Milestones

Part of the best practice that the CSM should have applied in earlier stages of the engagement is the documentation of the customer's outcome requirements together with the KPIs that will be used to measure progress toward their attainment. Readers will recall that the concepts relating to both outcomes and KPIs were discussed in Chapter 1 of this book. The will also recall that KPIs need to be selected carefully in order to ensure an accurate picture of current progress is portrayed, and that the measurements are meaningful in terms of how well they indicate progress toward attainment of objectives.

It is generally (though by no means always) the case that customers know *what* KPIs they want to measure. If the customer does not know this information then it may be useful for the CSM to arrange a discussion with a colleague who is an industry expert from the customer's industry to help them determine their KPI requirements. Where the CSM can often be of particular value however is in *how* to take KPI measurements. This is particularly the case when the measurements will be wholly or partly made by the CSM's company's own products and services. Advice from the CSM might include information about what types of activity or performance information is automatically measured and what additional measurements can be configured to be taken. Again if necessary the CSM might bring in additional expertise to help the customer, for example, from a product specialist or service manager who has the required knowledge and experience to assist the customer with understanding what options are available to them and how the system needs to be configured to attain these measurements.

The recommendation is that wherever applicable a *baseline measurement* should be taken prior to the new system being implemented. This measurement serves as a comparison point, so that future measurements taken after the new system is implemented can be contrasted to understand performance differences between before and after the new system. In addition, it is also

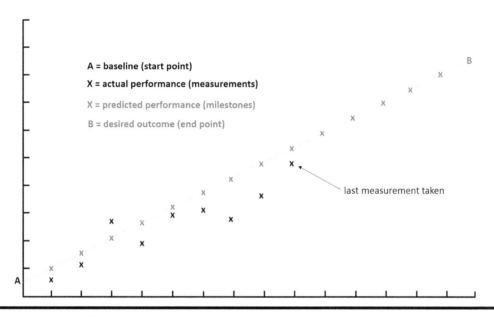

A = baseline (start point)

X = actual performance (measurements)

X = predicted performance (milestones)

B = desired outcome (end point)

last measurement taken

Figure 10.4 Tracking the journey from baseline to outcome.

recommended that the customer determine some interim targets to achieve en route to the overall and ultimate attainment of the outcome. These are generally referred to as *milestones*, and they serve as check points along the journey to make sure that progress is being made at an adequate rate to ensure that the long-term outcome objectives will be achieved, or if not to serve as advance warning of this so that appropriate corrective actions can be taken. The image below shows how these different components might look if displayed together on a simple chart (Figure 10.4).

In summary, CSMs should make sure that the customer is clear as to what KPIs are being measured, how they will be measured, how they will be documented and who will be responsible for making sure it happens.

10.4.5.2 Reporting and Reviewing Progress

It's all very well to take and document measurements, but those activities on their own will not be sufficient. The data that is collected needs to be turned into useful information, and that information needs to be reported to decision makers for them to analyze and determine whether or not any corrective actions need to incur and if so what those actions should be.

Even if all of the measurements that are being taken are automatically procured by the CSM's company's own services (for example, in the case of a software system that is being provided on an as-a-service basis), it should still be remembered that the data being measured is still the customer's data. Discussions should take place to determine in what format the customer needs to receive this data and how often it should be provided. It may well be the case that connector software needs to be configured to automatically and routinely transfer such data from the CSM's company's systems to the customer's own systems. This should be fairly routine for the CSM's company, and is likely to have already been discussed and agreed at the pre-sales stage; however, CSMs are well advised to make sure that these discussions have indeed taken place and that the relevant connectivity is in place. Also they (or a relevant colleague) may need to brief the SPL on this, since that individual may not have been involved in those pre-sales discussions.

Some considerations around reporting and reviewing progress are shown below:

- Schedule regular time for reviewing progress in your own and your SPL's diary
- Consider who else from the customer's company might need to, or might benefit from attending review meetings
- Consider who else from the CSM's own company might need to, or might benefit from attending review meetings
- Consider whether there is anyone from any third-party companies who might also need to, or might benefit from attending review meetings
- Find out if the customer's organization already has a suitable format for progress report documents and if so propose to use it for this initiative's progress reports
- If the customer's organization does not already have a format for progress report documents, find out if your own organization has a suitable template that could be used (a great port of call for this might be your service managers, who may well have report templates that they use to report to customers on service delivery which could be adapted to suit your purpose)
- Negotiate and agree with the SPL (and others if necessary) on the cadence and duration of ongoing progress meetings (i.e., how often to meet and for how long to meet)
- Negotiate and agree with the SPL (and others if necessary) on the location and format of ongoing progress meetings (i.e., where/how to meet and how the meeting will be conducted)
- Find out from the SPL who within the customer organization will not attend regular meetings but needs to receive regular update reports (for example, this might include senior level project sponsors)
- If required, help the SPL to determine what information to provide within the report, and how this information should be displayed. Try where possible to recommend representing detailed or complex information graphically (for example, using pie charts, bar charts, etc.).
- Try not to make the report overly long or complicated—be as succinct as possible and make sure any recommendations or actions that need approval are clearly marked
- Agree with the SPL what types of needs might trigger an additional, non-routine meeting (for example, if a risk occurs, or if there is a strategic change made by senior management to the initiative's outcome requirements) and how this will be handled

10.4.5.3 Dealing with Challenges

Challenges include anything at all that either actually or potentially disrupts the ongoing process of value realization. Challenges are bound to come along in one form or another, and so it makes sense for the CSM to anticipate them and to prepare for them.

Types of challenges include (but are not limited to):

- The occurrence of a previously identified risk
- The occurrence of a previously identified adoption barrier
- The occurrence of a risk which had not been previously identified
- The occurrence of an adoption barrier which had not been previously identified

In the case of previously identified risks or adoption barriers, the CSM should assist the SPL to follow the previously agreed upon activities to manage the risk or barrier. In the case of risks or adoption barriers that were not previously identified, the CSM should assist the SPL to follow the process of dealing with risks and adoption barriers outlined in Section 8 of Chapter 9.

10.4.5.4 Managing Change

Managing all of the activities in a complex project can sometimes feel overwhelming or even impossible. Stress levels can very quickly rise when faced with hundreds or even thousands of tasks to manage, many of them simultaneously. The basic rule of *divide and conquer* can be applied here,

- A change to the initiative's outcome requirements
- A change to the customer's senior personnel who have some involvement with or connection to the initiative
- A significant change to the customer's organization (for example, a merger or acquisition)
- A change to the initiative's products, services or solutions (for example, the release of a software upgrade)

Where there is a change to the customer's senior personnel, the customer's organization or the initiative's outcome requirements, these are all likely to be identified by the SPL or other key customer stakeholder and brought to the attention of the CSM.

Where there is a change to the products, services and/or solutions that the CSM's company is providing, it is up to the CSM to ensure they are kept updated by the relevant product, service and solution managers within their own company, and the CSM should be the one who brings these changes to the attention of the SPL. In this situation, the CSM should make sure they are well briefed by their subject matter expert colleagues on the implications to this customer of the changes that have occurred. If necessary, the CSM might decide to invite the relevant expert/s to meet directly with the customer to explain the changes and their implications. This might include a briefing to business decision makers such as the SPL, but it might also include more technical handovers or even training for relevant technical managers or workers within the customer's organization.

Whatever form the change takes, if a change occurs the CSM should propose a meeting to discuss the details of the occurrence and in the meeting determine the following:

- What positive and/or negative impacts (if any) the change will have on value realization
- What actions need to be taken to deal with the change
- How the actions will be taken, by whom and with what resources
- What approval (if any) needs to be given to sanction those actions, and who will be responsible for securing this approval
- How the actions will be measured and the measurements analyzed to ensure the change has been dealt with successfully

If the information needed to perform the above activities is not readily available then the CSM should agree with the SPL on a plan to research and identify the missing information first. A simple template called *Challenges_and_Changes_Checklist* is provided in the Downloads section at www.practicalcsm.com which can be used to assist with managing challenges and changes.

10.5 Maximizing Renewals

10.5.1 It's not ALL about Renewals, but…

…but if your company is selling its products and services on an as-a-service basis via monthly or annually renewable contracts then the importance of maximizing renewals (also referred to as minimizing churn) cannot be overemphasized. Ensuring that as many customer as possible renew their contracts each year (or month) can make the difference between a successful, profitable and growing business and an unsuccessful, unprofitable and failing one. It's as simple as that. For many CSM teams the core reason for their team's existence and the reason why the senior leaders have invested into customer success is in order to reduce churn and to increase both the renewal rate (the percentage of customers who renew their contracts) and the average renewal level (the increase or decrease in average contract size). We will refer to this simply as "maximizing renewals" in this section.

10.5.2 The Role of the CSM in Maximizing Renewals

Clearly, as the possible who is responsible for taking the lead in helping the customer to realize value from the purchase of the company's products, services and solutions, the CSM has a very important role to play in maximizing renewals. The essential concept is that if the customer can be shown to be attaining a good return on their investment from their contracts, they are highly likely to renew those contracts. The CSM helps to make this happen in a number of ways (Table 10.5):

Table 10.5 The Role of the CSM in Maximizing Renewals

Type of Help	Description
Defining customer outcome requirements	By ensuring that the customer has both completely and accurately defined their outcome requirements, the CSM ensures that there is an accurate target by which the ultimate success of an initiative can be measured in the long term, and by which progress toward attainment can be measured in the meantime
Defining milestones	In helping the customer to determine the key milestones along the way to ultimate outcome achievement, the CSM provides additional ways in which the relative success of the initiative can be measured during the value realization journey
Determining KPIs and measurements	Assisting the customer to select relevant KPIs and to work how (and how often) to take measurements, enables accurate and meaningful data to be collected, analyzed and reported on, to prove the level of progress being made and thus the level of ROI being generated
Assisting with onboarding activities	Providing a high-quality onboarding experience for the CSM's company's products, services and solutions enables customers to hit the ground running and start realizing value from them more quickly and efficiently
Assisting with adoption activities	The CSM's help in researching and analyzing adoption needs, creating a fully fledged adoption plan that comprises communication, training and support activities to fulfill users' KSA requirements greatly assist the customer in ensuring that the CSM's company's products, services and solutions get fully adopted and utilized

(Continued)

Table 10.5 (*Continued*)   The Role of the CSM in Maximizing Renewals

Type of Help	Description
Making process changes official	The work the CSM undertakes during the adoption implementation to ensure that changes are official, including things like updating job role descriptions, writing new process guidelines, providing changes to documentation such as FAQs, updating documentation used in external certifications such as ISO 9001, etc., helps to make it easier for the customer to continue to renew and harder to revert to the previous processes
Reporting and presenting information	The CSM's assistance in determining the best way to format and report on information and where necessary in actually reporting and presenting that information to sponsors and other senior leaders within the customer's organization assists with the transfer of information to the decision makers
Dealing with challenges	By helping the customer to manage and overcome hurdles such as project risks and adoption barriers, the CSM assist the customer to keep the initiative on track to realize its outcomes
Acting as a single point of contact	Finally, by making themselves available to the customer as a single point of contact for liaising with the CSM's company's and even other third parties' consultants, experts, assets and resources the CSM smooths the path for the customer and makes it much easier and more efficient to get hold of the people and resources they need
Leading, influencing and selling	While the CSM is not a salesperson, neither should they be shy of proactively communicating the value of their company's products, services and solutions to the customer's key stakeholders and positively influencing the decision to renew and continue using them
Acting as an ambassador and role model	Finally, as a customer-facing employee the CSM acts as an ambassador of their own company's culture, beliefs and attitude, and in so doing helps to forge deep and meaningful relationships with key customer stakeholders, many of whom may be involved in any contract renewal decision-making

10.6 Upselling and Cross-selling

10.6.1 Everyone Is a Salesperson

In my opinion, absolutely anyone and everyone who is customer-facing has a role to play and a contribution to make to the company's sales processes. To my mind, there are no exceptions to this rule. At the very minimum, every contact with the customer should be conducted in a manner that enhances the relationship between the company and the customer, and that shows the company in a positive light. It's good for being known for being friendly, professional, courteous and helpful and even if no specifically sales-related conversations take place, each contact we have with our customers either enhances or diminishes the overall impression the customer has of who we are and what we stand for.

10.6.2 The CSM's Sales Responsibilities

With that said, while the CSM does of course carry this general responsibility for acting in a way that sheds a positive light on their company and helps to improve the relationship with the customer, the CSM also tends to have specific duties around spotting potential sales opportunities, around communicating to customer stakeholders the potential additional value they could be getting from further purchases and from liaising and coordinating with the sales team to ensure that opportunities they do spot are followed up. This is often referred to as "expansion" or even just "expand" activity.

The CSM is in fact very often in a very privileged position with the customer. This is because they have had the opportunity to develop meaningful relationships with key customer stakeholders and to hold detailed conversations with those stakeholders about their vision and strategy, about their capabilities and processes, about the challenges and opportunities they face, about their business and technical requirements, and about the initiatives and projects that they are either planning or currently undergoing. Not only this, but they have conducted these conversations in the role of an adviser and consultant, rather than in the role of a salesperson. As such, if done well and assuming that the customer's stakeholders have been open to it, the CSM may well have forged very strong business relationships with some of these key stakeholders and learned a lot of useful and interesting information about their customer's desires and needs.

Next to the account manager, the CSM is probably the person who knows most about the customer as a whole and from a business outcomes perspective. Possibly they sometimes even know more than the account manager! Thus it is that the CSM should most definitely be given the responsibility of working closely with their sales team to spot and work on sales opportunities with each customer, though of course this must be done in such a way that does not negatively impact the relationship between CSM and customer stakeholders.

10.6.3 Understanding Upselling and Cross-selling

In short, *upselling* is when you sell the customer a more expensive version of a product, service or solution than that which they already have, whereas *cross-selling* is when you sell additional products, services and solutions that will work alongside the product, service or solution which they already have.

Turning to upselling first, this can take various forms depending upon what has been sold. Examples of upselling might include:

- Purchasing a larger-sized version of a product or service (e.g., the larger, higher capacity lathes instead of the smaller, smaller capacity ones)
- Purchasing more user licenses for software (e.g., 2,000 end-user licenses instead of 1,000 end-user licenses)
- Purchasing a version of a product or service that contains additional features or functions (e.g., the Gold version instead of the Silver version)
- Purchasing additional optional add-on features and functions alongside the basic product or service (e.g., the basic lathe plus rotating vise, three jaw chuck and auto tool presetter)
- (and arguably) Purchasing value-added services alongside the basic product or service (for example, support and maintenance, customization, integration with existing systems, insurance, financing, etc.)

Cross-selling is about adding further products or services to the purchase list. This could, for example, include:

- Managed services to operate and maintain a service or even an entire department
- Professional services such as consultancy to assist the customer with analyzing challenges and opportunities and formulating a strategy
- Complementary products or services that contain additional features and functions that work alongside the features and functions of the original product/service to provide enhanced results (e.g., selling a milling machine to work alongside the lathe, or selling security devices to work alongside networking devices)

10.6.4 Spotting Upselling and Cross-selling Opportunities

The first thing to say is that upselling and cross-selling go hand-in-hand together. There is no need to think of them as different or separate activities. Instead, both are done simultaneously and can just simply be thought of as "selling" in the overall sense, which incorporates both upselling and cross-selling.

It is a matter of having the mindset that keeps an eye open at all times for spotting needs within the customer organization that might be fulfilled by the CSM's company's products and services. At every conversation, and each time information about the customer is researched, the CSM has an opportunity to understand the customer's challenges, opportunities, strategies, capabilities and needs in more detail. At any moment the CSM might come across a requirement, a need, a desire to be able to perform a new task, or to be able to perform an existing task better—for example, to a higher quality, with reduced cost, more quickly, and so on. CSMs with a natural flair for spotting challenges and problem-solving to come up with solutions to those challenges are likely to be particularly good at spotting ways in which further products, services and solutions could potentially generate value for the customer.

10.6.5 Dealing with Upselling and Cross-selling Opportunities

It is not sufficient simply to spot a sales opportunity. That opportunity also needs to be dealt with in an efficient and effective manner. Each company will have its own policy on how sales opportunities are handled, and if the CSM is unsure what their company's policy is then they should make it a priority to find out as soon as possible.

In some companies, the CSM might be responsible just for spotting a potential opportunity and then communicating that opportunity to the relevant person within the sales team to deal with. However, it is increasingly the case that because CSMs are so well positioned within their role to talk to and influence the customer, they may now be required to play a more active role in the initial or even all sales conversations, acting almost as a customer advocate and providing contextual information about topics such as impacts to onboarding, adoption and value realization which the sales person may be less familiar with.

10.6.6 How Much CSM Sales Assistance Is Required?

Generally speaking, it comes down to relationships and circumstances. If, for example, the customer's account manager has been managing the customer account for 17 years, knows everything there is to know about the customer organization and is personal friends with the CEO then it may just be a matter of communicating any potential opportunity the CSM comes across to the account manager and letting them get on with it. On the other hand, perhaps, for example, the CSM has been engaged for quite a while with some of the customer's key business decision makers, working closely with them on the launch of an extensive and highly strategic initiative. Maybe in so doing they have themselves forged strong relationships with those key decision makers and learned very in-depth knowledge about certain aspects of the customer's capabilities, processes, challenges and opportunities. In this situation, it may be very important not just to pass on a sales opportunity to the account manager, but to work closely with the account manager to build a business case for it and then to present and communicate that business case to the customer's key decision makers.

In short as with many aspects of the CSM's role, the CSM needs to understand what is generally required and expected of them from their company, and then needs to adopt a flexible approach as to how they go about fulfilling those requirements and expectations, adapting to the specific needs of a particular situation in each circumstance.

10.7 Feedback and Advocacy

10.7.1 The Fear of Critical Feedback

Let's be honest, everyone's favorite topic is themselves. We all spend time over the course of an average day thinking about ourselves, and if we are asked questions about ourselves by an interested friend or acquaintance we are generally speaking only too eager to talk about ourselves for just as long as they are prepared to remain interested (or at least acting interested). It is not unreasonable for our own selves to be a topic that is dear to our hearts, after all we are very important to ourselves… in fact we rely on ourselves 100% of the time to do absolutely anything and everything, so no wonder the subject is an important one to us!

The high level of importance to ourselves of the topic of "oneself" is precisely why it can sometimes make us sensitive to receiving feedback from others about ourselves and/or our performance and capabilities. This of course is especially so if someone is already feeling vulnerable or emotionally sensitive for whatever reason, or perhaps for a combination of several reasons. If the feedback is at all negative, an emotionally vulnerable person may struggle to deal with it, and so of course they may think that it is safest not to ask for any feedback at all, or at least to choose to ask for feedback only from those people whom they think will give praise rather than criticism.

10.7.2 The Difficulty with and the Value of Critical Feedback

The high level of importance to ourselves of the topic of oneself and of the organization we work for is precisely why it can sometimes make us sensitive to receiving feedback from others about our or its performance and capabilities. The problem with this of course is that it can lead to a false understanding and perhaps to complacency. After all, if we never learn about our faults then how can we fix them? So it may be the case that those people who regularly ask for and receive feedback about themselves, their skills, their performance and any other aspect of who and what they are that they are interested to improve from a wide and diverse range of people might find themselves in a cycle of continual learning, development and improvement that over time leads to significant change in who they are and what they can do. On the other hand those people who do not receive any feedback at all or perhaps worse still only look for and receive praise from friends who are prepared to bend the truth a little in order to bolster and massage their friend's ego may find themselves either standing still rather than moving forwards in their lives or even making things worse because of the positive reinforcement they are receiving for their current performance level.

The above works on a personal level, but works equally on a corporate level. The better the organization truly understands its weaknesses as well as its strengths, the better enabled the business leaders of that organization are to take steps to deal with those weaknesses.

Critical feedback is therefore essential—perhaps even invaluable. It gives us perspective on our personal and our corporate lives and helps to guide our (and our organization's) thoughts, decisions and actions. It is a very important part of growth and development, and it is something that should most definitely be encouraged. In fact, it could be argued that while positive feedback or praise is nice to have (since it reinforces feelings of self-worth) it is only negative or critical feedback that actually helps us to change. This being the case, surely we should all be eager to receive critical feedback in order to be able to grow and mature as professionals and as human beings? Well you'd think so, but as we have said, just because it's good for us it doesn't mean it's comfortable to listen to.

10.7.3 Formal and Informal Feedback

Both formal and informal feedback can be very useful to receive, and one, the other or even both types of feedback can be asked for from the same person or company, depending upon the situation.

Formal feedback refers to written (or otherwise recorded) surveys. Formal feedback is great for gathering multiple responses to the same questions from multiple people or companies. This enables you both to compare the responses between different people or companies and also if you repeat the process over a longer term to compare answers from the same person or company over time to see what progress you are making. The potential disadvantage of the formal approach is that it may sometimes run the risk of capturing "the official stance" rather than "the reality of the situation" which customers may be willing to tell you off the record but less happy to have documented in any formal way.

Informal feedback can fill in these gaps by providing the opportunity to be more honest and open by being able to speak "off the record" in an unattributable way. It can also be useful simply where a formal approach is not feasible due to limitations such as time, or cost or where the person or company you want to get feedback from is unwilling to provide that feedback in a formal manner. Informal feedback does generally require both a good quality trust relationship between the customer-facing employee (for example, the salesperson or customer success manager) and the customer stakeholder, and also the opportunity to make the request, such as over lunch or a coffee break. Informal feedback can be as simple as asking "How am I doing?." It does not have to be "clever" to be valuable.

10.7.4 Unprompted Feedback

Sometimes the customer is the one that initiates the giving of feedback on their own and without being asked for it. This tends to only happen in exceptional circumstances which inspire this to occur. Those circumstances could either be exceptionally good or exceptionally poor.

If it is the former then that is great news, and this should definitely trigger the CSM not only to thank the customer for the positive feedback but also to ask them for advocacy, seeing as they are likely to be in a receptive frame of mind. This additional help might take various forms, depending upon the current need of the CSM's company. For example, the CSM might ask the customer if they can quote the positive feedback in marketing materials, or they might ask the customer if they would be prepared to refer the CSM's company to any colleague or peer who have a similar requirement that the CSM's company can fulfill.

If the unprompted feedback is negative then *regardless of how valid the CSM considers it to be* the feedback should always be taken seriously. The CSM should make sure that the feedback is acknowledged as soon as possible and the customer should be thanked for their time in providing the feedback and assured that their concerns are important to the company and the issues raised will be fully looked into. This initial step of reassuring the customer that their problems or criticisms are being taken seriously is a very important one. From a psychological standpoint, the customer who has complained is often not just looking to provide information, but wanting to have their issue *acknowledged*. Doing so in a prompt and polite manner and showing that you take their criticisms seriously may go a long way toward if not resolving any real problems, at least mending the relationship between the company and the customer. In fact, if done well, it sometimes even enhances this relationship so that it becomes stronger than ever before.

Of course, in addition to this, the complaint or criticisms should be carefully reviewed and any necessary actions swiftly taken to rectify any faults that are found to legitimately exist. It is good practice also to let the customer know that this is happening and also to communicate the results of any action to them afterwards, as again this reassures them that the company views them and their opinions as being important to the company. It also of course removes (or at least reduces) any potential objections that the customer might have to making further purchases in the future, since the issues can be shown to have been resolved.

10.7.5 Managing Feedback

The CSM's company will (or should) have a policy about and a documented process for handling feedback. CSMs who are not aware of their company's feedback policy and process should make sure they learn about it so that they know what their role in managing feedback is. Depending upon the type of feedback and in addition to their own work and any collaboration within the CSM team itself and with the customer directly, the CSM may need to communicate and liaise with various colleagues from other departments to explain, document and deal with the feedback. These departments might include:

- R&D (research and development) for future product/service improvement-related feedback
- Services management for all existing service-related feedback
- Sales and marketing teams for all feedback relating to sales and marketing
- Operational teams (e.g., customization, implementation, configuration, etc.) for all feedback relating to the work these teams have done
- Marketing (or whoever handles customer problems and complaints) for all problems and complaints

10.7.6 What Is Advocacy and Why Is It Important?

In general parlance, an advocate is a person who acts on behalf of another person. In the case of business advocacy, we want the customer (either as an organization or as an individual business leader within that organization) to act on behalf of our own company. What we specifically want them to do is to "speak up for us" in various ways to help promote our products and services to other potential customers. There are various ways in which customers can act as advocates. These include (Table 10.6):

Table 10.6   Ways in Which Customers Can Act as Advocates

Method	Description
Referrals	The very best type of advocacy is where the customer provides a direct introduction to another prospect who has the same or similar challenges as the customer and who may therefore wish to make a similar purchase. Referrals are very powerful sales opportunities that should always be followed up as soon as possible
Providing a sales reference	This is where the customer consents to being contacted by a prospect who is considering making a purchase and who wishes to talk to a previous customer to find out about their experience of the company and its products/services
Providing a marketing reference	This is where the customer consents to being mentioned or even directly quoted about their customer experience in the company's marketing materials
Speaking at a sales event	This is where an existing customer attends a conference or workshop of some kind and speaks to the prospects who have been invited to attend about their experience of purchasing and using the company's products/services
Acting as a case study	This is where the customer's initial challenges and the selection, purchase and utilization of the company's products/services together with the results attained are documented and published as an example for prospects to review. Case studies can range from a fairly brief and simple paragraph or so in a brochure or on a website to a fully produced "infomercial" with interviews from multiple stakeholders, videos of the products/services in action, and details of results attained and value gained

10.7.7 The Role of the CSM in Managing Feedback and Advocacy

Because the CSM works with the customer's stakeholders after the purchase has been completed to get the company's products, services and/or solutions implemented, configured, onboarded and adopted and then on an ongoing basis to assist with ensuring value gets realized over the entire ownership lifecycle, the CSM is ideally placed to request feedback and/or advocacy, and to liaise with and communicate to the customer about that feedback and advocacy.

10.7.8 Requesting Feedback and Advocacy

In terms of feedback and advocacy quantity it may seem trite to say it, but the best way—indeed the only way—to increase the amount of feedback and advocacy being received is to ask for more of it. The best way to maximize the amount of feedback and advocacy you are receiving is to build the request for feedback directly into the company's systems and processes so that it always occurs automatically at every appropriate occasion. This also has the benefit of making the request for feedback and/or advocacy less scary for those who struggle with asking for it, since it enables the requester to follow the system by rote rather than having to work out what to say and when or how to say it.

Trigger points for requesting feedback and/or advocacy could include:

■ At commencement of initial discussions.

It's never too early to mention that part of your ongoing improvement process is to ask for feedback from customers in order to learn what currently works well for customers and where improvements could be made, and to request advocacy from them if the customer finds that they are pleased with the results they ultimately obtain. Bringing up the topic of feedback and advocacy early on also softens the request when it is made later, since the subject has already been raised and discussed and the customer should therefore be expecting it to be asked for.

■ Upon negotiating and signing the contract.

It's a good idea to reinforce the idea of feedback and advocacy within the contractual discussions, explaining that it is a critical part of improving products and services so that you can better serve customers' needs in the future. If the customer negotiates a discount then a trade-off can be their agreement to provide comprehensive and honest feedback and certain types of advocacy in return.

■ Immediately upon implementation of the product, service or solution.

At this stage customers cannot give feedback on any value creation because this has not yet occurred, but they can give feedback on the sales process and on any subsequent processes such as customization, installation and configuration, and they may also know of others either from within their own company or who work in similar roles in other organizations who may have similar problems that the CSM's company may be able to help with. It's a good idea to ask for feedback and advocacy as soon as possible because the challenge that the customer was facing is more likely to be fresh in the customer's mind and also still at the top of their mind. If you wait until later you run the risk of them either forgetting some of the details of what happened that might be useful to know and secondly of them becoming distracted by other priorities that have now taken over in their lives and therefore either providing less details or not providing any feedback at all.

■ Upon the first business review following implementation.

Assuming you will have follow-up meetings with customers' post-implementation to report on performance and to track progress toward attaining the customer's target outcomes this is an ideal forum to ask for feedback and advocacy. Of course it's easier to make the request if the measurement figures you are reporting are positive, but as we have already discussed it may actually be more important to request feedback when things are not going according to plan so that you can learn how to fix the issues in the future.

■ Upon subsequent business reviews

Feedback and advocacy can be asked for more than once. In fact, if you build it into your template business review agenda then it becomes a natural thing for your customer success manager, consultant, service manager, sales person or whoever is conducting the review to always ask for it. Remember that this does not always have to be a formal thing, it can be as simple as asking the question "Do you have any feedback for us on how things have been going since you last provided us with feedback on date x?," or "would you be happy with us getting Person X from Company A who is thinking about making a purchase from us to give you a call to discuss your initiative, so they can understand how we helped you?."

- Upon outcome attainment

    If the customer has stated one or more specific outcome targets up front that they are hoping to attain from the implementation of your product, service or solution then it makes sense to ask for feedback and/or advocacy at the time that those outcomes are attained. This can of course be very powerful from a marketing perspective if the customer is pleased with the performance of your solution.

- Through an annual customer survey

    Feedback and advocacy can also be requested on a routine, cyclical basis, for example, once per annum. From a feedback perspective, this has the advantage of enabling comparisons between customers giving feedback at the same time, as well as comparisons of the feedback from the same customer over time. In terms of advocacy, this can be as simple as providing a space within the feedback survey for the customer to write a brief sentence or two that they would be happy to have published as a marketing reference. Again, it is a good idea to explain right from initial discussions onwards that gathering feedback in order to improve products and services and gaining advocacy in order to increase future sales opportunities are standard procedures within your organization, so that the receipt of something like a feedback survey questionnaire with a space for advocacy within it will come as less of a surprise. Prior to sending the survey questionnaire, it may be a good idea to get the customer success manager, salesperson or other relevant customer-facing person to prepare customers for it and if possible get their commitment to complete and return the questionnaire.

10.8 Has Everything Been Done?

10.8.1 An Opportunity to Ensure All Work Is Completed

A lot of the tasks and duties at this value realization phase relate to the overall management of all customers alongside each other, using a tool such as a health score system to do so. Additionally, there are some specific new tasks relating to renewals, cross-selling, upselling, feedback and advocacy that the CSM needs to take on. In addition to the above, when any specific customer engagement gets to this stage it is a good opportunity for the CSM to reflect back on the objectives, plans and activities for that engagement and to check to make sure that everything that ought to have been done actually *has* been done.

10.8.2 Using a Checklist

A good way to approach this might be to prepare a simple checklist that the CSM can then use with this and also with future engagements with very little modification. Items that the CSM might incorporate within their checklist include:

- Have we performed sufficient research and analysis to state that we understand the customer's organization, including its vision and strategies, its challenges and opportunities, its capabilities and its organizational structure and culture? If not, what is missing?
- Have we performed sufficient research and analysis to state that we understand the initiative we are supporting and the outcome requirements for that initiative, the products, services

and/or solutions that they have been sold, the stakeholders who are involved in decision-making and the users who are impacted by change? If not, what is missing?
- Is the customer fully onboarded? If not, what is missing?
- Has the adoption planning been completed? If not, what is missing?
- Has the adoption plan been implemented? If not, where are we in this process, and is this progress sufficient? If not, what should be done about it?
- Have relevant KPIs and milestones for measuring progress toward outcome attainment been identified? If not, what should be done about it?
- Are necessary measurements to determine performance being taken, and are these being analyzed and reported on and (if necessary) is any corrective action being taken to get the initiative back on track? If not, what should be done about it?
- Are we meeting the customer regularly to discuss and review progress and to deal with any challenges or changes that may come up? If not, what should be done about it?
- Are we sufficiently working toward ensuring the customer renews any as-a-service contracts? If not, what should be done about it?
- Are we spotting and dealing appropriately with any additional sales opportunities, including both upselling and cross-selling? If not, what should be done about it?
- Are we sufficiently asking for and getting feedback and advocacy from the customer? If not, what should be done about it?

A document called *Value_Realization_Activity_Checklist* has been created that provides this list in a Microsoft Excel worksheet format, which can be found within the Downloads section at www.practicalcsm.com.

10.9 Tools for Practical CSM Framework Phase 6: Value Realization

10.9.1 Tools for Implementing the Adoption Plan

When the CSM has reached the value realization phase with a customer, the majority of the intensive work around things like onboarding and adoption has already been planned and implemented. At this stage, it is mostly about keeping *all* customers on track and dealing with any problems or changes that arise for any one customer alongside all the needs of all other customers the CSM is responsible for as well as any non-customer-specific duties. As such the principle tools that the CSM needs to use are their corporate customer success management software system (including its health score tool) and other systems such as CRM tools, product databases, etc. In addition, the CSM should refer to their company's success management strategy to help prioritize their activities, and to each individual customer's *Customer_Research_Checklist* that the CSM created during Practical CSM Framework Phase 1: Preparation to refresh themselves as necessary regarding that customer's challenges, opportunities and outcome requirements.

Two tools have been created to assist specifically with value realization, and these are the *Challenges_and_Changes_Checklist* and the *Value_Realization_Activity_Checklist*. The *Challenges_and_Changes_Checklist* provides two checklists—one for changes and one for challenges presented as two separate worksheets within a Microsoft Excel workbook. Each checklist provides a way for CSMs to document and track progress toward dealing with each change and challenge that occurs.

10.10 Activities and Outputs for Practical CSM Framework Phase 6: Value Realization

10.10.1 Activities for Practical CSM Framework Phase 6: Value Realization

The Activities for Phase 6: Value Realization include:

1. Review your company's customer success software system and in particular the health score system to determine the health of all customer relationships and to understand which customers require help and assistance
2. For each customer that you identify as requiring your assistance, determine how much of your time to allocate to that customer's needs and perform the steps outlined below as necessary based on relevance to that company's needs:
3. Review the completed *Customer_Research_Checklist* for this customer (or other tool you use in handovers) which you created in Phase 1: Preparation.
4. If there are any information gaps that need to be filled or assumptions that need to be validated make a note of them and prepare questions for the customer
5. Review the completed *Customer_Engagement_Strategy* together with any other documents that have also already been created in the Central Repository for this customer to ensure you are up-to-date on requirements from the engagement
6. Assist customers toward realizing their value by ensuring that KPIs and milestones have been carefully thought through and identified, that measurements are being taken and that progress is being monitored and reported and (where necessary) corrective action taken to get the initiative back on track
7. Use the *Challenges_and_Changes_Checklist* to identify any challenges and/or changes that occur and to plan for taking actions to deal with each one
8. Make every effort to ensure that customers perceive the value of the existing products, services and/or solutions that they have purchased in order to maximize the likelihood of them renewing their contracts and renewing at the highest possible level
9. Keep an eye open for upselling and cross-selling opportunities and when such an opportunity is spotted deal with it quickly following your company's policy and process for doing so
10. Attend regular meetings with the customer to report on and discuss progress and to acknowledge and plan for any new challenges or changes that have been identified
11. Take every reasonable opportunity to ask for and obtain feedback and advocacy from the customer
12. Use the *Value_Realization_Activity_Checklist* to check to ensure that all activity that should have taken place has indeed occurred and if not, formulate a plan to ensure it happens now
13. Update the corporate customer success management software system to ensure that all information pertaining to each customer is accurate and up-to-date

10.10.2 Outputs for Practical CSM Framework Phase 6: Value Realization

The outputs for Phase 6: Value Realization include updated information that is documented on the corporate customer success management software system together with any completed changes and challenges checklists and/or value realization activity checklists. The CSM should store a copy of any documentation created during this phase in the Central Repository, together with lessons learned which should be documented within the *CSM_Activity_Tracking_Template*. By the end of this adoption planning phase you and the customer will be ready to move forward to PCSMF Phase 7: Engagement Evaluation.

Chapter 11

Practical CSM Framework Phase 7: Engagement Evaluation

11.1 The Importance of Reviewing CSM Activity

11.1.1 Every Customer Engagement Involves a Substantial Amount of Work

In Chapters 4–10 of this book, we have explored in depth the role of the CSM in helping customers to realize value from their initiatives. We have seen that there are many steps for the CSM to take, and a lot of activity required of the CSM to perform this role well. Each customer engagement therefore could represent many weeks, months or sometimes even years of hard work from the CSM to assist their customer in getting where they want to be, and in doing so in continuing to use and purchase the CSM's company's products, services and solutions (which of course is what it's all about from the CSM's company's perspective). Indeed, if performed well, the work of the CSM over the entirety of a customer engagement not only represents hundreds or thousands of hours of effort expended by the CSM but also generates potentially hundreds of thousands of dollars' worth of value returned to the CSM's company in terms of increased sales (Figure 11.1).

11.1.2 Learning Lessons from Previous Engagements

Given the above, all CSMs should of course be well rewarded for their hard work by their employer. But in additional to that, this quantity of work should also be treated as a valuable source of further knowledge and insight which can be applied to future, similar engagements. Each customer engagement should be treated as a potential diamond mine, from which the "diamonds" of information about the customers themselves but also about best practices and process step improvements for managing and working with customers can be extracted and used within

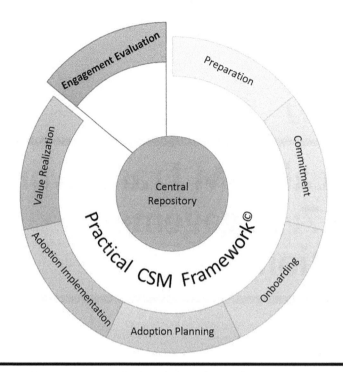

Figure 11.1   Practical CSM Framework Phase 7: Engagement Evaluation.

future, similar customer engagements. In this way, both the individual CSM and the customer success department for which they work can grow and enhance its body of knowledge and understanding, and can increase its library of best practices, processes, templates and tools. This is how the CSM and the customer success team as a whole can mature as a department and become more useful and relevant to customers. In so doing of course they also become more valuable to their own company, and therefore it becomes easier for senior business leaders to justify their continued investment (and perhaps even increased investment) in customer success operations.

11.1.3 Rewarding Success

As an additional point, tracking and recording each CSM's activity and the results of that activity is also necessary in order for businesses to remunerate their CSMs with any performance-related portion of their overall salary package. While most CSMs are not directly rewarded through sales commissions as a sales person would be, most CSMs do still have a significant part of their overall salaries awarded if personal and/or team targets are met or exceeded. These targets most commonly relate to increases in as-a-service contract renewal rates, increases in product utilization and increases in customer satisfaction and advocacy. Typically, targets are set for the team rather than each separate individual, and typically they are set both quarterly and annually, although of course each company differs in the detail of its remuneration scheme, and some organizations may have a very different system to that which is described here. Obviously, if the CSM is not aware how their company's remuneration works they need to make sure they find out, since this will (or should) also tell them what outcomes their company is looking for them and their colleagues to attain for it.

11.2 Increasing the Customer Success Management Knowledge Base

11.2.1 The Point of a Knowledge Base

A knowledge base might mean different things to different people. Here I am just using it as an overall expression to mean "everything that the customer success department knows." Increasing the customer success management knowledge base therefore increases the ability of the customer success team—and perhaps especially new recruits to the team—to perform activities to help customers realize the value they desire from the CSM team's company's products, services and solutions. At its heart it is a very simple relationship—the more we know, the more we can do and the better we can perform—or to use the words of Francis Bacon: *"Knowledge is power."*

11.2.2 The Concept of the Central Repository

It's of no use *having* knowledge if this knowledge is not made *available* to those who need it. Information needs therefore to be stored in a location from where it can readily be accessed, and stored in a way which means it is not difficult to find what one is looking for, and when found is easy to digest and understand and can be easily updated and shared with others. The small, newly formed customer success team might get away with a simple shared folder structure on a centrally managed server for a time, but as the team's size and the sophistication of their needs grow there is likely to come a time when this simple method will no longer suffice. On the other hand, a larger organization such as a regional, national or multinational company may determine that they wish to "do things properly" right from the get go. There are many information management software systems out there, and each has its own features, advantages and benefits. Whatever tool or system the CSM team uses to store its information, it should have the ability of being accessible by the people who need to access it from wherever they need to access it from, while at the same time ensuring that the information is secure from those who should *not* have access to it and is appropriately backed up in order to ensure continuity of its availability in the event of a system malfunction. In larger organizations, it may also be necessary to think about how the customer success team's information integrates and works with other corporate systems to ensure that data is not being stored unnecessarily in multiple locations and is available to *everyone* who needs it.

11.2.3 Adding to the Central Repository

The "rules" by which new information can be added to the central repository is another aspect of knowledge management that may need to differ based upon the size of the CSM team and the sophistication of that team's needs. Giving everyone Read/Write access to all information is the simple route and this may well be the most effective way forwards for smaller teams. However as the team grows and as the size and complexity of information stored in the central repository grows, so the need for "proper" management of this repository also grows. At some stage it may be prudent for one person (or a very small team) to take on the specific role of managing and controlling the team's information, while still of course allowing each individual CSM to control and manage their own personal information. This approach helps to prevent loss of or damage to important information, and negates problems, for example, Person A amending a document that outlines the process steps for a particular activity in the way they think is best, and then Person B amending the same document to put it back to how it was before because they disagree with the way Person A believes the process should be undertaken.

As a general rule therefore, centralized information requires centralized management and control. Rules and procedures might need to be put in place for how information should be stored and when and how it can be modified, and of course by whom. These rules and procedures do need careful thinking about however, since it is important that bureaucracy and administrative red tape is kept to a minimum, and that CSMs and others do not become frustrated by being prevented from performing their jobs. The contributions of *all* CSMs toward the growth of the customer success team's knowledge need to be welcomed and supported, so it is important not to place obstacles in the way of this occurring.

11.3 Updating Personal and Team Best Practices

11.3.1 The Power of Applying Best Practices

One basic rule in life is that the more you perform a particular task or activity, the better you tend to get at it. This is perhaps particularly true for skill-based tasks such as playing the violin or performing open heart surgery, but it is also true for more knowledge-oriented activities such as researching, consulting and project management that a CSM will get involved in. Better still of course is not to have to start from scratch on one's own and work things out from first principles, but instead to build upon the existing knowledge, skills and experiences of others who have been there before you by learning lessons from *their* experiences and applying those to your own situation. Of course that is precisely what this book has been all about—attempting to take all of the knowledge that I have learned both from my own direct experiences and from training courses, books, conversations and other such interactions to learn from others, and distilling it into a *best practice framework* for other CSMs to read and to adapt and use in their own specific circumstances.

11.3.2 Learning from Others and Learning from Yourself

The advantage of reading a book such as this one and then applying the information within it to your own work situation is that with any luck, you will find that you will be able to operate more productively and provide higher quality results than beforehand. That at least is my intention and of course I very much hope it proves to be the case for you! However, because you and I have never met and therefore I do not know exactly what role you have, what tasks you undertake or what needs you have, and also because in any case the book is intended for a wide and diverse audience of CSMs from any background and working for any type and size of company, and not least because it only contains ideas and principles that come from one source—namely me—it can of course only take you so far, regardless of how useful it may be. The remainder of the journey is yours to take, and while other books, training courses, workshops and coaching sessions will all no doubt play a part in your ongoing development, so too should learning directly from your *own* experiences and from those of your close colleagues. This type of learning is especially important, since it is learning *in situ*, i.e., it relates directly to the customers, the activities, the products and services, the customer success strategy and the resources and capabilities of your own circumstances, and therefore are more directly applicable to those circumstances than any other source of learning can be.

11.3.3 The Formal Approach to Creating and Updating Team Best Practices

I am of the opinion that the ongoing development of every individual CSM's and the overall team's knowledge and skills is a critical component of *any* customer success team's growth. It therefore makes sense for the team's best practices to be agreed upon as a team and formalized into some kind of best practice framework (for example, by taking my own *Practical CSM Framework* that is laid out for you within this book and adapting it to meet your organization's requirements), and then by creating a process for regular review and maintenance of this framework so that updates can be applied over time as new information is learned and new ideas are discovered. In most cases it should probably be the head of the department who is ultimately accountable for ensuring that this happens to a consistently high enough standard and to meet the strategic needs of the company, but probably with the responsibility for the management of it being appointed to one or two specific people within the team, and with *all* team members being both consulted and informed on proposed and actual changes (see the RACI matrix for an explanation of these different roles).

Once any changes to the team's best practices have been made, it is vitally important to ensure that these changes are disseminated throughout the team. It's also important to make sure not only that all team members are aware of any changes but that they start to *use* them as well.

11.4 Templating Common Process Steps

11.4.1 I'd Rather Work It Out Once and Then Do It Many Times

It is my experience that having to work out both *what* to do and *how* to do it every time you perform a particular task is expensive and time-consuming and often quite frustrating as well. Far better to *already know* what to do and how to do it, so that you can just get on and perform the task with a minimum of fuss and bother. The "what to do" part comes from the best practice framework. It should explain in a simple, step-by-step format what tasks or activities need to be performed, in which order they should be performed and to what quality or standard they should be completed. In terms of "how to do it" this is where the templates come in.

You will have seen numerous tools alluded to throughout those chapters of this book that deal directly with accomplishing each phase within the Practical CSM Framework. These tools are pre-created templates that list out what information is needed to be researched, analyzed and/or documented at each step along the way and that help the CSM to ensure they perform a task efficiently, completely and well. They can of course be first of all adapted to suit a specific CSM or customer success team's circumstances and needs, and indeed this is something that I would definitely encourage.

11.4.2 Creating Your Own Templates

Alongside the tools you find within this book and elsewhere you may also decide to create your own templates for performing specific tasks that either are not covered at all by the material you find here and elsewhere, or where you have quite specific and/or unusual requirements around those tasks that might make it more simple to create a tool from scratch instead of amending an existing one.

11.5 Improving Your Own CSM Practice

11.5.1 You Are Responsible for Your Own Success or Failure

All sorts of things can happen in life that are outside of our own control including accidents, illnesses, situations at work and situations in our personal life. Fatalists might therefore take the view that there is little point in trying to improve their lot in life, since circumstances will dictate the level of their success or failure. They will of course be found to be true. Pragmatists on the other hand, will see that while not *everything* is under their control to change, many things *are*, and that the best course of action therefore is to do all that they can to influence things in order to ensure positive outcomes are attained as much as possible. They also will be found to be true. In other words, regardless of what actually ends up happening, the best approach is to do whatever we can to help ourselves (and indeed others) to get where we (and they) want go to. This of course applies equally in all aspects of one's life including the professional. It is therefore important that we do indeed take responsibility for our career development and do not leave it in the hands of fate or of others. If you want to get anywhere in life you *have* to take responsibility for undergoing the journey.

11.5.2 Creating a Personal Development Plan

It's not a bad idea to treat oneself as if you were a business, and to go through a similar process about defining yourself and your goals and planning for the accomplishment of those objectives in a similar (though perhaps less formal and less detailed) was as might the board of directors of a company.

1. Create a personal vision statement

    If that sounds like an appealing idea then why not start with a vision statement? Take an afternoon or so to think about where you want to be in say 5 years' time, and then try to distill that down into a simple paragraph of no more than two or maximum three sentences that really speak to you about where you want to be, what you want to be doing how you want to be living your life at that time. The more vivid and meaningful you can make this vision statement, the more powerful it will be as a tool to keep you on track as you work toward its fulfillment.

2. Determine four to six CSFs that will help you to attain your vision

    Once you have your vision statement, determine perhaps four, five or six (not too many more—keep it relatively simple) core strategic things that you will need to do in order to achieve your vision. These are your CSFs—critical success factors—since they are the things that you *must do* in order to attain your goal. CSFs should be qualitative in nature and should be aspirational. The point of the CSFs is that while you cannot just "do" your vision, you *can* get on and take actions to attain these qualities, and by doing so you *will* ultimately attain your vision as well—always assuming of course that you have selected the right CSFs.

3. Determine two or three activities for each CSF that will help you to achieve them

    Now take each CSF and decide how best to go about attaining it. This might include activities you undertake alone and through your own personal efforts and expense as well as those that you can persuade your company to sponsor you to do (much the best way of course, so long as you can show there is value for your company in doing so).

4. Determine KPIs and measurements for each activity

    Now you need to decide what "success" will mean in terms of a specific quality, quantity and deadline—just as we discussed earlier in the book when we reviewed the topic of KPIs—and decide how you will measure your progress toward their attainment.

5. Create a roadmap and then take the action

Finally, schedule the necessary activities into a roadmap and if necessary (for example, if the overall vision is a long-term one) consider creating some significant milestones along the way. Then it's simply a case of working the plan and taking the measurements to ensure you stay on track with it. You should of course review and adjust your vision, CSFs and activities occasionally to make sure they are still relevant to your current needs. You might also decide to celebrate your successes along the way, as a great way to motivate yourself to keep going.

11.5.3 An Example of a Personal Vision with CSFs

For example, let's say that an important part of someone's vision is "…to become the CEO of a major, international company." Depending upon that person's current situation and circumstances this may be a goal that while achievable in the long term is not going to happen in one step or overnight. Perhaps one CSF that this person might have is "…to be an excellent communicator and an inspiring leader." And maybe another one might be "…to be able to handle tough negotiation situations to gain the best possible outcomes for my company." A third one might be "…to have great entrepreneurial skills that will help to drive my business forwards in new and exciting directions." Perhaps their fourth CSF might be "…to have an in-depth understanding of financial decision making best practices." While it might be difficult to just "do something" to go from wherever they are to becoming a CEO in one go, this person probably *can* think of ways in which they can work on their communication and leadership abilities, their negotiation skills, their entrepreneurialism and their ability to understand business finance and financial decision-making. While achieving these qualities will not on their own turn them into a CEO, they will most certainly increase their chances over someone who does *not* have those qualities.

Now what this person needs to do is to work out their activities, KPIs and measurements for each CSF and then put it into a plan and work that plan to attain the results.

Remember that this plan can include components from all of the following:

- Formal learning from outside sources (e.g., training, workshops, etc.)
- Informal learning from outside sources (e.g., books, websites, etc.)
- Learning from colleagues (e.g., coaching, mentoring, ideas sharing, etc.)
- Learning from your own experiences

11.6 Working with Quarterly Activity Targets

11.6.1 The Power of Regular, Formal Progress Reviews

I have found that I work best if I have some structure to my work and if I have some specific goals to work toward achieving. I also find I work best where in part at least those goals are relatively short term. So while I have a long-term vision for my career which I am slowly working toward, I also have a quarterly plan for my activities which I am taking immediate action on. I find this combination motivates me and also helps me to stay on track and to be able to measure progress effectively.

In particular, I find that having someone else—a trusted person whose views and opinions I respect—involved in a more formal quarterly review process is very helpful, since it provides valuable insight and guidance that I would otherwise not have. The obvious candidate for this role is the CSM's line manager, since they have the experience and knowledge that makes them useful as coach and counselor, and they also have the authority to sanction and approve activities and resources. If (like me) you do not have a line manager then select someone who has an knowledge and experience of the work you do and whose opinions you trust. Perhaps you can offer to act as their reviewer in return for them acting as yours.

11.6.2 The Quarterly CSM Review Format

Just as we may have a quarterly business review with our customers, we should also have regular—for example, quarterly—reviews of our own strategy and activities. The quarterly review should be formal in the sense that it happens on a regular quarterly schedule and that it follows a pre-specified agenda or format. It does not have to be formal in terms of where it takes place or how the two of you communicate and work together. For example, a quarterly CSM review could be equally effective in a coffee shop, or over an Internet virtual conferencing tool as in a meeting room in an office. It is important to try not to be interrupted or overheard too much, but otherwise the style and setting is immaterial.

The review meeting does not need to be onerous in length—perhaps an hour to an hour and a half would be a good duration to aim for. The agenda or format that I recommend is very simple and would include the following components:

■ Review of previous quarter's measurements and goal attainment
■ Discussion on previous quarter's activities and any problems or difficulties encountered
■ Discussion on upcoming quarter's work required, goals to attain and resources needed
■ Agreement on and documentation of upcoming quarter's activities and goals and how they will be measured

If working with a peer rather than a line manager it may work well to perform the role of a reviewer and reviewee on a back-to-back basis so that you both get reviewed at the same meeting, one after the other.

11.7 Improving Your Team's Practice

11.7.1 The Power of Teamwork

For millennia, people have come together to accomplish mutual goals. This is because people have found the old adage that *the whole is greater than the sum of the parts* to be true. More can be done by a well selected and organized team than can be accomplished by those same people each working separately and alone.

There are multiple potential benefits of working with and as a team. These include:

■ Practical support to perform tasks that require more than one person to accomplish, or that need completing more quickly than could be done alone
■ Creative problem-solving using collaboration to come up with the best ideas
■ Specialist knowledge of other team members that can be utilized by all on an as-needed basis
■ Best practice processes, tools and templates that can be developed by one team member and shared between all team members

- Stakeholder management tasks, negotiation tasks and other tasks that can be carried out by a team member but which would be difficult to perform oneself because of the relationship formed with the other party
- Training, coaching and mentoring from team members to increase knowledge and skills
- Emotional support and encouragement to keep you motivated, energized and mentally strong

11.7.2 Creating a "Team Player" Culture

The true success of a team is often found in the way the members of that team come together to help each other not because it's "their job" to do so but because they desire to help a team mate out, and because they know that a strong and supportive team benefits *everyone*—themselves included.

This culture of being there for the team and expending effort to help one's team mates doesn't happen by accident. The start point of course is in the selection of people to recruit into customer success roles, and alongside technical skills and experience, a high EQ (emotional intelligence quotient) and the ability and desire to get along with and help others are highly desirable traits to seek in each potential recruit. The team manager principally and indeed all team members secondarily are then responsible for setting and contributing to the team culture. Care should be taken to cultivate this culture and to create a strong, well-knit and supportive team. Further discussion on this topic is beyond the scope of this book, but team managers are most definitely recommended to look into best practices for creating and managing strong, supportive teams if they have not already done so.

11.7.3 Specialist Roles within a Customer Success Team

As a customer success team grows in its size and sophistication, there may come a time when it starts to make sense to divide up the overall work into different types and to start using specialist roles to accomplish the work more effectively. The need for this is likely to vary considerably between different organization's customer success team, dependent upon their companies' industry, products and services and customers, but the specialist roles that individual CSMs might start to take on may include:

1. Product Specialist

    This would typically be someone with a more technical background and who may have particular qualifications and or experience in deploying, configuring, supporting or selling a specific product or service or product/service range or portfolio. They are called in to help customers understand the products or services they have purchased and to provide advice on the use of features and functions of these products or services to improve business capabilities.

2. Industry Specialist

    This is a person with a strong background and experience within that industry itself—typically having worked within the industry prior to their current role. They are brought in to help the customer understand how a particular product or service might be utilized within their organization and what the challenges and opportunities and consequences of doing so might be.

3. Account Specialist

    This is a person with more generalist knowledge of customer success but who is selected to permanently manage the relationship between the CSM's company and the customer.

They may only be given a small number of important customer accounts to manage, so that they can divide their time in such a way as to give sufficient of that time to each customer. They have the opportunity therefore to build strong trust relationships with key customer stakeholders and to build up an intimate knowledge of the customer's business including its customers, its products and services, its strengths and weaknesses and its vision, strategy and supporting initiatives.

4. License/Contract Renewals Specialist

This is someone who understands the options (and often the very great complexities) for license and/or contract renewals. This might include, for example, information pertaining to changes to what is included within a particular license or contract, changes to how licenses or contracts are sold, for example the introduction of or change to an ELA (enterprise licensing agreement), ways of applying discounts, options for selecting and combining licenses and/or contracts to gain most value, and so on.

5. Change Management and Adoption Specialist

This may include people with a formal qualification and/or background in change management best practices. They are brought in at the adoption planning stage to help formulate the best possible adoption plan for the customer and may also be involved in managing or overseeing adoption implementation.

6. Project Management Specialist

This may include people with a formal qualification and/or background in project management best practices. They are also brought in at the adoption planning stage to help formulate the best possible adoption plan for the customer and will then take the lead alongside customer project managers in managing or overseeing adoption implementation.

11.8 Celebration of Success

A short note to end the discussions on the Practical CSM Framework. One final recommendation is to make sure that in all the stresses and strains of managing and completing the hard work that needs to somehow be fitted into ever more tightly compressed personal schedules, time is still found for both the individual CSM's and the team's successes to be acknowledged, rewarded and celebrated.

11.9 Activities and Outputs for Practical CSM Framework Phase 7: Engagement Evaluation

11.9.1 Activities for Practical CSM Framework Phase 7: Engagement Evaluation

The Activities for Practical CSM Framework Phase 7: Engagement Evaluation include:

1. Review the work you have completed for a customer engagement on a regular basis to determine lessons learned both for self and team
2. Capture any best practice processes, tools and templates that you have developed for this customer engagement and save them in a format that makes them accessible for either yourself or the customer success team as a whole as appropriate

3. Determine any mistakes made or lessons learned about how things could be done better in future similar engagements and plan how this can be achieved

4. Develop your own vision for your personal career success, determine the CSFs for attaining this vision and then design and plan activities for achieving those CSFs and work the plan to do so

5. Meet on a regular basis (for example, quarterly) to formally review progress made in the previous period and determine activities and targets for the upcoming period. This can be done with your team manager where possible but otherwise select a colleague or peer to work with

6. Contribute as appropriate not just to the content within your customer success team's central repository but to the management and maintenance of it

7. Act as a team player by helping team members when opportunities arise to do so, and do not be afraid of reaching out to fellow team members for their assistance when you need it

8. Celebrate your own and your team's successes as often as you have the opportunity to do so

11.9.2 Outputs for Practical CSM Framework Phase 7: Engagement Evaluation

The main Output for Phase 7: Engagement Evaluation is a better *you*. This is achieved through learning the lessons of the experiences you encounter as you engage with each customer and help them on their journeys toward value realization. In addition to this, the best practice processes, tools and templates that you and your team members have available to them will be improved as your body of knowledge and experience matures and evolves.

Chapter 12

Concluding Thoughts

12.1 Who Benefits from Customer Success Management?

12.1.1 Is Customer Success Management Worthwhile?

Why bother? As we have seen it's a lot of effort, so why take all the trouble? Would it not be simpler and cheaper *not* to provide customer success management services? After all, we survived for years without the need for a formal customer success management role, and the important stuff is already being done by our customer services staff, right?

I hear the above questions fairly often, both from those outside *and* inside the customer success management profession. In all honesty the answer is not an unequivocal "Yes" for every situation. It really does depend upon the company in terms of what it sells, how it sells it and who it sells it to. The four main factors that will dictate the level of return on investment that a company can expect to attain from owning and operating a customer success management team are provided below:

1. Amount of revenue coming from renewals of as-a-service contracts
   Customer success management provides an excellent way to reduce churn and increase both renewal rates (the percentage of customer that renew their contracts) and renewal levels (the value of each contract that gets renewed). If the amount of revenue from renewals of as-a-service contracts is sufficiently high, and especially where this amount is a significant proportion of *all* revenues and/or where the company's strategy is to grow as-a-service contract revenues, then owning and operating a customer success management team is likely to make financial sense.

2. Complexity of products, services and/or solutions sold
   If the company sells complex products, services and/or solutions that require a high level of planning and activity to implement (for example, customization, installation, configuration, integration with other corporate systems, training and support of end users, changes to business capabilities and processes) then customers will have a higher need for the type of onboarding, adoption and value realization-related assistance that customer success managers can provide.

3. Customer loyalty and lifetime customer value

If customer loyalty is important to the company in terms of expectations of a high total revenue value coming from multiple sales of products, services and solutions sold to an average customer over the customer's entire lifetime as opposed to a relatively few number of sales to any one customer, then the company may desire to put more effort into customer success management activities as a part of an overall customer experience strategy aimed at maximizing customer retention.

4. Average deal size

If the customer's investment in the company's products, services and/or solutions then customers will be likely to have a higher expectation as to the value returned by their purchases, and an equally higher expectation as to the type and level of post-sales support they receive from the supplier.

12.1.2 Summary of Benefits to the Customer

The benefits that customers might expect from being provided with a CSM from their supplier are many and varied; however, the most common items on the list might include (Table 12.1):

Table 12.1 Common Customer Success Benefits for Customers

Benefit	Description
Improved onboarding experience	Customers are likely to receive a better onboarding experience when CSMs with both product and customer knowledge are involved, and when the CSM is able to consult with the customer to understand their organization's specific onboarding requirements. This enables the customer to "get going" with adopting and using the solution faster and more effectively
Access to useful assets and resources	CSMs with a good knowledge of both their own company's and third parties' assets and resources (such as, for example, generic training content, user guides, installation instructions, etc.) can act as a useful conduit for recommending and providing access to these assets and resources based upon their understanding of the customer's needs
Access to technical (and other) expertise	CSMs with a good knowledge of both their own company's and third parties' human resources (including not just those with technical expertise but also subject matter experts in topics such as business consulting, change management, project management, training and so on) can act as a useful conduit for recommending and providing access to these human resources
Increased and enhanced solution adoption and utilization	CSMs can help customers increase solution adoption by providing the benefit if their experience of other customers' adoption of the same or similar solutions, and by recommending best practice processes and tools for both planning and implementing an adoption plan that enables solution users to utilize the solution to its maximum potential

(Continued)

Table 12.1 (*Continued*)   **Common Customer Success Benefits for Customers**

Benefit	Description
Improved understanding of ROI	CSMs help their customers to better understand the return on their investment by assisting them to determine appropriate KPIs and by helping with analyzing and reporting on the measurements in ways that make sense to business decision makers
Better management of change	CSMs can use their solution knowledge to help customers manage both change coming from within their own organization (such as strategic direction changes, for example) but also changes to the products and services they have purchased (such as a "dot x" upgrade, for example)

12.1.3 Summary of Benefits to the CSM's Company

The benefits that the CSM's own company might expect from deploying CSMs to work with and assist their customers to realize value from the solution they have purchased are also many and varied, and the most common items on this list might include (Table 12.2):

Table 12.2   Common CSM's Company Benefits from Customer Success

Benefit	Description
Increased renewal rates	Customers who are helped to generate and then realize (i.e., understand) the greatest possible value from the solutions they have purchased are more likely to renew their service contracts, and are also more likely to renew at an increased level
Increased renewal levels	Customers who are helped to understand how they can attain additional value from the solutions they have purchased are more likely to renew their service contracts at an increased level to enable this additional value to occur
Improved customer understanding	By working closely with the customer in a post-sales role to help the customer with onboarding, adoption and value realization, the CSM learns much information about the customer that can help their company to understand how to become more useful to the customer
Improved customer stakeholder relationships	Again, by working closely with the customer in a post-sales role to help the customer with onboarding, adoption and value realization, the CSM helps to strengthen and deepen relationships with key stakeholders that can, in turn, lead to increased sales and longer total customer lifetimes
Enhanced product/ service R&D	Because the CSM is on the ground with the customer observing and learning how the CSM's company's solutions are adopted and utilized, they can provide valuable feedback to the R&D team about how to improve future iterations of products and services to make them more applicable to customers' true needs

(Continued)

Table 12.2 (*Continued*)   Common CSM's Company Benefits from Customer Success

Benefit	Description
Increased advocacy from customers	Because CSMs extend the relationship past sales and on into adoption and ultimately into value realization, they are ideally placed to request advocacy from the customer at this later stage when value has been measured and realized, including, for example, requests to act as a reference, provide referrals and be used in a written-up case study.
Additional sales opportunities	In addition to maximizing renewal rates and levels for the existing solution, the CSM can gain sufficient knowledge of the customer's business challenges, opportunities, initiatives and needs that they can potentially spot additional "expand" opportunities for selling further solutions to the same customer

12.2 Common CSM Traps and Pitfalls

12.2.1 Things That Go Bump in the Night

There are many things that can go wrong in business just as in one's personal life. Sometimes these things are unavoidable either because we cannot foresee them in time to take any corrective action or simply because it is beyond our control to affect them. However, there are *some* ways in which savvy CSMs can prepare themselves so that they both reduce the likelihood of these challenges occurring in the first place and reduce the negative consequences of them if they do still occur. The list below provides some common traps and pitfalls that the knowledgeable and self-aware CSM can either avoid entirely or take mitigating actions for if they happen (Table 12.3):

Table 12.3   Common Traps and Pitfalls for Unwary CSMs

Trap	Consequence	Action
Doing too much for each customer	Not enough time to perform your role properly, leading to reduced productivity	Make sure the customer has the information it needs to be as self-sufficient as possible. Try to act as an adviser, consultant and project manager rather than saying "yes" to performing longer tasks. Understand the key roles of colleagues and stakeholders and get them involved as appropriate
Not leaving time for continual professional development	CSMs gradually become less useful and relevant to customers' needs	Use the 80/20 rule to allocate 80% of your time to working *in* your role as CSM but 20% of your time working *on* your role. This enables you to keep up-to-date on your own company's products and services, your customers' businesses and industries and your own knowledge and skills

(Continued)

Table 12.3 (*Continued*)   Common Traps and Pitfalls for Unwary CSMs

Trap	Consequence	Action
Not understanding your own company's customer success strategy	Not optimizing your time on performing those tasks which align best with this strategy	Make sure you are absolutely clear as to what is being expected of you as a CSM. For example, how important are expand opportunities compared to renewals? What priority should be put on helping customers with poor health scores compared to obtaining advocacy from those with good scores?
Focusing on technical issues instead of business issues	Reduces the potential value of the help that the CSM offers the customer down a level to just technical assistance	Keep the conversations with customer stakeholders as focused on business issues and business outcomes requirements as much as possible. Pro-actively develop relationships with business-related key stakeholders. Where possible pass technical enquiries to subject matter experts to deal with (even if you could deal with them yourself)
A lack of insight into your customer's business model, strategy, capabilities, challenges and outcomes	Prevents the CSM from gaining trusted business adviser status with the customer and reduces the value of the help they can offer	Learn how to create and analyze business models and spend time asking high-quality open questions about the customer's business vision, strategy, capabilities and challenges and especially the outcomes they desire so that you have a strong context from which you can understand them and thus help them
Too much time spent on "the paperwork" and routine administration	A lack of productivity and effectiveness due to insufficient time spent with customers	Tools such as CRM and health score systems are important assets that need to be used to understand the customer and to record activity so that it can be measured. But they must also not serve as a barrier that prevents CSMs from performing the "real" customer-facing activities that actually generates customer success
Lack of best practice resources such as a framework and tools/templates	A lack of productivity and potentially a lack of quality due to having to work out *what* to do and *how* to do it each time	Employ a best practice framework and either use existing or create your own checklists, tools and templates that enable you to get on with performing the tasks themselves in a consistently high-quality manner, rather than wasting time working out what to do and how to do it each time. Collaborate with your line manager and team members to create best practices across the team

(*Continued*)

Table 12.3 (*Continued*) Common Traps and Pitfalls for Unwary CSMs

Trap	Consequence	Action
Lack of ongoing communication with customers	Weakened stakeholder relationships, reduced importance in the eyes of the customer and less opportunities for renewals and expand	Make sure you have regular contact with each customer you are responsible for as that customer's CSM. This should include a regular cadence for business reviews which should at a minimum occur on a quarterly basis

12.3 Customer Success Is the Jewel in the Customer Experience Crown

12.3.1 Are We Measuring Happiness or Success?

When discussing the concepts behind customer success management it is important to recognize that "customer success" is not the same thing as either "customer happiness" or "customer satisfaction," though it is certainly closely related to them. Generally speaking "customer happiness" or "customer satisfaction" refers to the overall level of contentment that the customer feels about their entire experience of our company, including the quality and usefulness of its products and services, the friendliness and expertise of its people, its marketing and selling techniques, its level of after-care support and anything else that relates in any way to their relationship with us.

I am not suggesting that customer happiness is not important—obviously it *is* important—but there is a difference that needs to be acknowledged. Customer happiness/satisfaction is a measurement of overall customer experience. Customer success, on the other hand, is something slightly different and more specific. As the word implies, customer success occurs when the customer successfully obtains whatever value from the products and/or services they purchased that they had hoped to obtain. Success is therefore a measurement of value where the more value the customer gets as a return on their investment in our products and services the more successful the purchase of those products and services can be said to have been.

In summary, I would describe customer happiness or satisfaction as being a measurement of the *overall experience that customers receive from their relationship with our company*, whereas I would describe customer success as being a measurement of the *overall value that customers realize from the utilization of our products and services to generate their desired business outcomes*.

12.3.2 Customer Success Is a Subcomponent of Customer Experience

If we are defining and/or measuring the overall customer experience then it makes sense that we talk in terms of customer happiness or satisfaction, whereas if we are more specifically defining and/or measuring customer value realization then it makes sense that we talk in terms of customer success. Customer success (which measures customer value realization) is one aspect of customer experience (measured in customer happiness or satisfaction). Everyone in the company who touches the customer in any way has a part to play in overall customer experience. The focus of CSMs (customer success managers) is specifically on helping customers increase the value they received from the products and services they have purchased from us, although in successfully

customer experience					
marketing	sales	professional services	product support	managed services	customer success
Profiling customers, raising product awareness, evangelizing & educating	Understanding needs, creating sales proposals & negotiating deals	Additional paid for services that create extra value for the customer	Answering customers' questions and fixing product related problems	Delivering a specific service to the contracted quality and availability	Helping customers to maximize the value they attain from our products

Figure 12.1   Customer success is a subcomponent of customer experience.

performing this role they will also of course be contributing to the overall customer experience (Figure 12.1).

So to sum up, customer success is a measurement of the *value* that customers gain from using our products and services. Increasing levels of customer success for customers is what customer success management is specifically tasked with achieving. In doing so, the CSM's efforts will also have the effect of increasing the level of customer happiness (or satisfaction) since the customer experience will be a more positive one.

12.3.3 Why Customer Success Is Critically Important

It is my opinion that customer success management is the trump card within the customer experience card deck. Of course, all aspects of customer experience are essential—you cannot have a decent business without marketing, sales, customer support and (where applicable) service management and professional services activities– and I am not for one moment suggesting that they are not all important. However, what I *am* proposing is that customers will put up with a lot and still remain loyal if you get the customer success right, but conversely will be much less likely to remain anywhere near so loyal if you do not get the customer success right *even if you are fantastic in every other aspect of your customer experience.*

Let's turn things around for a moment and view things through the eyes of our customers. If we place ourselves in our customer's shoes, what would we say is most important in terms of their relationship with us? Or to put it another way, why do they buy our products, services and solutions and what makes them come back and continue to buy them? I would suggest that ahead of whether or not they find our marketing information to be excellent or cringe worthy, or our sales processes to be simple or frustrating, or our product support service to be helpful or inadequate what is most critical to them is whether or not our product, service or solution solves their problem or meets their needs. If our products and services generate measurable and provable value for our customers then those customers will be far more forgiving of all other aspects of the customer experience. Conversely, if our products and services do not generate measurable and provable value for our customers then those customers will most likely cease to be our customers regardless of how nice we are to them or how easy we are to work with.

12.3.4 Customer Success—Where the Rubber Hits the Road

In essence, what I am saying is that customer success is where the rubber hits the road. It takes a *lot* of effort to win a new customer. Anyone in sales or marketing knows just how hard it is to win a new customer compared to winning further business from an existing customer. On a dollar-for-dollar basis, the research shows that it makes sense for most businesses to focus more efforts on growing existing customers' lifetime value (CLV) than on acquiring new customers, and for many businesses it only takes a small improvement in that CLV to gain significant profitability increases.

12.3.5 How to Improve Customer Experience?

As with customer success, customer experience is also very much a buzzword at the moment and the concept of improving customer experience is something that many companies are focusing on. Organizations who are wondering how they can improve their customer experience need to ask themselves which aspects of customer experience they are currently strongest in and which they are weakest in. From this, it should be clear what it is they need to invest in to bring it up to an appropriate level to make the overall customer experience a good one. In many cases, the investment may need to be in customer success, since this is the aspect of customer experience which is often the weakest.

12.3.6 The Value of Helping Existing Customers to Maximize Success

Customers are like diamonds, they are precious things that should be nurtured and cherished. All of the different aspects of customer experience contribute to that nurturing and all of them are important, but to my mind the most critical question *for the customer* is whether or not they obtain a positive ROI from their purchase (however that might be measured, and it's not always in dollars). That is why customer success management is so critical to get right. Either our products, services and solutions perform for our customers or they do not. Assuming we already have some great products, services and solutions and some existing customers using them, the most important thing we can do to increase the profitability of our business is to help our customers to maximize the value they get from those products and services so we can keep them as customers and continue to sell more to them.

12.4 The Future of Customer Success Management

12.4.1 Where Does Customer Success Go from Here?

Customer success management is still a relatively new profession, although as we have seen, a lot of the functions and activities that relate to the CSM role have been around for a long time and were fulfilled by a variety of different customer-facing roles including sales, service management and support professionals. We have seen that the rise of customer success as a specific role in and of its self has largely been generated by the need for the supplier to provide its customers with increased agility by providing flexible as-a-service offerings that enable those customers to make lower risk purchasing decisions.

Customer success is now most definitely "a thing" and it certainly looks like it is here to stay. So where does it go from here and how will it change and adapt over time? Naturally, just like anyone else I do not have a crystal ball that lets me see the future, but I do have a few ideas to share about where I think customer success management is likely to be headed, which I present below for your consideration.

12.4.1.1 Customer Success Will Become More Widely Adopted

The need to differentiate on value, combined with the increased demands from customers for agile and flexible as-a-service style contracts and shared risk models will continue to drive growth within the customer success profession. Customer success concepts that were initially worked out for the larger players within the SaaS industry will increasingly become normal for companies of all sizes and from all industries. For example, the wife of a close friend of mine is successfully applying customer success management techniques to the dental practice that she owns and runs as a small business with excellent results in terms of both revenue growth and customer retention.

12.4.1.2 Customer Success Will Become More Integrated within the Business

At the moment customer success management can sometimes feel like an after-thought that has been added on to the business but that doesn't quite fit anywhere. Much discussion has been had both within specific companies and more generally within the customer success profession as to "where customer success management belongs." Is it a part of Sales and Marketing? Does it belong with Professional and Managed Services? Or should it be a function of a brand new organizational unit called Customer Experience? In some companies such as Salesforce.com the Chief Customer Officer sits at the same organizational level as the Chief Finance Officer and is responsible just for the Customer Success Group.

While the reporting structure and organizational hierarchy might differ still in the future from company to company based upon need, what I do think will happen is that concepts of customer success will be embodied within *all* functions of a business from initial R&D through to manufacturing, marketing, selling and customer support operations. Eventually, we will see organizations that put customer success concepts first throughout the *entirety* of their business.

12.4.1.3 Customer Success Will Mature as a Profession

As with every new idea there is a lifecycle for customer success management, and I think it is safe to say that we are currently seeing customer success just beginning to move out of the "early adopter" phase of this lifecycle and starting to move into the "early majority" stage. This trend is likely to continue through to the "late majority" phase and ultimately even the "laggards" will take on board its concepts and values, although this may take quite a while to occur. But in the meantime, the transition that I believe we *are* seeing into the "early majority" will see the development of clearer guidelines and standards for the profession. This will include the development of industry-wide best practice frameworks and tools such as those presented here within this book that will help to standardize how customer success management works and ensure conformity to requirements for quality, efficiency and productivity.

12.4.1.4 Customer Success Will Be Automated in Order to Scale

Not every business sells million-dollar solutions to its customers. Some businesses sell hydro-electric dams and some sell crayons, but arguably customer success management is still required whether the customer is purchasing a strategic software system or a packet of paperclips. The problem, however, is that while it is relatively straightforward to provide a small number of CSMs to assist a small number of high-value customers, it becomes very difficult to afford the provision of a very large number of CSMs to assist tens or even hundreds of thousands of customers each of which having a lower net worth. The only way to scale customer success to reach these lower net worth customers will be to automate customer success activities in order to provide a service that remains valuable for the customer but is also affordable for the supplier.

12.5 Glossary of Essential Customer Success Management Terminology

This glossary is not intended to be comprehensive. Its aim is to list some of the more commonly used terms within the customer success profession and also to explain how they are used both within the context of this book specifically and within the field of customer success management more widely. Many words have multiple definitions, so even if you are familiar with a term I recommend that you review the definition anyway so you know how I am using it in this book. Likewise, if there are some terms that are new to you and do not make complete sense to you at this stage do not worry, each term is explained fully at the appropriate place within the book and where necessary examples are provided to ensure the reader fully "gets it" (Table 12.4).

Table 12.4   Glossary of Customer Success Terminology

Term	Definition
X-as-a-Service (XaaS)	"Anything" delivered as a service, usually where the customer pays for the service on a monthly, quarterly or annual contract basis, but sometimes provided on a "pay as you go" basis
Customer success	Refers to customers gaining measurable value from the purchase and use of our products and services
Customer experience	Refers to the overall happiness or satisfaction that customers feel from all of their interactions with us
Professional service	A separately billable service that may be sold alongside the core product or service. These might include consultancy, management, development and so on
Support service	A service that provides technical and/or end-user help and assistance for customers after they have purchased our product or service
Value added service	A service that is sold or provided at no charge which is delivered alongside the main product/service and which enhances that main product/service's value to the customer
Revenue	The income which is generated by all or by a particular part of an operation (for example, the use of a product, service or solution), usually calculated annually.
Capital Expenditure (CAPEX)	The up-front costs associated with purchasing and implementing a product, service or solution

(Continued)

Table 12.4 (*Continued*)   Glossary of Customer Success Terminology

Term	Definition
Operational Expenditure (OPEX)	The ongoing costs associated with managing and maintaining a product, service or solution and supporting its users
Total expenditure	The total costs associated with a product, service or solution which is calculated by combining CAPEX and OPEX
Profit	The revenue generated from using a product, service or solution, minus the combined capital and operational expenditure. Calculated by subtracting total expenditure from Revenue (technically this is called gross profit). The term ROI is sometimes used to describe profit (see below)
Return on investment (ROI)	Used correctly, ROI refers to the level of efficiency of an investment (i.e., how hard the investment "worked" for us), usually expressed as a percentage where a higher percentage reflects greater efficiency. ROI is calculated by subtracting Total Expenditure from Revenue and then dividing this by Total Expenditure. In non-financial circles however, ROI often simply means the same as Profit (see above)
Onboarding	The provision of information and assistance to the customer to ensure they are able to start using the product or service they have purchased
Value proposition	A description of the intended value that our customers will get from using a particular product or service
Research and analysis	The acts of uncovering information and studying it to understand its meaning and/or value
Planning	The act of determining what activities need to be done and how they should be done in order to achieve a goal
Project or program management	The act of managing activities and measuring progress to guide and direct efforts to the successful achievement of a goal
Change management	The process of managing change in order to reduce its negative impact on the business and to ensure the change takes place completely
Adoption	The process of bringing a new system, process, product or service into use such that it is generating its intended outputs
Expansion or expand	The process of selling further products, services and/or solutions to an existing customer
Output	The direct result of performing an activity, which can be measured to determine the value of that activity
Outcome	The desired end result of an initiative, which is usually attained by the accumulation of multiple outputs over time (for example, each sale of a product is an output that contributes to the outcome that the annual revenue target is reached)

(*Continued*)

Table 12.4 (*Continued*) **Glossary of Customer Success Terminology**

Term	Definition
Incentivizing	The provision of positive or negative rewards for users in order to motivate them to do (or not do) something
Validation	The process of checking to ensure sufficient accuracy of information or agreement on opinions
Activity	A task that can be described as a discrete "thing" which needs to be completed
Framework	Best practice guidance that breaks down complex goals into a series of steps containing activities and provides help on how those activities should be performed
Agility	The quality of being able to change what is currently happening without too much cost or difficulty
Risk	A measurement of uncertainty, based on the consequences that may arise if an unplanned event occurs
Persona	A group of users who share the same adoption needs
User group	A group of users who perform the same tasks or duties
Senior authority figure	A person who commands authority and respect and whose requests and orders will therefore be listened to and obeyed
Senior decision maker	A person who makes (or contributes to) high-level decision-making that has far-reaching consequences. Commonly manages a budget
Senior project lead (SPL)	The person who is responsible for the day-to-day management of a project, often appointed by and/or reporting to the senior decision maker
Key stakeholder	A person who influences the decisions made by a senior decision maker, usually by virtue of their seniority, experience or position
Stakeholder	Anyone who is interested in and/or impacted by the project
End user	A person who is or will be performing activities that are impacted by the project (and may therefore need to be communicated with and provided with appropriate training, support and incentives)
"C" level executive	A senior executive, usually (but not always) with the word "Chief" in their job title, such as chief executive officer (CEO)
View	The opinion of an individual or group of people who share a common perspective by virtue of their position in the company and/or role in the project
Viewpoint	The perspective from which an individual or group of people form their view (i.e., it defines their position in the company and/or their role in the project)

(*Continued*)

Table 12.4 (*Continued*) Glossary of Customer Success Terminology

Term	Definition
Subject matter expert (SME) or "specialist"	Someone with specific expertise who can provide advice and guidance related to that expertise to help decision-makers make informed decisions
Vision	A high level and aspirational description of what your company desires to become in the future
Goal	One specific aspect of the vision (the vision divided into goals)
Objective	One specific aspect of a goal (a goal divided into objectives)
Mission	A high level and aspirational description of what your company will do to turn its vision into a reality
Strategy	A mid-level plan to achieve a goal
Tactic	A detail-level plan to achieve an objective
SMART objective	An objective which has the qualities of being specific, measurable, actionable, realistic and time-bound
Initiative	A specific project or undertaking that the customer is working on in order to fulfill a tactic or strategy
Roadmap	A high-level plan that covers a medium- to-long time frame and which typically divides the pan into phases that contain building blocks and milestones
Building block	A component of a roadmap that can be discretely described and measured
Milestone	A mid-way target that helps to measure progress toward desired outcomes
Project	The entire activity that takes place to attain a desired result
Solution	Multiple products and services that have been combined and packaged together as one purchase to solve a common problem or overcome a common business challenge
Customer engagement	A specific instance of the CSM working with a customer to help them realize value from the products and/or services they have purchased. Each customer engagement should be treated as a separate project by the CSM and should be measured and managed as such
Engagement strategy	The overall plan for engaging a particular customer that the CSM develops for their own benefit
Engagement strategy roadmap	The CSM's engagement strategy for a particular customer, summarized and formatted into a simple-to-follow document
Customer initiative	A project that the customer is working on within their own business that is the underlying reason for their purchase of products and/or services. Initiatives may be large and corporate-wide or smaller in scope and only impact one team, department or process.

(Continued)

Table 12.4 (*Continued*)   Glossary of Customer Success Terminology

Term	Definition
Health score	A metric that is commonly used in customer success management to determine the relative health of the relationship between the CSM's own company and each customer
Net promoter score (NPS)	A metric that is commonly used to determine the overall level of satisfaction customers perceive, which is calculated by asking them how likely they would be to recommend the company to a friend or colleague
Critical success factor (CSF)	A strategic quality that must be attained alongside all other CSFs in order for the initiative's outcomes to be attained
Key performance indicator (KPI)	A measurement that is designed to indicate the level of progress being made toward achieving and outcome. Multiple KPIs may need to be used in order to fully understand overall progress toward outcome attainment.
Customer retention	The act (and the measurement) of keeping existing customers—especially important where customers are on annual or monthly renewable contracts for services
Customer churn	The measurement of customers who do not renew their contracts, usually expressed as a percentage of the total number of customers. For example, a churn rate of 14% would indicate that 14% of existing customers do not renew their contracts
Value realization	The process of attaining value for the customer from the CSM's company's products, services and/or solutions, which occurs through their utilization over time to assist with the attainment of the customer's outcomes
Adoption barrier	A challenge or issue that presents a potential barrier to the successful adoption of the company's products, services and solutions and which must therefore be overcome
Use case	A step-by-step "walk through" of how the customer's processes are used to generate a specific output
Renewal	The renewal of a service contract at the end of the existing contract's term (for example, on an annual basis)
Customer lifecycle	The entire length of time in which a particular company or individual remains as a customer of the company
Engagement lifecycle	The entire length of time in which the CSM is engaged with the customer to assist them with a specific initiative for which products or services have been purchased
Product/service lifecycle	The entire length of time in which a product or service is used by a customer before it is replaced

Please Provide Your Feedback

Writing this book has been both a pleasure and an honor, and I sincerely hope that it has brought fresh concepts and new ideas to you that you can apply to your own unique situation to generate more value for your customers, your company and yourself.

I am very keen to get feedback from readers, since feedback is the essence of how we learn and improve our game. Whatever you have to say—whether that be a simple rating out of five, a general comment on what you thought of the book, or a specific suggestion for a way the book could be improved in upcoming editions—I am eager to hear from you. Please take a moment to go to www.practicalcsm.com/feedback to leave me your comments and suggestions, or indeed just to say hi. I promise that all feedback will be read with interest. Thank you.

If you purchased this book on Amazon then I would be very grateful for a review on Amazon's website as it is very helpful for other potential purchasers to see what previous readers have thought of the book, in order to know whether or not to purchase it for themselves.

You Still Want More?

If you have enjoyed this book and would like to take things a step further either for yourself as an individual or for your entire customer success team then please visit my website at www.practicalcsm.com where you can find information about the range of customer success-related newsletters, articles, training courses, certification exams, coaching, consulting, online tools and other services that I offer and which complement this book and help you to take the concepts behind the Practical CSM Framework to another level.

Index

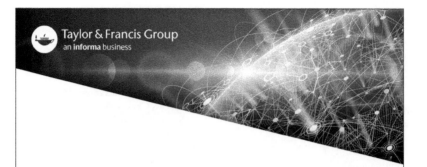

For Product Safety Concerns and Information please contact our EU
representative GPSR@taylorandfrancis.com
Taylor & Francis Verlag GmbH, Kaufingerstraße 24, 80331 München, Germany